Manifest Destiny and the Expansion of America

Other titles in ABC-CLIO's

TURNING POINTS—ACTUAL AND ALTERNATE HISTORIES

series

Books in the Turning Points in History series ask the question: What would have happened if . . . ? In a unique editorial format, each book examines a specific period in American history, presents the real, or actual, history, and then offers an alternate history—speculations from historical experts on what might have happened had the course of history turned.

If a particular event had turned out differently, history from that turning point forward could be affected. Important outcomes frequently hinge on an individual decision, an accidental encounter, a turn in the weather, the spread of a disease, or a missed piece of information. Such events stimulate our imagination, accentuating the role of luck, chance, and individual decision or character at particular moments in time. The examination of such key turning points is one of the reasons that the study of history is so fascinating.

For the student, examining alternate histories springing from turning points and exploring What would have happened if . . . ? gives insight into many of the questions at the heart of our civilization today.

Manifest Destiny and the Expansion of America

Rodney P. Carlisle and J. Geoffrey Golson, *Editors*

A B C 🞉 C L I O

Santa Barbara, California
Denver, Colorado
Oxford, England

Copyright 2007 by ABC-CLIO, Inc.

Library of Congress Cataloging-in-Publication Data
Manifest destiny and the expansion of America / Rodney P. Carlisle and
J. Geoffrey Golson, editors.
       p. cm. — (Turning points : actual and alternate histories)
   Includes bibliographical references and index.
   ISBN-13: 978-1-85109-833-0 (hard copy : alk. paper)
   ISBN-13: 978-1-85109-834-7 (ebook)
   ISBN-10: 1-85109-833-X (hard copy : alk. paper)
   ISBN-10: 1-85109-834-8 (ebook)
  1. United States—Territorial expansion. 2. United States—History—
1783-1815. 3. United States—History—1815-1861. 4. Imaginary histories.
I. Carlisle, Rodney P. II. Golson, J. Geoffrey.

   E179.5.M33 2007
   973.5—dc22   2006102133

11 10 09 08 07   1 2 3 4 5 6 7 8 9 10

Media Production Coordinator: Ellen Brenna Dougherty
Media Resources Manager: Caroline Price
Production Editor: Anna A. Moore
Editorial Assistant: Alisha Martinez
Production Manager: Don Schmidt
Manufacturing Coordinator: Paula Gerard
Text Design: Devenish Design

This book is also available on the World Wide Web as an eBook.
Visit http://www.abc-clio.com for details.

ABC-CLIO, Inc.
130 Cremona Drive, P.O. Box 1911
Santa Barbara, California 93116-1911

This book is printed on acid-free paper. ∞
Manufactured in the United States of America

Contents

Contributors

Introduction

I . . . regard the chief utility of all historical and sociological
investigations to be to admonish us of the alternative possibilities
of history.
> —Oscar Jaszi, *The Dissolution of the Habsburg Monarchy*

There is nothing new about counterfactual inference. Historians
have been doing it for at least two thousand years.
> —Philip Tetlock and Aaron Belkin, *Counterfactual*
> *Thought Experiments in World Politics*

The question, What would have happened if . . . ? is asked all the time
as historians, students, and readers of history examine past events.
If some event had turned out differently, we are often reminded that
the whole course of history from that particular turning point forward
could have been affected. Important outcomes frequently hinge on an
individ-ual decision, an accidental encounter, a turn in the weather, the
spread of a disease, or a missed piece of information. Such events stimulate our imagination, accentuating the role of luck, chance, and individual decision or character at particular moments in time. The examination
of such key hinge points is one of the reasons that the study of history is
so fascinating.

"Alternate history" has become a fictional genre, similar to science
fiction, in that it proposes other worlds, spun off from the one we live in,
derived from some key hinge point in the past. Harry Turtledove, among
others, has produced novels along these lines. Turtledove has written a
widely sold sequence of books that follow an alternate past from a "counterfactual" Confederate victory at the battle of Antietam, resulting in the rise of
the Confederate States of America as a separate nation, with consequences
well into the twentieth century.

Alternate or counterfactual history is more than a form of imaginative
speculation or engaging entertainment, however. Historians are able to
highlight the significance of an event they examine by pointing to the consequences of the event. When many significant consequences flow from a
single event, the alternate history question is implicit—the consequences
would have been different, and a strange and different history would have
flowed from that time forward if the specific event in question had turned

out differently. Those events that would have made the most dramatic or drastic alternate set of consequences are clearly among the most important; thus key battles in wars are often studied in great detail, but not only for their own sake. The importance of such battles as Gettysburg and Antietam is not simply military. Instead, those battles and others are significant because such deep consequences flowed from their outcomes. The same could be said of General Erich Ludendorff's offensive in 1918—had it been successful, the Allies might have been defeated in World War I, and the map of Europe and the rest of the twentieth century would have been very different from the way they actually turned out. Similarly, if for some reason the nuclear weapons used at Hiroshima and Nagasaki in 1945 had failed, the outcome of World War II could have been very different, perhaps with a greater role for Russia in the dissolution of the Japanese Empire. Others have argued that had the bombs not been used, Japan would have been defeated quite promptly even without them.

Every key event raises similar issues. What might the world have been like if Christopher Columbus and his sailors had failed to return from their voyage in 1492? What if Hernán Cortéz and Francisco Pizarro had been soundly defeated in their attempts to defeat the Aztecs and the Inca Empire? What if John Wilkes Booth had failed in his assassination attempt against Abraham Lincoln? What sort of world would we live in if any of the other famous victims of assassination had survived, such as John F. Kennedy, Martin Luther King, Jr., or Malcolm X?

For the student, examining alternate histories springing from multiple turning points and exploring what would have happened if . . . gives insight into many of the questions at the heart of history. What were the roles of specific individuals, and how did their exercise of free will and choice at a moment in time affect later events? On the other hand, to what extent are the actions of individuals irrelevant to the larger outcomes? That is, in any particular period of history, were certain underlying forces at work that would have led to the same result, no matter what the individual did? Do underlying structures and deeper causes, such as economic conditions, technological progress, climate, natural resources, and diseases, force events into a mold that individuals have always been powerless to alter? Do certain ideas have such importance that they would spread, even if particular advocates had never lived to voice them?

The classic contest of free will and determinism is constantly at work in history, and an examination of pivotal turning points is key to understanding the balance between deep determining forces and the role of individuals. Frequently, it seems, no matter what individuals tried to do to affect the course of events, the events flowed onward in their same course; in other cases, however, a single small mistake or different personal decision seems to have affected events and altered the course of history. Close study of specific events and how they might have otherwise turned out can illuminate this challenging and recurrent issue.

Of course, when reviewing what would have happened if . . . , it is important to realize exactly what in fact really did happen. So in every chapter presented in this series, we are careful to explain first what actually happened, before turning to a possible alternative set of events that could have happened, and the consequences through later history that might have flowed from an alternate development at a particular turning point. By looking at a wide variety of such alternatives, we see how much of history is contingent, and we gain greater insight into its specific events and developments.

Alternate histories would have flowed, had there been different outcomes of a great variety of events, many of them far less famous than the outstanding battles, and the lives and deaths of explorers, conquerors, statesmen, and political leaders. Seemingly obscure or little-recognized events in the past, such as legislative decisions, court cases, small military engagements, and even the lives of obscure minor officials, preachers, writers, and private citizens, frequently played a crucial part in shaping the flow of events. It is clear that if any of the great leaders of the world had died as infants, the events in which they participated would have been altered; but we tend to forget that millions of minor players and less famous people take actions in their daily lives in events such as battles, elections, legislative and judicial decisions, sermons, speeches, and published statements that have sometimes altered the course of history.

Alternate histories are known as "counterfactuals," that is, events that did not in fact happen. Some counterfactuals are more plausible than others. A few historians have argued that all counterfactuals are absurd and should not be studied or considered. However, any historical work that goes beyond simply presenting a narrative or chronological list of what happened and begins to explore causes through the use of such terms as "influenced," "precipitated," or "led to," is in fact implying some counterfactual sequences. A historian, in describing one event as having consequences, is by implication suggesting the counterfactual that if the event had not occurred, the consequences would have been different.

If history is to be more than a chronicle or simple listing of what happened and is to present "lessons" about statecraft, society, technology development, diplomacy, the flow of ideas, military affairs, and economic policy, it must explore how causes led to consequences. Only by the study of such relationships can future leaders, military officers, business people and bankers, legislators and judges, and, perhaps most important, voters in democratic nations gain any knowledge of how to conduct their affairs. To derive the lessons of history, one has to ask what the important causes were, the important hinge events that made a difference. And once that question is asked, counterfactuals are implied. Thus the defenders of the approach suggest that counterfactual reasoning is a prerequisite to learning lessons from history. Even many historians who resolutely avoid talking about "what might have been" are implying that what in fact happened was important because the alternative, counterfactual event did *not* happen.

Two scholars who have studied counterfactuals in depth, Philip E. Tetlock and Aaron Belkin, in an edited collection of articles, *Counterfactual Thought Experiments in World Politics* (Princeton University Press, 1996), have concluded that counterfactual reasoning can serve several quite different purposes in the study of history. They define these types of counterfactual work:

1. Case-study counterfactuals that "highlight moments of indeterminacy" in history by showing how things might have turned out differently at such hinge points because of individual free choices. These studies tend to focus on the uniqueness of specific events.

2. "Nomothetic" counterfactuals that focus on underlying deterministic laws or processes, examining key events to show how likely or unlikely it was for events to have turned out differently. The purpose of this type of study is to test how powerful an underlying law or process is by imagining alternative situations or decisions.

3. A combination of types one and two above, blending the test of theory or underlying law approach with the unique event approach.

4. "Mental stimulation" counterfactuals that highlight underlying assumptions most people have by showing how causes that most people believe are inconsequential could have major effects, and other causes that most people believe are very important might have little or no effect in changing the course of history.

The reader will recognize aspects of each of these different models in the accounts that follow. Moreover, the reader can find the contrasts between actual history and alternate history quite puzzling and thought provoking, as they are intended to be. As readers study the cases, they may want to keep asking questions such as these:

What was the key hinge point on which the author focused?

Is the altered key event a plausible change—something that could easily have happened?

Was the change "minimal" in the sense that only one or a few turning point events had to turn out differently from the way they did?

Did the alternate outcome seem to develop in a realistic way; that is, does the alternate sequence of events seem to be one that would be likely, once the precipitating change took place?

How plausible is the alternate long-term outcome or consequence that the author suggested?

Was the changed key event a matter of an individual person's choice, an accident, or a change in some broader social or technological development?

Does the counterfactual story help us make judgments about the actual quality of leadership displayed in fact at the time? That is, did key actors in real history act more or less wisely than they did in the counterfactual account?

Does the outcome of the episode suggest that despite the role of chance and individual choice, certain powerful forces shaped history in similar directions, in both the factual and counterfactual account?

Does the account make me think differently about what was important in history?

Does the counterfactual story challenge any assumptions I had before I read it?

Remember, however, that what really happened is the object of historical study. We examine the counterfactual, alternate histories to get a better understanding of the forces and people that were at work in what really did occur. These counterfactual stories will make you think about history in ways that you have never encountered before; but when you have explored them, you should be able to go back to the real events with fresh questions in mind.

Introduction to the Manifest Destiny Volume

In the first sixty years of the nineteenth century, the United States expanded from its original boundaries between the Atlantic coast and the Mississippi River to become a continental nation, one of the largest in the world (in terms of land area). With lands that were purchased from France, acquired by war and purchase from Mexico, and in the case of Oregon, settled by negotiation with Britain, the country extended to the Pacific Ocean on the west and to the Rio Grande River on the south. Borrowing a phrase from journalists, politicians asserted that the expansion of the United States was the fulfillment of its "Manifest Destiny."

That expansion came with a cost. Native Americans who found their lands overrun by miners, ranchers, settlers, and soldiers from the east sometimes rebelled. While they won a few notable engagements, some of the battles led to slaughter of whole villages of Native American men, women, children, and babies. American settlers in the Mexican province of Texas soon rebelled against Mexican control, partly because the Mexican government disallowed slavery, and the American settlers, mostly from slave states, sought to preserve that institution. After Texas gained its independence from Mexico and became a self-governing republic, it sought admission to the United States as a state.

Controversies over the admission of Texas revealed the depth of disagreement in the United States over the issue of slavery. After Texas joined the country, the United States fought a short war with Mexico and negotiated a boundary dividing the Oregon Territory. In the short period from 1838 to 1848, the United States suddenly became a continental power. Heady with conquest and expansion, some leaders were already looking across the ocean for other lands to acquire, in the Caribbean, in Central America, or northward in Canada or Alaska.

However, the question of whether slavery would be permitted in the newly gained territories severely divided the nation and Congress. Southerners argued that the lands had been won at the cost of Southern as well as Northern money and lives, and that the "peculiar institution" of slavery should not be barred in the newly acquired territories. Divisions over this issue wracked the country over the following decade, finally resulting in the secession of some of the slave states and the Civil War (1861–1865).

As we read of the conflicts and crises in this turbulent period we often are struck by the hinge points or turning points when things might have turned out differently. The whole future of the nation would have been altered at many points if certain individuals had died earlier, if specific battles had turned a different way, or if different political decisions and compromises had been made. In this volume of the series of Turning Points, we explore a variety of events of the period of Manifest Destiny, asking such questions as these:

What might have happened if the original exploration by Lewis and Clark, which aroused the interest of Americans in the West, had been a miserable failure instead of a qualified success?

What might the nation have looked like if the British had retained control of Washington, D.C., after the War of 1812?

If the Monroe Doctrine (which was intended to limit European influence in the Western Hemisphere) had never been developed, how would that have changed the developments in the period?

If key technologies in transportation had been delayed, how would that have affected westward expansion?

If Mexico had won the Mexican-American war, how would that have shaped future American history?

Through the 1850s, the issue of slavery threatened an impending crisis, and many opportunities for compromise and political resolution were explored. What might have happened if one or more of those compromises had succeeded?

Abraham Lincoln rose to national prominence partly because he argued very well against Stephen Douglas in Illinois's 1858 race for U.S. senator. If he had not done so well in that debate, he probably would not have won the nomination for the presidency two years later, and the election of 1860, which sparked the secession of slave states, might have turned out quite differently.

When would slavery have ended in the United States if the Civil War had been avoided? What sort of nation would the United States have been if that war had never been fought?

In the following chapters, such scenarios are explored, and alternate histories are considered. Such "might have beens" lurk behind all the great events of the period, including others not covered in this volume. As you think about such issues, you have to start raising questions and finding out information about broader aspects of U.S. history. So, while this collection of articles starts with and presents issues about the period when the American Republic expanded to become a continental nation, it raises many deeper questions about history and about the long-term consequences of individual actions.

WARNING!

You are probably accustomed to reading a book of history to find out what happened. We offer this book with a major warning. In this volume, the reader will see and be led to think deeply about what actually happened, and that part of history is always designated ACTUAL HISTORY. However, the last part of each chapter presents a history that never happened, and that is presented as the ALTERNATE HISTORY.

To be sure that it is clear that the ALTERNATE HISTORY is an account of what would have happened differently if a TURNING POINT had turned out differently than it really did, the ALTERNATE HISTORY is always presented against a gray background, like these lines. The ALTERNATE HISTORY is what might have happened, what could have happened, and perhaps what would have happened if the TURNING POINT had gone a little differently. Think about this ALTERNATE HISTORY, and why it would have been different. But don't think that it represents the way things actually happened!

Each chapter is also accompanied by informative sidebars and a few discussion questions that take off from the ACTUAL HISTORY and the ALTERNATE HISTORY and that allow readers to think through and argue the different sides of the issues that are raised here.

We also want to warn readers that some may be surprised to discover that history, when viewed in this light, suddenly becomes so fascinating they may never want to stop learning about it!

Rodney Carlisle

TURNING POINT

The explorations of Lewis and Clark encouraged westward expansion. What if the famed explorers had not reached the Pacific coast?

INTRODUCTION

When Thomas Jefferson began his first term as president in 1801, his agenda included an exploration of the interior of the continent of North America. The purpose of this exploration was simple: to find an all-water route—the fabled Northwest Passage—across the continent to trade with Asia. Part of this route was already mapped and well known: the entire area from the Atlantic Ocean west to the Mississippi River; the Missouri River from its confluence with the Mississippi in St. Louis north to the Mandan native villages (about forty miles north of present-day Bismarck, North Dakota); and the Columbia River from the Pacific Ocean east to present-day Portland, Oregon (approximately one hundred miles from the Pacific). The area from the Mandan villages to the last one hundred miles of the Columbia was a mystery for those of European descent. There were, of course, the Native American inhabitants who knew the "unknown" regions well.

It was believed, in Jefferson's time, that a journey by water from the Atlantic Ocean to the Pacific Ocean could be accomplished by using the Delaware, Susquehanna, Mississippi, Missouri, and Columbia river systems and two short portages. The first of these portages was an often-performed crossing of the Appalachian Mountains. The other, thought to be as easy as the Appalachian crossing, was the portage over the Rocky (or Stony) Mountains.

At the time it was assumed that the Rockies were of the same height (short) and the same layout (one long chain) as the Appalachians. This belief was bolstered by an overland journey made by a Canadian explorer who crossed the Rockies in Canada at a point at which their height was similar to that of the Appalachians. When Jefferson conceived his plan, this was the most up-to-date information available. No one from the United States had yet crossed the Rocky Mountains south of the Canadian border, but armed with this geographical knowledge, Jefferson thought that crossing would be a mere formality.

KEY CONCEPT Why Lewis *and* Clark?

The man President Thomas Jefferson selected to execute this planned exploration was Meriwether Lewis, whom Jefferson had selected as private secretary. First and foremost, Lewis had been an officer in the army, and Jefferson's position as commander in chief gave him the authority to send a military expedition across the continent. This eliminated the potential problem of requesting money from Congress for a civilian-led mission.

However, it was a military expedition only on the surface. Jefferson began composing a document that contained instructions for Lewis. In addition to commanding a group of ten to twelve soldiers, it enumerated a host of duties Lewis was expected to carry out, including (but not limited to) constructing a map; establishing friendly contact with the native tribes he met en route; collecting plant, animal, and geological specimens; recording weather data; and noting ideal locations for trading and military outposts.

Jefferson groomed Lewis for the position. As private secretary, Lewis lived with the president both in Washington, D.C., and at Monticello, Jefferson's home in Virginia. Jefferson instructed Lewis in the basics of geography, stellar navigation, pressing plants, and preserving animal skins. In the winter of 1803, Jefferson sent Lewis to Philadelphia for further training with several of the most learned members of the American Philosophical Society. In addition, Lewis met with Benjamin Rush, the best physician in the United States, for some basic medical training.

Even with this extra tutelage, Jefferson's instructions were too much for one man to carry out. After consulting with the president, Meriwether Lewis sent a letter to his former commanding officer, William Clark, asking if Clark would co-command the expedition. Clark was an ideal choice: He was an experienced field commander (Lewis had never had his own command); had been trained in surveying (not cartography, as is sometimes reported); and was an experienced waterman who had grown up along the Ohio River (Lewis was a planter from Virginia).

When Clark received the offer, he immediately accepted. Not only did the letter from Lewis paint the expedition in glowing terms, but it also gave Clark the chance to get away from his aging older brother George Rogers Clark, noted general of the American Revolution, whose personal affairs the younger Clark had been trying to straighten out for some time.

Further simplifying the exploration was the United States' purchase of the Louisiana Territory from France in 1803. The purchase comprised most of the land between the Mississippi River and to the Rocky Mountains, but it did not include most of present-day Texas. Spain was none too pleased with the sale. Although the French legally controlled the territory, it had been in the hands of Spain until 1800, when a treaty returned control to France. However, the Spanish still were running day-to-day operations in the territory and felt that if France was going to sell the Louisiana Territory, Spain should have had the first chance to purchase it. Regardless of the Spanish position, however, the purchase was good news for Jefferson: the expedition would be doing most of its traveling on land "owned" by the United States. There was, however, an important question to be answered.

Who owned the area from the Rockies to the Pacific Ocean, particularly the region known as the Pacific Northwest (the present-day states of Washington, Oregon, Idaho, western Montana, and the Canadian province of British Columbia)? Several countries could claim ownership: Britain, Spain, and Russia all had potential interests there. Britain and

Russia had trading posts in the Pacific Northwest, and Spain had explored the area. Although Pacific Ocean trading provided an economic incentive to take control, none of these countries assumed a dominant role. This left the door open for the United States, but Jefferson's expedition would have to reach the Pacific Ocean, then return home and present their report before the president could take further steps to add the land in the Pacific Northwest to the United States.

The exploration party, called the Corps of Discovery, numbered approximately forty-five men. It left St. Louis on May 14, 1804, under the command of William Clark. Jefferson's hand-picked leader, Meriwether Lewis, remained in St. Louis to finish up last-minute business. Lewis joined the rest of the group a few days later in St. Charles, about twenty-five miles upriver.

The group traveled by keelboat, a type of river barge fifty to sixty feet long and about eight feet across, commonly used during the time period. Additionally, two oversized canoes, known as pirogues, were paddled upriver by a dozen French *engagés* (hired rivermen). The pirogues would replace the keelboat after the expedition reached the Mandan native villages, where the Missouri River was known to be too shallow for a large keelboat.

After leaving St. Louis and before reaching the Mandan villages in October 1804, the Corps of Discovery made contact with several native tribes, including the Missouris, Omahas, Yankton Sioux, Teton Sioux, and Arikaras. The atmosphere at the councils held between the white explorers and the natives was friendly at best and nonconfrontational at worst. Only the meeting with the Teton Sioux in September 1804, near present-day Pierre, South Dakota, presented major difficulties, however; the Teton Sioux controlled that particular geographic section of the Missouri River and demanded a toll from Lewis and Clark for the expedition to pass along the river. The captains refused and a standoff ensued. After four tense days, the situation was resolved when the captains paid the token toll of some tobacco. No blood was spilled, but much of the fault for this potentially expedition-ending conflict fell on Lewis and Clark and their lack of understanding of native protocol.

Meriwether Lewis as portrayed in a painting by C. W. Peale in Independence Hall, Philadelphia. (Library of Congress)

A C. W. Peale watercolor painting of William Clark, who started the expedition on May 14, 1804. (Library of Congress)

The expedition spent the winter of 1804–1805 among the Mandan and Hidatsa tribes and added three new members: Toussaint Charbonneau, his Shoshone wife Sacagawea, and their baby Jean-Baptiste, born during the winter. On April 7, 1805, the Corps of Discovery, now numbering thirty-three, continued up the Missouri River in the two pirogues and six dugout canoes, while the keelboat returned to St. Louis with a small detachment of soldiers, official reports, natural history specimens, and two soldiers who had been court-martialed and dismissed from the expedition.

After their journey through the northern plains of present-day North Dakota and Montana, the Corps of Discovery reached the Great Falls of the Missouri in June 1805. The Mandan and Hidatsa natives spoke of a one-day portage around the falls. As it turned out, the eighteen-mile portage took more than three weeks. The group endured sweltering temperatures, torrential rains, hail, and grizzly bears during the ordeal, but they survived.

Following the portage, the group traveled south along the Missouri and eventually arrived at its headwaters. Sacagawea's people, the Shoshones, lived just south of this region in the vicinity of present-day Dillon, Montana, and Tendoy, Idaho. It was essential for the expedition to make contact with this tribe: the Shoshones had horses, which were needed to cross the Rocky Mountains.

TURNING POINT

After several failed attempts, the expedition finally made contact in August 1805. The Shoshones, as it turned out, lived in fear of other Great Plains tribes and hid in the mountains. War parties had taken many Shoshone women and children as prisoners and incorporated them into enemy tribes, and Sacagawea came to live with the Hidatsas after one of these raids. Because of the danger from neighboring tribes, the Shoshones could not hunt with any great frequency and were undernourished, a condition that would soon affect the members of the Corps of Discovery.

In order to reach the Pacific Ocean, the Corps of Discovery needed to make its way to the Columbia River drainage, which lay on the western side of the Rocky Mountains. Horses would carry the group and their most important gear over the mountains; nonessential items, along with a supply of gunpowder, were buried in caches before the crossing. With Sacagawea's help, Lewis and Clark were able to trade with the Shoshone for the required number of horses. Some of the animals were of marginal quality, but the Salish natives, who would swap some of the expedition's poorer horses for others of superior quality, would alleviate this problem as the expedition traveled northward from the Shoshone homeland.

The corps planned to cross the mountains on the Nez Percé buffalo route, also known as the Lolo Trail, which had been used by the Nez Percé for centuries on their annual trek to the Plains to hunt buffalo. Lewis and Clark asked their Shoshone hosts if any among them had ever traveled on this route. One man, whom the captains referred to as "Toby" in their journals, had done so years before, and along with his son, agreed to serve as guides for the expedition.

Although the problem of a guide was solved, the problem of a stable food supply remained. The availability of game had decreased significantly as the Corps of Discovery had made its way into the land of the Shoshones. The Shoshone informed Lewis and Clark that the mountains contained little, if any, game. The chance of starvation during the crossing was a real possibility. Among the horses Lewis and Clark acquired were three colts, which were to be used for food if all else failed.

After leaving the Shoshone homeland and traveling north, the expedition almost immediately got lost, but Toby rediscovered the trail and crossed what Lewis and Clark named Lost Trail Pass. Once over the pass, the northbound journey along the Bitterroot River was relatively uneventful, save for the meeting with the Salish. With the Bitterroot Range of the Rocky Mountains always in view to the west, the expe-

A Shoshone chief. The Shoshone provided guides for the expedition. (Library of Congress)

dition was keenly aware of the journey ahead. The group made camp at a location dubbed Traveler's Rest. Hunters were sent out, but they returned with little game. Preparations were made for the mountain crossing.

Having fought the elements and won during the Great Falls portage, the Lewis and Clark Expedition would be facing greater foes this time: mountains, starvation, and—though they did not know it while camped at Traveler's Rest—a rare early-September snow. If the expedition was overpowered by the Rocky Mountains, the United States would have little claim to the Pacific Northwest, and Britain, Russia, and Spain could remain the major forces in the region for many years to come.

ACTUAL HISTORY

The expedition walked along Lolo Creek, climbed to Lolo Pass (on today's Idaho-Montana border), and then descended the west slope along the Lochsa ("rough water" in the Nez Percé language) River. Food supplies had dwindled to almost nothing. The three colts had been killed for the party's nourishment, and the group had to eat candles made from buffalo tallow. The group then once again ascended to the ridgeline, and the snow began. As the need for food grew and the snow deepened, Clark agreed to take a small team to find the end of the mountains and, with any luck, a supply of game to feed the party. The remainder of the group followed under Lewis's command.

Clark and his men emerged from the mountains and almost immediately came upon a Nez Percé village. The Nez Percé gave their visitors dried salmon and roots. Clark's party ate heartily but paid the price: the oily salmon and the fibrous roots wreaked havoc on the men's digestive systems. Lewis and his party arrived two days later, but they ignored Clark's advice to not overindulge in the abundant food. As a result, the entire party—except for Sacagawea—was ill for a week. The Nez Percé did not kill the group, even though doing so would have been simple: too sick to defend themselves, the expedition was an easy target. The natives would have been able to take possession of the arms and ammunition the men carried. These guns would have given them a great advantage over Blackfoot groups that regularly harassed the Nez Percé on their annual journey to the Great Plains to hunt buffalo with the Salish.

The expedition survived thanks to the only member of the tribe who had previously had contact with Europeans. Watkuweis, an older woman, had been taken prisoner by a rival tribe when she was much younger (a situation identical to Sacagawea's story of how she came to live with the Hidatsas). She was freed by two Canadian men and eventually made her way back to her homeland. Watkuweis instructed her people that when the white men came, the Nez Percé should do them no harm. Thus the first major contact between the Nez Percé and whites was exceptionally friendly. Two of the chiefs offered to serve as guides as well as keep the expedition's horses until the Corps of Discovery returned in the spring.

After recovering, the corps descended to the Clearwater River, built canoes, and began to head downstream for the first time since leaving St. Louis. Following the Clearwater to the Snake River, and then the Snake to the Columbia River, the Corps of Discovery made friendly contact with many tribes related (by language) to the Nez Percé, including the Yakimas and the Walla Wallas. The two chiefs left the group once the expedition moved into territory down the Columbia that was occupied by tribes unrelated and unfriendly to the Nez Percé.

In November, the expedition reached the Pacific Ocean. The group remained near the coast for the winter of 1805–1806, at their winter quarters, Fort Clatsop, named for their Clatsop native neighbors. The chosen location, on the south side of the Columbia River in present-day Oregon, was selected because of easy access to fresh water and a good food supply (a large herd of elk). The weather that winter mainly consisted of rain. According the journals, there were only twelve days with no rain during the time the Corps of Discovery spent at Fort Clatsop. The daily hunting party wanted to endure as little of the rain as possible, and so killed the elk closest to the fort first. This meant that as the winter progressed and the rain continued to fall, the hunters had to travel farther and farther for food. As the hunting became more difficult and the members of the expedition tired of eating elk for every meal, another food source was needed. Once again, Native Americans came to aid the Corps of Discovery, trading salmon and domestic dog (a traditional food source for the natives of the area) with the expedition.

On March 23, 1806, the corps began its eastbound journey. Because of the fierce rapids on the upper Columbia River, the group traveled primarily on foot. Along the upper Columbia, the expedition once again made contact with the Walla Walla tribe. Because of their haste to reach the Pacific, Lewis and Clark had declined an invitation to stay for a few days, but they promised a visit on the return trip. At the time of their arrival, the Corps of Discovery was once again low on food. They had nothing left to trade, except their knowledge of medicine: on their brief stop with the Walla Wallas the previous fall, Clark had treated one of the natives who complained of sore eyes. Upon the expedition's return, it seemed that the entire village had learned of the efficacy of the eyewash in the expedition's medical kit. A few drops of the liquid for each patient was exchanged for food for the entire party.

Upon returning to the Nez Percé village, the Corps of Discovery found their native friends to be as good as their word. Almost all of the expedition's horses were still there. Furthermore, the Nez Percé offered to send guides to lead the group back over the mountains. It had taken eleven days to cross the mountains on the westbound trip. With the guides, the eastbound crossing was made in six days.

The decision to divide the Corps of Discovery into smaller groups to gather additional information about the region had been made during the winter at Fort Clatsop. The bulk of the party traveled with Clark to explore the Yellowstone River. One small group unearthed the caches of goods buried before the westward crossing of the Rocky Mountains and traveled back along the Missouri River. And one group of four, commanded by Lewis, explored an area in present-day Montana twenty to thirty miles east of the land that is now Glacier National Park. This time, the contact with the natives almost proved fatal to Lewis and his party. From his discussions with the Mandans, Hidatsas, and Shoshones, Lewis knew that he was headed into Blackfoot territory, and these natives had a reputation for indiscriminate killing. Still, after meeting a few members of the Blackfoot tribe, Lewis and his men camped with them. During the night, one of the natives tried to steal a rifle and another tried to drive off the group's horses. A fight broke out; one of the Blackfoot men was stabbed to death, and Lewis shot another. Lewis and his men managed to ride to safety, meeting the small group that was returning along the Missouri River. This combined group met Clark's party near the confluence of the Yellowstone and Missouri rivers.

A Blackfoot Native American: Lewis's encounter with the Blackfeet proved fatal. (Library of Congress)

Jefferson had been explicit in his instructions to Lewis regarding the treatment of natives who were going to be encountered along the journey. He had instructed Lewis to treat the Native Americans with kindness and to avoid violence at all costs. The expedition's safety was Jefferson's primary concern, but he also wanted to bring the natives under American influence, since the British, French, and Spanish had influenced the native tribes for well over a century. In the report that Lewis sent from Fort Mandan in the spring of 1805, Jefferson would have learned of the conflict with the Teton Sioux. Lewis's conduct in the situation with the

Mandan Native Americans helped resupply the Lewis and Clark expedition. (Library of Congress)

Blackfeet was far more serious. By taking just four men into known hostile territory, Lewis had risked the lives of those with him. Furthermore, he had been involved in a violent incident that could have been completely avoided had the entire Corps of Discovery stayed together as a single unit.

The expedition stopped at the Mandan villages, where it reunited with the Mandans and Hidatsas who had supplied Lewis and Clark with detailed information about the region to the west during the winter of 1804–1805. After a friendly reunion came unwelcome news: the peace that Lewis had negotiated between several of the area tribes had fallen apart just days after the Corps of Discovery left in April 1805.

During their return journey along the Missouri, the Corps of Discovery encountered many American traders and trappers on the Missouri River. The reports sent back from Fort Mandan in 1805 had circulated: the Louisiana Territory was a trapper's paradise. Settlers would follow in the coming decades, driving the Native Americans from their lands in the Great Plains and the west.

The Corps of Discovery arrived in St. Louis exactly six months after leaving Fort Clatsop. In their report to Jefferson, Lewis and Clark had to admit failure. They had not accomplished their primary objective: to find an all-water route across the continent (the Northwest Passage), but they had found the most practical route.

A Bicentennial commemorative map of the Lewis & Clark expedition produced by the U.S. government. (NGS/NOAA)

After Jefferson's presidency, the War of 1812, and a treaty with Britain in 1819 (which did not address the issue of natives already living in the region), the Pacific Northwest was in the hands of the United States. Events in the eastern part of the country would have enormous consequences for the natives in the eastern United States. In 1830, President Andrew Jackson implemented his policy of removal: all natives east of the Mississippi River were relocated to Oklahoma.

The western natives fared no better. Mid-nineteenth century treaties, both legitimate and fraudulent, drove Nez Percé and Salish from much of their home territory. The first governor of the Washington Territory, Isaac Stevens, was the principal force behind these treaties. Stevens sought a route for a transcontinental railroad between Minnesota and the Washington Territory, and his relentless pressure on the natives included threats and bribery. Stevens's ultimate prize was the "purchase" of native lands in present-day Oregon, Washington, and Idaho for three cents per acre. When white settlers arrived to areas guaranteed to native tribes by treaties, the settlers immediately broke the agreements.

The tension between whites and natives continued for two decades, until 1877. In that year, an attack (based on faulty information) was launched by U.S. military forces on a group of nontreaty Nez Percé, led by Chief Joseph, that was peacefully moving to a reservation. Joseph's group retreated north and east toward Canada and mounted a counteroffensive at Big Hole (in Montana), but they eventually surrendered. By this time, there was nothing left of the positive initial contact with the Nez Percé made by Lewis and Clark seven decades earlier.

The British had signed a treaty giving the United States possession of present-day Washington and Oregon. The Russians and the Spanish,

IN CONTEXT   William Clark and Andrew Jackson

In the actual history, thirty-five-year-old Meriwether Lewis committed suicide in 1809, but William Clark had a long career in government service until his death in 1838 (at the age of sixty-nine). One of Clark's jobs was head of the Bureau of Indian Affairs. He held this post during the presidency of Andrew Jackson, meaning that Clark was in charge of implementing Jackson's policy of removal of Native Americans. Although it is not known for certain, this situation may have been quite troubling for Clark.

He had acquired a reputation as an even-handed native agent and was called "The Red-Headed Chief" by some tribes in the Great Plains—a compliment indeed.

In the alternate history, William Clark perishes during the journey. Clark would have had no career in public service. This begs the question: how would someone else have treated the Native Americans? Would their complaints have gotten a hearing at all, let alone a fair one?

---

however, appeared to pose potential threats to sovereignty. Russian patterns of settlement and Spanish economic practices prevented these threats from materializing. The Russians never amassed large populations in their settlements in Alaska, Washington, Oregon, and California. Total Russian populations numbered in the hundreds, not thousands. In the mid-nineteenth century, Russia transferred control of Alaska to the United States. Perhaps, like Napoleon, the Russians foresaw the expansion of the U.S. population into the unoccupied regions.

The economy of Spain revolved around the Spanish Crown. All colonial revenue (including plunder, in the form of gold and silver) was sent to the king. The Spanish army represented the Crown's interest. With no incentive for private ventures, permanent settlers never arrived in any great numbers. Although the Spanish had been the first to thoroughly explore the Pacific Northwest coast, they were not a factor in the region's final settlement. While Spanish cultural influence continues into the twenty-first century, Spain's dominant position as a world power was severely diminished by the nineteenth century.

In the end, the U.S. population's continuing growth required much more land than that purchased by Jefferson. Native Americans paid the ultimate price, however. European settlers during the Early Colonial era frequently took land from the native people; they labored under the false assumption that the natives were not using the land to its fullest potential. While the rationalizations changed, the result did not: the native populations were pushed, pulled, and squeezed from their lands, activity that had a detrimental effect on Native American culture.

Though Native American culture had nearly vanished—even from some reservations—it is now undergoing a revival. By the end of the twentieth century, many reservations had instituted programs to teach traditional native language, rituals, and crafts to their young people. Elders of each nation, who in some cases were the last to learn the traditional ways, often served as instructors. The recovery of ancestral lands has been a continuing uphill battle, but there is the realization among these nations that native culture must not only persist but also thrive.

ALTERNATE HISTORY

If the Lewis and Clark Expedition had never reached the Pacific Ocean and had not returned safely to St. Louis, the final story of westward expansion would read much differently. The outcome in the twenty-first century would most likely be similar (but not identical), but the process of Northwest settlement would have taken much longer. Without a strong claim to the Oregon Territory, the United States might never have acquired parts of the region.

After crossing Lolo Pass and descending to the Lochsa River, Lewis and Clark would have led the party back up to the ridgeline. Having eaten the last of the three colts purchased from the Shoshone natives, the group would have had virtually no food left. The snow would have begun and grown heavier, and the trail would have been nearly impossible to follow. The packhorses would have lost their footing, and several would have tumbled down the steep slope. Valuable ammunition would have been lost, including extra rifles. The cold would have begun to take its toll on the men. Hungry and tired, many of the soldiers could not have kept marching and would have collapsed in the snow, where they would have died of exposure. Over the next two days, Lewis, Clark, and Sacagawea would have all met the same fate. Sergeant John Ordway and the few others remaining would have died the next day.

After the snow melted in the late spring of 1806, the Nez Percé would have begun their annual trip east across the mountains. Once in present-day Montana, they would have joined the Salish and hunted buffalo in the Great Plains. As they began their journey, the Nez Percé would have come upon the bodies of Ordway and the last survivors. Taking the rifles, sidearms, and ammunition, the natives would have continued their trek. As they proceeded, the Nez Percé would have found the other members of the expedition and their weapons. The dead packhorses would also have been spotted and relieved of their cargo. The Nez Percé would have completed the mountain crossing and met the Salish.

After hearing of how the Nez Percé acquired the weapons, the Salish would have replied that these were most likely the white men that they had encountered and traded with the previous fall. Their common enemy, the Blackfeet, would then have had to show respect, given the new arsenal acquired by the Nez Percé. A test of the guns would have perhaps shown that only 70 percent of them still worked, but the Blackfeet would not have known that. All of the weapons would have been carried openly, as a deterrent to an attack. The bluff would probably have worked, and the Blackfeet would have ceased their harassment of the two tribes.

As a consequence of this freedom, the Nez Percé and the Salish would have been able to hunt more successfully and for a longer period of time. Both groups would have seen an improvement in their diet and overall health, which in turn would have led to larger populations of Nez Percé and Salish. The sheer numbers of these tribes would have kept the Blackfeet away, guns or no guns.

News of the fate of the Corps of Discovery would have reached Jefferson in Washington, D.C., in the fall of 1806. By the end of his second term, Jefferson would have presided over two failed westward explorations: In actual history, Zebulon Pike's journey into the southern portion of the Louisiana Territory was also unsuccessful. Pike was captured by the Spanish, and although he was freed, his journals were confiscated.

The Spanish would have been pleased by the news that the explorers of the Corps of Discovery had died. In actual history, after the expedition left St. Louis in May of 1804, the Spanish—who were still upset over not being given a chance to purchase the Louisiana Territory—sent two different groups of soldiers to kill Lewis, Clark, and the rest of the men. Both missions failed. Still, Spain would not have aggressively tried to win control of the Louisiana Territory from the United States. Had Spain seized the opportunity and brought strong military force to bear on the Louisiana Territory, much of the region west of the Mississippi River would have likely remained in Spanish hands for decades. However, Spain would have maintained its policy of bringing few soldiers and fewer emigrants to North America.

Unlike the Salish, the Nez Percé would still have not made contact with whites by the time Andrew Jackson was elected president in 1828. Since the unsuccessful end of the Lewis and Clark Expedition, no exploration of the Pacific Northwest would have been attempted. The Louisiana Territory was, by Jackson's time, thoroughly explored and mapped. The Rocky Mountains were the biggest obstacle between the two sides of the country.

In 1830, Jackson implemented his policy of Native American removal, and at the same time he might have sent a military expedition to cross the Rockies to reach the Pacific coast. With no country in true control of present-day Oregon, Washington, and Idaho, Jackson would have seen a chance to establish the United States as sovereign, both politically and economically. Jackson would have wanted an estimate of native populations in the west, as well as an estimate of how much land would be needed to implement a similar removal policy in that region.

Unlike Jefferson, Jackson would not have cared if the soldiers traveled by land or water, but he would have cared about results. However, by that time, prior British expeditions and settlers would have weakened any claim by the United States to the territory. Without Lewis and Clark's rich descriptions of the resources of the area, mountain men from the American West would have been less likely to conduct independent exploration and establish private fur-trading stations and private forts in the region. In a broader sense, the two failed expeditions might have somewhat disillusioned the general American population about the idea of westward migration.

The British, who technically controlled the Oregon Territory, would have retained that control and would have been in stronger position to deny any claims made by the United States to the territory. Thus when President James Polk sought to make claims on the territory in the 1840s, he would have had fewer arguing points, and the

British would have been able to retain all of the territory, not just the section above the 49th parallel that they continued to control in actual history. With British control of the more than 288,000 square miles that are now the states of Washington, Oregon, Idaho, and the western part of Montana, those regions would have become several provinces of Canada, probably with different names. Presuming that the United States and Mexico fought the same war that occurred in actual history, Mexico would have ceded the same territories to the United States, including lands now occupied by California, Arizona, New Mexico, Nevada, Utah, and about half of Colorado. The question of slavery in the newly acquired territories would have continued to be the focus of North-South disagreement and for attempts at compromise in Congress, regardless of the fact that the Pacific Northwest remained in British control.

During the Civil War, officers and some troops from Washington and Oregon fought on the Union side (in actual history). If the British controlled the Pacific Northwest, these officers and troops would not have been available to fight in specific battles, and this might have affected the outcome of several engagements in the war. However, since such participation was in fact limited in scale, the overall outcome of the war would probably have not been affected.

Following the Civil War, Secretary of State William Seward would have been in a much weaker position to argue for the purchase of Alaska from the Russians. Although he might have attempted to do so, the bill authorizing funds for the purchase would have failed in Congress without support from representatives from Oregon and Washington. As a consequence, it is possible that the Russians would have retained Alaska for another decade or so, though they would probably have ceded it to Britain at some point in exchange for funds or diplomatic concessions.

With the 1897 Klondike discovery of gold in the Yukon Territory of Canada, the development of the lower panhandle of Alaska would have proceeded much as it did in actual history. In this alternate history, however, the international population of Chinese, Australians, Americans, and others would have been under British administration rather than American administration, and they would have become Canadian rather than American citizens. The total area of Alaska, including inland waters, is over 656,000 square miles, and this would have brought the Canadian total (with the Oregon Territory included) to about 4.8 million square miles. By contrast, the United States would occupy less than 2.6 million square miles if both the Oregon Territory and Alaska had become part of Canada.

Thus, by the early twentieth century, unified Canada would have been much larger in territory and population and would have been a much more economically powerful part of the British Empire. As an ally of Britain in World War I from August 1914, Canada would have provided even more economic assistance to the Allies in that war. Canadian troops from the western provinces would have participated on the Western Front and at Gallipoli in greater numbers. With the establishment of Dominion status following World War I, Canada,

IN CONTEXT The British in India

Experience in managing an empire had already taught Britain a lesson. After their defeat in the American Revolution, the British concentrated on building a new economic empire with India as its centerpiece. The same mercantilist principles that drove the triangular trade (Britain, America, and Africa) were reinvigorated into a Britain-India trade zone. The East India Company was chartered to control the day-to-day operations. Unlike the massive settlements in America, very few British went to India, thus leaving the problem of policy enforcement to locals. To that end, the company coerced and bribed Indians to join a mercenary army. The company became, in effect, India's de facto government, and India's people were subjugated to a foreign power. Officials within the East India Company were growing rich by skimming profits and setting up side businesses. After years of such abuses, the Crown and Parliament dissolved the company and took direct control of India. Administering India left little time for a concentrated effort in the Canadian Pacific Northwest. Thus, if the British had retained control of the Oregon Territory and later acquired Alaska, the development of the region would have followed the same patterns as the rest of Canada.

with its Alaskan and Pacific Northwest provinces, would have been an even more influential Pacific rim nation than it is in actual history. With major seaports in Seattle and Portland (cities that might have had different names under British and Canadian developments), with a timber export business, and with hydrodynamic electric power from the Columbia River providing sources of foreign exchange and revenue, the political balance of power within Canada would have shifted westward. With cattle ranching, apple and pear orchards, vineyards, and other crops, the region would have provided economic benefits, taxes, and a solid base for further population growth.

Given the fact that British Columbia is in fact the most politically liberal of the Canadian provinces, it is likely that Canadian politics would have shifted noticeably to the left during the 1930s and 1940s. Canada's very liberal immigration policies would have allowed the Pacific Northwest and Alaska to be populated with a different ethnic mix, drawn from all over the British Empire and other nations, so that the populations of Fairbanks, Anchorage, Sitka, Portland, Seattle, Tacoma, and other cities of the region would resemble those of Toronto and Vancouver. As the price of petroleum increased in the late twentieth century, Alaskan oil reserves would have made Canada a major oil producer, perhaps ameliorating the effect of OPEC on world oil prices.

Although settlement patterns and immigration policies would affect population growth and figures in ways that are difficult to predict, Canada would be home to many more people than it has in actual history. With provinces carved from Alaska and the Oregon Territory, Canadian population in the early twenty-first century might be about 44 million (rather than 33 million, as it is in actual history), while U.S. population might be around 284 million (rather than 295 million).

Without the territories of Alaska and the Pacific Northwest, the United States would also have been a somewhat different nation. Settlers and immigrants who moved to the Oregon Territory in the

1840s, 1850s, and later would perhaps have opted to move to California or other parts of the U.S. West instead. Some who moved west to become Oregon and Washington settlers in actual history would have remained at home and raised crops similar to those grown in the Midwest.

In 1898, during the Spanish-American war, the United States would have been less capable of naval operations in the Pacific without the naval facilities in the Puget Sound, perhaps not acquiring the Philippines and Hawaii. If the United States had not fought in the Pacific in that war, the country would have had less incentive to secure the Panama Canal, and it is likely that without aid from the United States, Panama would not have become independent from Colombia. Without the political influence of Washington and Oregon, some American national elections would have turned out differently, and the generally liberal influence of those states would have been missing. Tensions between the United States and Canada might very well have been much greater, and the two countries might have clashed over such issues as territorial disputes, labor union policies, and American concerns about threats from the political left during the 1920s and 1950s.

In many ways, Canadian control of the Oregon Territory and Alaska would have affected twentieth-century political, military, and economic events and developments. When the Manhattan Project developed the American nuclear weapon in World War II, the production reactors (needed to make plutonium) built at Hanford, Washington, (in actual history) would probably have been constructed elsewhere, most likely in California. During World War II, Canadian aid to Russia might have been as significant or even more significant than American aid and would have included regular flights via Alaska. The Alcan highway, which was built by the U.S. Army Corps of Engineers in World War II (in actual history), would have been constructed by the Canadians to provide for Canadian defense of Alaska against Japanese threats. Twentieth-century corporations such as Olympia Beer, Boeing, Starbucks, Weyerhaeuser, and Microsoft might never exist, and if they did they would have developed along entirely different lines and in different locations. In addition to North Slope petroleum, Canadian export items would include Tillamook Cheese, Hood River Apples, Alaskan king crabs, high-quality plywood, and Northwest canned salmon.

Paul A. Sivitz

Discussion Questions

1. Without the claims established by Lewis and Clark, the United States might have tried to rely on the fact that John Jacob Astor had developed a trading post at the mouth of the Columbia River to make a claim to Oregon during Polk's administration. Which activity provided more justification in claiming territory: priority of exploration or trade? If Lewis and Clark had been killed by Native Americans

during their exploration, how do you think that might have affected European American attitudes toward the native population in the early nineteenth century? Would it have led to greater hostility or to greater respect?

2. If Canada existed today with provinces in Alaska and the former Oregon Territory, exactly how would the boundaries of the United States and Canada look?

3. How would Canadian-American relations differ today if the two countries had evolved along the lines suggested in this alternate history?

4. How would the absence of the Oregon Territory as open to American settlers have affected Manifest Destiny? Would the westward movement and the myth of the American West have been as influential in American culture as it was in actual history? To what extent do you think disillusionment in westward migration might have hampered the settlement of California?

Bibliography and Further Reading

Allen, John Logan. *Lewis and Clark and the Image of the American Northwest*. Mineola, NY: Dover, 1975.

Ambrose, Stephen E. *Undaunted Courage: Meriwether Lewis, Thomas Jefferson, and the Opening of the American West*. New York: Simon & Schuster, 1996.

Cronon, William. *Changes in the Land: Indians, Colonists, and the Ecology of New England*. New York: Hill & Wang, 1983.

Josephy, Alvin M. *The Nez Perce Indians and the Opening of the Northwest*. Boston: Mariner Books/Houghton Mifflin, 1997.

Moulton, Gary E. *The Lewis and Clark Journals: An American Epic of Discovery*. Lincoln: University of Nebraska Press, 2003.

Richter, Daniel K. *Facing East from Indian Country: A Native History of Early America*. Cambridge, MA: Harvard University Press, 2001.

Ronda, James P. *Lewis and Clark among the Indians*. Lincoln: Bison Books/University of Nebraska Press, 1988.

Taylor, Alan. *American Colonies*. New York: Penguin Books, 2002.

TURNING POINT

During the War of 1812, the British burned and then left Washington, D.C. What if they had remained and the American capital was relocated to New York City?

INTRODUCTION

In the decades immediately following the Revolutionary War, two principal trends defined American foreign policy: the need to be recognized as a sovereign nation by other countries and expansion across the frontier. Britain presented itself as an obstacle in both instances, and the Anglo-American conflict led to several skirmishes and incidents before coming to a head in the War of 1812, which was declared in June and fought until 1815. It remains one of the only major wars the United States has lost, and it seems little remembered, except for the composition of the "Star-Spangled Banner."

The 1783 Treaty of Paris had ended the Revolutionary War, and while its primary purpose had been to recognize American independence, it also established boundaries between the United States and British North America (the Dominion of Canada and the colony of Newfoundland; Florida was ceded to Spain) and access to bodies of water (fishing rights, for instance, and access to the Mississippi River for transport). Although Vermont had established itself as the Vermont Republic in 1777 and had dealt diplomatically with both the United States and Britain as that entity, the boundaries drawn up in the Treaty of Paris implied that Vermont would be considered part of the United States—and eight years later it became the fourteenth state without fuss.

But recognizing independence is not the same thing as acting accordingly. Britain never surrendered its forts in western North America (as it promised to do in the Treaty of Paris), and the continued illegal presence of such a powerful enemy made Americans nervous, as did their suspicions that the British were arming the Native Americans of the northwest and encouraging them in anti-American violence. Worse and more disruptive was the behavior of the British Royal Navy and Britain's naval policies during the Napoleonic Wars.

During the wars between France and Britain that straddled the end of the eighteenth and first two decades of the nineteenth centuries, Americans

IN CONTEXT   The Napoleonic Wars

In contrast to the American Revolution, the French Revolution of a decade later was messily unsuccessful. The French Revolution was fought not against an external power but between factions in France; the French Revolution saw drastic changes wrought by the National Constituent Assembly. A feudal monarchy with strong ties to the Catholic Church—outside of Italy, no country had been more important to the history of the Catholic Church than France—France found itself stripped of its monarchy, its nobles and aristocrats, and even its Christian ties, as the clergy lost any special privileges and Church property was confiscated. The violence and extreme changes of the Revolution made it wildly unpopular with the rest of Europe and led directly to war with Austria and Britain.

Out of these wars came Napoleon Bonaparte, a successful general who became first consul—and later emperor—of France in the coup that overthrew the revolutionary Republic. The wars continued without pause, though the period we call the Napoleonic Wars was specifically expansionist. The wars were marked by the first major use of mass conscription and newly advanced artillery—in some sense, then, the Napoleonic Wars can be considered a nineteenth-century world war. The French resented the Jay Treaty, which took the attitude that "the friend of my enemy is my enemy"; this treaty led to the so-called Quasi-War, an undeclared war fought from 1798 to 1801 in which French warships and privateers attacked American merchants and seized their goods.

Because the division between the French Revolutionary Wars and the Napoleonic Wars is somewhat arbitrary, the period is sometimes collectively referred to as the "Great French War"; it lasted twenty-three years.

almost universally supported noninterventionist policies; as a young, nearly newborn, nation, the United States was concerned first with its own organization and economy. The Eleventh and Twelfth Amendments to the Constitution were made in this time, and they clarified the federal judicial and electoral systems. It is significant that the Constitution would not be amended again until the abolition of slavery sixty years later: these early amendments were adjustments to the structure of government based on the rough draft provided by the Constitution. America was still finding itself and strove for neutrality in foreign affairs—as long as its rights were protected.

Where America's two political parties disagreed was in the means to this end, and the War of 1812 would be their final dispute. The Federalists, who were in power in these early years, followed President George Washington's example: preserve the peace by being ready for war and espouse a pro-British foreign policy. The Jay Treaty, named for Chief Justice John Jay, was a Federalist attempt to assuage Anglo-American wounds during Washington's second term. While some reparations were made for British confiscations during the Revolution, impressment was not even addressed, a problem that spurred pro-France Thomas Jefferson—future president and Washington's secretary of state—to form the Republican Party (later called the Democratic-Republican Party; now the Democratic Party).

Impressment, which angered so many Americans, was the British practice of taking sailors from American ships at sea—ostensibly British citizens in American employ, but often Americans unable to prove they were not British subjects—for the thinning ranks of the Royal Navy. As the Napoleonic Wars heated up, impressment became a bigger problem—and the Jay Treaty inadvertently contributed to the problem. As improved trade between Britain and the United States bolstered the American economy (exports tripled over the next seven years), merchant ships suffered a shortage of labor. Even more British subjects found work with American ships, and this gave the Royal Navy even more of a reason to forcibly board them in press gangs. The American ships so boarded were often left with dangerously small crews on the high seas and sometimes lacked critical personnel. The United States issued certificates of citizenship in 1796 to protect these sailors, but to little effect.

In 1801, the Republicans took office: Jefferson was elected president, and a number of his political allies were elected to Congress. Reversal of Federalist policies was an explicit goal, along with financial and budget reforms. Jefferson was also the first president to begin his presidency in the White House, which finished construction at the end of 1800, ten years after Washington, D.C., was established as the national capital (the city was created as a federal district unaffiliated with any state and placed roughly between the industrial North and agrarian South). In 1806, Jefferson rejected another treaty that failed to end impressment: the Monroe-Pinkney Treaty, named for diplomats William Pinkney and future president James Monroe. The treaty offered little concession to the United States but promised to end the commercial sanctions the American government had called for in response to impressment and other problems. Jefferson rejected it out of hand, not even bothering to submit it to the Senate.

The early nineteenth century, under the presidencies of Jefferson and his successor (and secretary of state) James Madison, was marked by increasingly violent conflicts between Britain and the United States. In 1807, shortly after the rejection of the Monroe-Pinkney Treaty, the British HMS *Leopard* encountered the USS *Chesapeake* at sea. The *Chesapeake* counted at least four Royal Navy deserters among its crew, and the *Leopard* demanded that a boarding party be allowed to retrieve them. When the *Chesapeake* refused, the *Leopard* opened fire and took its subjects back, inspiring enough outrage among the American people that Jefferson ordered all British ships out of American waters while waiting for the official British response. Britain did nothing but to disavow the attack, claiming it could not be held responsible for the actions of a single ship, and anti-British sentiment soared in the United States as a result. Four years later, in 1811—as a precursor to war, we might see it now—the USS *President* attacked the HMS *Little Belt* to deter it from impressments. Americans celebrated this as deferred revenge for the British attack on the *Chesapeake*.

By now, pro-war sentiment was high. Nearly a generation after the Treaty of Paris had been signed, Britain still treated the United States with too little respect for Americans' taste. The Federalists strongly opposed any talk of war and believed diplomatic solutions had not been explored thoroughly or competently enough; some Republicans agreed, but their voices would be lost in the cacophony of the Twelfth Congress.

The Twelfth Congress—the "War Congress"—convened November 4, 1811. Republicans had overwhelming majorities in both houses—75 percent of the House seats and 82 percent of those in the Senate. They had in the past been hampered by factional differences within their party. Some of these factions were more closely allied with the Federalists than the main body of their own party: the agrarian Old Republicans espousing simple and limited government, the northern Clintonians seeking greater trade protections, and the Invisibles, a small group of senators who favored military preparedness and were known for speaking out against President James Madison.

The War Congress also saw a new faction, the War Hawks, which included freshman Representative Henry Clay of Kentucky, who was elected speaker of the House. Influenced by Clay's charisma and intelligence, the War Hawks dominated the House in practice if not in numbers, as Clay packed the most relevant committees—such as the Foreign Relations Committee—with representatives who sought war with Britain.

In late 1811, four years after the incident, the British finally agreed to settle the *Chesapeake* matter by paying reparations and returning two of the survivors to the United States (a third had died in the interim). Most Americans considered this to be too little too late. The following spring, the Royal Navy began exercising greater care in dealing with Americans, and several commanding officers ordered their ships to avoid the U.S. coast. That May, Britain offered to split with the United States its licenses for trading with the Continent, but by this point the United States did not want its economy to be so intricately involved with Britain, nor did it want to be viewed as one of Britain's trade partners in dealings with Europe. In June, two days before war was declared, Britain suspended the Orders in Council—and a week later the blockades and licenses were abolished. But it took weeks for this news to reach North America, by which time the War of 1812 was under way. In a message to Congress, President Madison indicted Britain for invading American waters, establishing illegal blockades under the auspices of the Orders in Council, attempting to subvert the Union, and instigating anti-American sentiment and actions among the Native Americans of the Northwest.

The Federalists united against the war once its specifics became clear—their hopes of including France in the conflict and of limiting it to naval battles had been ignored, their objections to a new tax system that disproportionately taxed the North overruled. The Federalists saw no point in a war against Canada, nor did they believe such land battles had any connection to the goal of ending Britain's illegal and unethical actions against the United States at sea. Many among the pro-war faction actually welcomed this opposition—it was, to them, evidence of Federalists' "Tory" tendencies, and their "traitorous" nature. The war, said this faction, would weed out anti-patriots.

Baltimore—the third-largest city in the nation, with some forty thousand people—was a particularly pro-war city, and anti-Federalist feelings ran high there. When Alexander Hanson, editor of the *Federal Republican* (a Federalist paper) and lieutenant in the militia, came out against the war, he knew there was a chance of violent reprisals. The next night, a crowd of hundreds of men tore apart the frame building housing the newspaper's offices, with little reaction from local law officers: rather than summon the militia, the mayor addressed individual members of the crowd personally, politely asking them to stop—and then went home. For

The 1813 Battle of Lake Erie, in which the Americans defeated the British and ensured control of the lake and the northwest. (Library of Congress)

his part, Hanson hired a Georgetown printer to print and ship the paper to Baltimore, and he resumed publication a month after the attack.

Once more the *Federal Republican* was targeted by pro-war mobs determined to permanently silence Hanson. It began with young boys gathered outside the new offices to throw stones at the building. They were joined by adults, who continued the assault until the windows and shutters were broken, and who taunted those inside, daring them to fire. A Federalist inside fired a warning shot, which scattered the crowd only long enough for them to retrieve their own weapons and reassemble under the urging of a local doctor, Thadeus Gale, who claimed (with no apparent reason or evidence) that the warning shot had been intended for him because of his pro-war views. Gale was killed when he and the mob stormed the doors, and the Republicans retreated but kept the building under siege until early the next morning, when the militia was finally called. By the time the mob was dispersed, with two dozen Federalists put in protective custody, the crowd of Republicans, Federalists, and onlookers had swelled to two thousand—or 5 percent of the entire city population (and all of this before five in the morning).

Almost inevitably, the jail was stormed, and the Federalists were lynched. Nine were beaten for hours until they died, and their eyes filled with hot candle wax to make sure they were not "playing possum" (faking death). One of the Federalists, a Revolutionary War general, was stabbed repeatedly until he finally died while pleading for mercy. At the time, it was one of the most controversial incidents in American history. Only one man was found guilty of any charge related to the Baltimore riots, and he was issued a modest fine.

The support for the war was not nearly as passionate as the opposition to anti-war factions. Military enlistment was low, and the rate of desertion was high (enough that Madison, in a desperate attempt to rebuild some of the ranks, was forced to offer pardons to any deserters who returned within four months). Conditions were terrible—to save costs, the commissaries were eliminated and the task of feeding troops fell to third-party contractors, who made their own profits by providing food of such low quality that rancid, rotting meat was shipped, and there were reports of excrement being found in bread. To attract men, pay and bonuses for soldiers skyrocketed to the point that, as a signing bonus, a new recruit was given over 300 acres of land and as much money as an unskilled laborer could expect to make in a year (in addition to wages competitive with labor jobs).

TURNING POINT

Although many—especially the Federalists—hoped the war would be largely, if not exclusively, fought at sea, the war was bound to come to land, even without the attempted conquest of Canada. The Canadian campaign was hampered from the start by the same sort of overconfidence that led Napoleon to invade Russia, albeit of a lesser magnitude: ex-President Jefferson predicted seizing control of Canada would be nothing but "a matter of marching," and many Congressmen believed they would be welcomed with open arms by Canadians eager to join the republic. The mission was not nearly as easy—or successful—as anticipated, and the United States suffered multiple incursions by northwest Native Americans allied with the British as well as the British occupation of Detroit. The Americans finally surrendered to a significantly smaller British force at the Battle of Beaver Dams, ending much of the attempt at Canadian conquest.

In the east, the British occupied Maine—then the northernmost district of Massachusetts—and remained there until war's end, the largest territory of prolonged occupation throughout the war. But it is the Chesapeake campaign and the destruction of Washington, D.C., that are the best remembered of Britain's attacks. The Chesapeake campaign began with the Battle of Craney Island on June 22, 1813, when seven hundred British soldiers attacked and were defeated by a smaller force at Craney Island off the coast of Virginia. The British commander, Admiral George Cockburn, was then defeated again further up the bay at the shipyards of St. Michaels, Maryland, but he persevered.

In Europe, Napoleon's defeat and exile to Elba had freed up British troops to be sent to the North American lines for the planned invasion of

A drawing of the U.S. Capitol after British attempts to burn it during the War of 1812. (Library of Congress)

the United States. The United States considered Baltimore, not Washington, D.C. (a minor port of less than ten thousand people, despite its significance to the federal government), the most important target, and so focused their defenses there. General William Winder was charged with the defense of Washington, D.C., positioning himself at the nearby town of Bladensburg. While he had at his command more troops than the advancing British forces, he was handily defeated—he had given no instructions for retreat or regrouping, and so his militia retreated in all directions.

President Madison, meanwhile, fled to a nearby town with his cabinet; his wife, Dolley, gathered valuables from the White House—not personal items but those of historic significance. Unopposed, the British army entered Washington, D.C. Baltimore, though, was not far away—the commander of the British ground troops, General Robert Ross, did not believe he had enough men at his disposal to occupy the city, so he destroyed it instead in revenge for the Americans' burning and pillaging of York (now Toronto) earlier in the year. Cockburn approved, believing the effect on both military and civilian morale would be staggering.

The buildings housing the Senate and House of Representatives were burned, along with the Library of Congress, the Treasury, and many other public buildings. Dolley Madison escaped from the White House literally moments before the British arrived to burn it to the ground—though the thick sandstone walls survived. Superintendent of Patents William Thornton convinced the British to spare the Patent Office because of the technological importance of patent documents not simply to a government but to the world's scientific community—but in the rest of the city, more fuel was added to the fires, and they might have burned for days had thunderstorms and tornadoes not put them out the next day.

A cartoon depicts British King George III getting a bloody nose from U.S. President James Madison. (Library of Congress)

ACTUAL HISTORY

The British continued north to Baltimore, with Ross leading the ground attack at North Point, where he was killed in battle by an American sniper. His command fell to Colonel Arthur Brooke, who halted his advance two miles outside of Baltimore in anticipation of the sea campaign. The naval attack led by Vice Admiral Alexander Cochrane came at Fort McHenry on the Locust Point peninsula that juts into Baltimore Harbor.

The British fleet bombarded the fort with rockets and mortar shells, mostly from outside the range of McHenry's cannon fire. At night, after a day filled with explosions and bombardment, a landing party attempted to divert the American army away from the planned British land assault but failed. Francis Scott Key, a lawyer watching the battle while detained on a British ship, would write a poem about it that, when set to the music of the English song "To Anacreon in Heaven," became "The Star-Spangled Banner," which was adopted a century later as the national anthem. Brooke, meanwhile, withdrew his troops while Cochrane prepared the fleet for their next assault—the Battle of New Orleans.

With a population of twenty-five thousand people, New Orleans was the largest city west of the Appalachians and a major port then (as now). Its defense fell to General Andrew Jackson, an Indian fighter from

Tennessee who had spent much of the War of 1812 fighting the Creek War—a virtually unrelated conflict with the Creek tribe over land in Alabama. With the Creek War over, Jackson attacked Pensacola, Florida—a Spanish outpost that willingly housed British soldiers as they prepared for the Gulf Coast campaign. Jackson's 4,100 troops outnumbered Pensacola's eight to one, and he took the city with little more than a dozen casualties on both sides. Sure that the British would next strike Mobile (now in Alabama, then in West Florida), Jackson marched there, found it unthreatened, and advanced to New Orleans, which he found thoroughly unprepared.

Public funds had been raided and squandered, and the Louisiana and city governments had little money available. The citizenry—still largely a mix of French and Spanish settlers and their descendents—had little interest in the war, and a spirit of apathy and pessimism permeated the city. The charismatic and no-nonsense Jackson quickly attracted a great deal of attention and support as he set to work establishing the city's defenses and blocking the water entrances. The Baratarian pirates—who had previously been attacked by American naval forces but were probably willing to take any side if it meant fighting the British—volunteered to join with Jackson, and their leader, Jean Lafitte, became his unofficial aide-de-camp.

Determined to engage the British outside the city and before they were at full strength, Jackson, supported by two ships, led his troops in a surprise nighttime attack on an occupied plantation eight miles south of New Orleans on the Mississippi River. Although British reinforcements arrived the next day, their leaders had been too surprised by the attack to assess the Americans' numbers, and they failed to realize that the British had an advantage of manpower. Over the next week—Christmas 1814 through the new year—Jackson strengthened his defenses and established artillery batteries. The fighting was so intense that British reinforcements were told to bring more cannonballs with them, one in each soldier's knapsack, to replenish diminishing supplies—and when a boatload of these troops overturned on Lake Borgne, the soldiers inevitably sank to the bottom.

Despite these two weeks of fighting leading up to it, the true Battle of New Orleans did not occur until January 8, 1815, when the main British force attacked under cover of fog. The fog lifted before they made much progress, and though the British outnumbered the Americans, they were vastly outfought. Jackson's command was almost flawless—he lost only thirteen men, while another sixty Americans were killed under the command of other officers. The British suffered some 1,500 casualties, with another 500 captured—a staggeringly unbalanced result, especially given that their force was twice the size of the American force. Ironically, what no

Andrew Jackson, victor of the Battle of New Orleans. (Library of Congress)

The Battle of New Orleans in 1815, which was actually fought two weeks after the peace treaty was signed. (Library of Congress)

party could know was that on December 24—while Jackson prepared his nocturnal attack on the encroaching British—their respective governments had signed the Treaty of Ghent in Belgium. Even aside from the slow speed at which news traveled, though, the treaty needed to be ratified for the war to end, an event that occurred on February 17, 1815.

The Treaty of Ghent did nothing more than restore the *status quo ante bellum*—everything went back to the way it was. Boundaries were restored to their prewar limits, more or less—Maine and New Brunswick continued to dispute their boundary until the Aroostook War (1838–1839), and other minor adjustments were made in other regions. Frustratingly for the Americans, impressment still was not abolished—but with Napoleon in exile and the Napoleonic Wars drawing to a close, the issues that led the Royal Navy to seize British subjects from American ships were fading anyway. Nevertheless, to many it seemed that a prolonged and complicated war had been fought to no side's benefit.

However, even reestablishing the status quo was a gain for the United States, as an important aspect of that status quo—sovereignty and protection from European interference—had been in jeopardy. Although the War of 1812 did not bring the nation any new rights, it did bring new respect from the international community, and this bettered the chances of those rights being honored. The Battles of New Orleans and Baltimore strengthened American morale and patriotism—even those who opposed the war were pleased at how well American forces fared toward the end of it. The Army Corps of Engineers took over the responsibility of fortifying New Orleans as a result of the British attack there, and the corps continues to retain the responsibility for the levees and other related works in the city. Finally, a general feeling of professionalism had begun to pervade the military, especially among its officers, who had often been criticized by the British for being uncouth and disorganized.

In other words, what we might call a physical status quo was restored, but feelings of nationalism and unity increased in the United States. James Monroe succeeded James Madison as president, and his presidency extending through most of the Era of Good Feelings: a time when politics were actually *boring*, with virtually no partisan conflicts except over slavery, a fight that was subdued by Henry Clay's 1820 Missouri Compromise, in which slavery was prohibited in the Missouri Territory but allowed in the part of the territory that became the new state of Missouri. The Federalist Party did not survive long after the war, but the Whigs rose in support of a strong legislature over a strong presidency, and their members included famed lawyer and Congressman Daniel Webster.

The Monroe Doctrine—suggested by British Foreign Minister George Canning and supported by Jefferson—was adopted by Monroe in 1823 and forbade further colonizing activities by Europe in the Americas. The New World would now govern itself. As the most able nation in the New World, the United States appointed itself an unofficial protector, one that viewed any war with a sovereign nation in the Americas as a hostile action against the country. This was a huge step forward from the policies of the postconstitutional era leading up to the War of 1812; it was a dictating of terms by a sovereign nation, the United States, that had proved its ability to contend militarily with Europe.

The Era of Good Feelings ended with the election of 1824, when Jackson accused John Quincy Adams of winning the presidency through corrupt methods. Jackson's reputation as a war hero had been sealed, and the legend of the Tennessee Indian fighter now included pirates, sneak attacks, sinking British soldiers, and the hundreds of freed Haitian slaves who had fought at his side. He lost the 1824 election, in which no candidate received a majority of votes and the House of Representatives was required to choose between Jackson and Adams. Jackson's loss added to his image as a man of the people dogged by bureaucrats. Jackson won the 1828 election and transformed his party—the Republicans now (and to this day) better known as the Democratic Party. This newly refreshed party of Jacksonian Democrats was marked by a belief in the strength of the executive branch and the encouragement of public participation in government: not only was Jackson himself a strong proponent of voting rights and representation for all men regardless of property, but he also set a controversial example by appointing his supporters to important positions, a tactic he suggested would improve the common man's participation in politics by providing a motivation.

It was under Jackson that Congress passed the Indian Removal Act in 1830, which gave the president the power to (often unethically and coercively) negotiate treaties that relocated Native Americans to the West in exchange for their eastern tribal lands. The most famous of these is the Trail of Tears, the arduous 1838 journey taken by the Cherokee. More and more, the federal government began to treat Native Americans as foreigners, people whose positions could be shifted when they became inconvenient. The westward expansion into the territory acquired through the 1803 Louisiana Purchase and beyond led to the settlement of Kentucky, Utah, Oregon, and other future states—and to gold rushes, wars with Mexico, and the transcontinental railroad. The official borders of the country expanded, and European holdings were slowly but inexorably absorbed even as Mexico and Canada gained independence from Spain and Britain (in 1810 and 1867, respectively, although not until the Canada Act of 1982 did Canada gain the right to alter its own constitution, and Mexico's sovereignty was not recognized until 1821).

By 1853, most of the modern-day contiguous United States were under American control, even if they were not yet official states; Alaska was purchased from Russia in 1867, and Hawaii was annexed in 1898. Throughout the twentieth century, various islands were acquired as territories, and the Mexican border was adjusted twice—but we can essentially think of the modern-day United States reaching its geographical maturity by the end of the nineteenth century, just as the frontier closed in 1890. In part as a response to all this territorial expansion, the modern-day Republican Party formed in 1854 in opposition to the institution of slavery in new territories—though few sought to abolish the practice in existing states, at least at first. Abraham Lincoln was elected the first Republican president six years later, and two-thirds of American presidents since then have come from that party. Since the two current parties have persisted longer than any others in American history, modern American politics traces a good deal of its precedents to the Civil War and to Reconstruction.

Increased immigration reached enormous levels from the 1840s to the 1920s; it provided cheap labor in the northern industrial cities and helped to settle the sparsely populated western lands—while at the same time giving rise to the image of the United States as predominantly Anglo-American and putting still more distance between the United States and Britain. The influx of immigrants—and the development of faster transportation, communication, and national news syndicates—contributed to Americans' awareness of world events, and the late nineteenth and early twentieth centuries were marked by opposing views of foreign policy: the "new imperialism" quickly took hold and accounted for many of America's Pacific territories and wars. However, isolationism, the notion that Americans ought to deal only with their own country and leave foreign affairs alone, drew enough support that President Woodrow Wilson had considerable difficulty convincing the people to enter the Great War (now called World War I). The League of Nations, a precursor to the United Nations, likewise failed to entice the support of the American people.

The mingling of heritages created by immigration led to some problems. During World War I, many German Americans anglicized their names to avoid sticking out, sauerkraut was renamed "liberty cabbage," and German Americans who opposed American involvement in the war were harassed and arrested. Far worse things happened to the Japanese Americans sent to internment camps during World War II. Many Irish Americans opposed the United States' alignment with Britain during the world wars. In general, shifting alliances across the decades meant shifting attitudes toward Americans of different heritages: Russian immigrants

KEY CONCEPT   Nativism

Nativism is a hostile reaction to immigration, generally (though not always) recent influxes of immigration. It is different from racism; the emphasis is not on the inferiority or superiority of a particular race but on the validity of "native-born" citizens—in the United States, white European Americans or Anglo-Americans, those who can trace their ancestry to the original colonies—versus more recent immigrants such as Italians, Irish, and so on. Nativism manifested itself most strongly in the wake of the waves of immigration from the mid-nineteenth century to the early twentieth century and was not always stigmatized: the American Party, which organized in 1854, was a nativist political party, and men often attained public office at the local level by running on nativist platforms.

Nativism often includes anti-Catholic sentiments, perhaps because the founding population of the United States was Protestant, and Catholicism became associated with the new immigrants, many of whom were poor and spoke English badly or not at all. Italians were the object of lynchings in New Orleans in the 1890s; the Irish at the turn of the century faced much persecution in the Northeast, and the stereotype of the "Irish cop" comes from Irish men taking jobs on the police force because no one else wanted them; the Ku Klux Klan, which formed in the 1920s, was a staunchly anti-Catholic organization, formed at a time when seemingly sane and respectable people passed out pamphlets accusing Catholics of eating babies; and as recently as 1960, John F. Kennedy's Catholic faith was believed to be an obstacle to his run for president. (He remains the only Catholic president.)

Whatever the relations were between the United States and Britain at any given time, citizens in the two countries always felt connected by the belief that Americans of British descent were the "true" Americans by virtue of their earlier arrival.

were perceived much differently before the rise of communism than afterward, whereas Catholics remained the subject of prejudicial treatment for decades because of their association with immigrants.

Even these fears, though—along with the Red Scare of 1918–1920, when Americans feared that radical and communist subversives would sabotage the war effort; Senator Joseph McCarthy's paranoid investigations into alleged communist corruption of the U.S. government; and the resurgence of the Ku Klux Klan as an anti-Catholic, anti-Semitic, nativist hate group—belied the fact that Americans now feared threats from within as much as or more than direct threats from other countries. The War of 1812 was and remains the second and last time the United States had been invaded, and to say that it is unusual for a country to be involved in a dozen wars without facing a serious danger of invasion or occupation is an understatement. The popularity of the Temperance Movement and the constitutional amendment prohibiting the sale of alcohol from 1920 to 1933 shows just how seriously "social ills" were taken, especially during the prosperous 1920s, when President Warren Harding promised a "return to normalcy" after the chaotic years of the Great War—a normalcy subverted somewhat by the meteoric rise in popularity of automobiles, radio, jazz, and movies, and of dancing and socializing among teenagers.

The 1920s saw a dramatic change in the American relationship to Europe. America's late participation in World War I and subsequent prosperity made it the economic superior to the war-torn, deeply indebted European nations. When Mark Twain went to Europe in the late nineteenth century, he did so to make money on lecture tours, but he was received as a sort of primal American, a spokesman for the culture of his country. The writers of the 1920s, on the other hand, were not merely touring lecturers: the Lost Generation included Ernest Hemingway, F. Scott Fitzgerald (leading chronicler of flappers and other movements among young people), and Gertrude Stein. They were generally cynical, disillusioned, and discontent with the Victorian morals inherited by their elders, and horrified by the events of World War I.

Against this background, it is important to note that some early Hollywood movies were racier, more "adult" than they would be again until the 1960s and 1970s and that many jazz and blues lyrics sung in nightclubs were much more explicit than anything that would be heard on the radio (even today). There was a general perception, though, that the United States was a more socially conservative, uptight nation than the countries of Europe—and the new fashions took their cue from overseas: jazz became at least as popular in France as in the United States (and arguably more "respectable"), the flapper look was based in no small part on the appearance of German actress Marlene Dietrich, and so on. Although the United States had a stronger economy, the idea persisted that *culture* still came from the Old World, particularly from continental Europe.

The Great Depression was instigated by the stock market crash of 1929—and exacerbated in no small part by the 1930 Smoot-Hawley Tariff Act signed by President Herbert Hoover, which imposed an extraordinary tax (effectively 60 percent) on goods imported into the United States. At its highest, unemployment reached a staggering 25 percent. By necessity, American concerns turned or remained inward, as President Franklin Delano Roosevelt's administration ushered in the New Deal Era of government programs aimed at saving Americans from starvation, sickness, and irrecoverable economic doom. World War II, then, was something of a shock—the first World War was meant to be "the war to end all wars," the war that ended imperialism. War had even been outlawed by no fewer than sixty countries.

Although the home front was more peaceful and calm during World War II than it had been during the first world war, World War II had just as profound an effect on American foreign policy. The unprecedented levels of destruction in Europe, the bombing of Pearl Harbor, the fear of other attacks on American shores, and the use of the atomic bomb in Japan clearly showed how serious war could now be, and the involvement of so many countries likewise made it seem unlikely that many wars could be contained simply between two nations. The United Nations formed without the resistance met by the League of Nations, while North American capitalist and Eastern European communist countries factioned off into NATO (the North Atlantic Treaty Organization) and the Warsaw Pact, respectively. Despite the Soviet Union's inclusion among the Allied powers in World War II, the lines of the Cold War were clearly and starkly drawn between communism and democracy, with the Soviets and Americans as team captains.

Under President Dwight D. Eisenhower, a project called Operation Solarium reconfigured American foreign policy in the mid-1950s. Eliminating communism and converting the countries of Eastern Europe to capitalist democracies seemed impractical—to do so would be an endeavor larger than World War II, from which America's allies had not yet fully recovered—and so containing communism was made the top priority in foreign policy. This marked a change from previous eras, which had been principally concerned with defending American sovereignty or acquiring territory. President Harry Truman had, however, talked about "the containment of communism" when communist revolutions seemed possible in Greece and Turkey. Arguably, Eisenhower's advisers would have said there was no change from previous foreign policy frameworks: communism was perceived as inherently expansionist, as a political system that needed to convert or conquer other nations. Containing communism, Solarium's proponents would argue, was the same thing as protecting American sovereignty.

Despite this climate, Eisenhower feared overspending on defense concerns, especially during peacetime; considerably more was spent on preparing for a Russian threat (even discounting the costs of wars in Vietnam and Korea) than was spent combating an actual Axis powers threat, and this says much about the intensity of the Cold War. Eisenhower told his cabinet he was concerned that a bloated military-industrial complex—the term he coined for the combination of the military, the defense industry, and associated political and business groups—would force the United States into war simply because it was so prepared for it, a concern that was even graver considering that it came from a veteran of two world wars who was a widely respected military commander.

Almost immediately, and certainly by the middle of the 1950s, the pervasiveness of the Cold War turned a once-isolationist nation into a superpower, one that seemed to represent a new sort of imperialism or at least feudalism: the United States had military bases all over the world, was instrumental in creating the state of Israel in the Middle East, fought wars against communist powers in Southeast Asia, and intervened all over Latin America to prevent communist revolutions or keep right-wing governments in power. The necessity of any of this is still a valid matter of debate, but there is no question that it represented a huge change in Americans' attitudes toward their place in the world. This new attitude also encouraged the occasional diplomatic role the executive branch of the United States sometimes played, particularly in the Middle East: the role of negotiator.

Secretary of State Henry Kissinger's "shuttle diplomacy"—in which a third party mediates between two opposing parties by speaking to each privately and then relaying communications—was one prominent example of this negotiator role at work, a technique Kissinger used not only to help reopen relations with the People's Republic of China (closed since the communist takeover) but to negotiate the end of the 1973 Yom Kippur War. This latter war, fought between Arab armies led by Egypt and Israel, was especially notable, since it did not directly involve American interests. President Jimmy Carter would, five years later, negotiate the Camp David Accords to ensure peace between Egypt and Israel. The Camp David Accords were enormously significant in Middle East relations: Egypt's separate peace with Israel destroyed any chances of a unified Arab alliance, but it also led to Egyptian President Anwar Sadat's assassination and a power vacuum that Saddam Hussein sought to fill. As president of Iraq, Hussein tried to consolidate power first by invading Iran (leading to the Iran-Iraq War of 1980–1988, in which he had the backing of the U.S. government) and later by invading Kuwait (leading to the Gulf War).

Throughout all of these changes, Britain remained America's strongest ally. While the two countries share perhaps the most history—even with the waves of immigration of the nineteenth and twentieth centuries, a great deal of American culture derives from British culture, as do the legal and governmental systems—the Revolution and the War of 1812 had put enough distance between them to avoid the narcissism of small differences that encouraged such violent disputes between the Irish and the British, the Basques and the French, the Arabs and Israelis. Indeed in the 1980s, the United States and the United Kingdom developed almost in parallel as President Ronald Reagan and Prime Minister Margaret Thatcher propagated their compatible versions of conservatism during especially strong terms of office.

When the Cold War ended with the fall of the Berlin Wall in 1988 and the disbanding of the Soviet bloc in 1991, the United States responded accordingly. NATO—not an American organization but certainly dominated by the United States—expanded to include several formerly communist Eastern European nations, and the effort the United States once put into containing communism has instead focused on peacekeeping (as in Somalia), human rights abuses (in Bosnia-Herzegovina), and terrorism (in Afghanistan and Iraq). While Britain has remained a staunch ally, in recent years the British people have become less enthusiastically pro-American, and Prime Minister Tony Blair came under heavy criticism for what his critics perceived as a willingness to follow President George W. Bush's lead in diplomatic affairs.

ALTERNATE HISTORY

But what if the British had occupied Washington, D.C. instead of burning it down?

The capital was undefended. There would have been no immediate threat to any occupying force, and Ross's concern was his doubt that he could hold the city indefinitely. What if he had commanded a larger force? He could have held the city for a couple of weeks while waiting for reinforcements, or he could have left a small complement to hold Washington while the rest of the British troops attacked Baltimore and attempted to divide the American forces between the two cities. While Brooke—Ross's temporary replacement when he was killed at North Point in the attack on Baltimore—was competent, Ross was more so. What if Ross had left Brooke in charge of the occupying forces in Washington, D.C., and—with a larger force at his disposal—survived a successful siege on Baltimore, instead of the two-pronged failure of actual history?

An occupied Washington, D.C., would have led to a very different war. It was a pivotal time in the morale of the people: while the burning of the capital was psychologically hurtful, Baltimore's survival considerably raised hopes. With Washington occupied, not only would morale have taken a hard hit, but the federal government would have had to relocate, and in this day and age doing so was not a fast process: several months would have passed before the federal government would have been fully reassembled and functioning in its new site in New York City, the city best able to accommodate it. The British would have had little chance of occupying Baltimore for a prolonged period, and would have realized this: consequently they would have destroyed the city's forts (as they later did in Pensacola), pillaged supplies, and burned the rest in retaliation for York.

A southern expansion from Washington, D.C., would have been Britain's next step; they would have used the minor port as a staging ground to capture Norfolk, Virginia, which lies closer to the coast and is more accessible and practical. (Washington, D.C., is accessible from the Atlantic via the Potomac River, which in time of war would be more easily blockaded than the seacoast or Norfolk's harbor.) Norfolk had been destroyed before by the British during the American Revolution only a generation earlier, and resentment would still have been strong. The fight against the invaders would have been passionate, and British forces already weakened by the attack on Baltimore and thinned by the occupation of Washington, D.C., would have struggled. In time, though, the British Navy would overcome Norfolk's defenses (but not without casualties). Thus, the force fighting the Battle of New Orleans would have been weaker than it was in actual history, and Andrew Jackson's victory would have been even more decisive.

Still, however, the British would have controlled Washington, D.C., during the treaty negotiations at Ghent in Belgium. Possession of the American capital would have given the British bargaining power they simply did not possess in actual history, and while it may seem that they would not have needed it, they too initially sought more than the *status quo ante bellum*. Just as the Americans were denied their desire to prohibit impressment, the British had to table their hopes for a Native American territory occupying land between Canada and the United States. British negotiators, in actual history, abandoned these hopes when diplomat Henry Clay declared he would leave Ghent with the negotiations unfinished if they pressed this request.

A trade for Washington, D.C., would have made the British braver, and they would have continued to press the issue. Would Americans really have given up their capital? The idea would seem unthinkable to the British, who had centuries of history, major landmarks at every turn, and a deep a loyalty to the soil. The United States is a younger nation, a nation composed as much of ideas as roads and houses. The burning of Baltimore—the site of such pro-war violence in the early months of the war—would have made the Americans even less willing to negotiate, and to British amazement, Washington, D.C. might have been abandoned, ceded to the British by default in the final treaty. Opposition to the "native territory" idea would have simply been too strong: too many Americans feared attacks by the Native American tribes, not only on their own but under British instigation. After all, poor relations with the northwest tribes were a contributing factor to anti-British sentiment in the decades leading up to the war.

The British would have kept Washington, D.C., and Maine, and they would have enlarged the boundaries of Canada and created a small British "island" in the midst of the United States—a small port positioned between the North and South. The cash-poor United States would have been paid respectable war reparations in accordance with standard international practice, and trade relationships would have been restored, at least in theory. The resentment would have remained, though—whereas many of the benefits reaped by the United States in actual history persist in this scenario, the loss of Washington, D.C., and Maine would have been a real blow to the aims represented by the Monroe Doctrine.

Just as New Amsterdam was renamed New York when it became a British colony, the name of Washington, D.C., would have changed—Britain would certainly not have retained the name of the American president. The new city—New Britain, we shall call it—would have adjusted its borders several times in the next few decades, in exchange for Britain's granting the United States most-favored nation status. The borders of Canada would eventually be readjusted, with Maine and parts of western Canada given to the United States in return for expanding New Britain's borders to something more useful for Britain—a controversial move during a time when the United States would have been more concerned with the growing North/South conflicts than with Europe.

The events leading up to the Civil War would have been a little different, though New Britain would have taken a role in the underground railroad, with slaves smuggled out of the South and into New Britain, where they could be sent to Europe or Canada, out of reach of their owners. Although Britain and New Britain would have remained officially neutral in the disputes between the North and South, the ordinarily pro-British Southerners would have felt increasing resentment toward this cavalier treatment of what they considered their property. And once the Civil War was under way, another key difference would have come about: New Britain, and by extension Britain itself, would have allied with the Union.

In actual history, the Civil War was a rare thing: a prolonged war, one that had impact on the world economy through its effect on New World trade, without direct foreign involvement. The British considered supporting the Union just as the French considered a Confederate alliance; both remained neutral, however, and no other European power gave the matter serious consideration. No one wanted to make an enemy of the eventual victor, or worse, somehow alienate both. But with the strategically and economically important port of New Britain right in the middle of the North and South—nominally a northern city, perhaps, but just north of Dixie—this neutrality would have been untenable. Both the Union and the Confederacy would have felt too much temptation to invade New Britain and put its fort and port to their use; the governor, perhaps the prime minister, would have foreseen this and built an alliance first, creating a friend rather than an enemy.

Once New Britain had allied with the Union—because Britain would have been strongly anti-slavery by this point, and a Confederate alliance would have been too unpopular to consider—Britain proper would have had to throw her lot with the Union, and while the war itself would have progressed in much the same way, the psychological effect would have been profound. Consider the difference between a war between two brothers, and a war in which one brother enlists the help of a mutual friend to fight the other. The sense of betrayal in the latter, of persecution and oppression, is far greater—it becomes more than a family dispute. The Union would still have won, Lincoln would still have been assassinated, Reconstruction would have begun in much the same way—but Southern resentment would have reached almost hysterical heights.

The South would have responded: Reconstruction would have been met with steady, enraged, and violent resistance, and it would not have been limited to vigilante groups. Indeed, racial violence would have been the exception, not the rule, because the true targets of anger would have been the Northerners and their British allies. Passengers on trains from the North would have been lynched—not often, not every time, but often enough. Carpetbagger teachers, businessmen, and government officials would have been ridiculed, attacked, their homes burned. The original Ku Klux Klan would have garnered a great deal more support, even public support, than it received in actual history. When the Redeemers—southern politicians "redeeming" the South from the northern interference of the War and Reconstruction—came into power, their actions would have been even more severe, and they would have limited not just the rights of African Americans but of anyone without southern roots. Voting rights in some local elections would have been limited to those whose grandparents were citizens of southern states, for instance; in other places, taxes would have been substantially increased, with deductions offered to homesteaders with the appropriate background. Northerners would have been barred from the highest public offices in southern states and would have encountered difficulty in business dealings, though money would still have opened many doors.

Nativism would have been on the rise, but the British would not have been immune to it as they often were in actual history. Instead, it would have focused on anything non-Southern: Europeans and Northerners especially. Federal peacekeeping actions against the South would have been necessary periodically through the end of the nineteenth century, with army troops sent in to deal with lynchings and presidential pardons forced through for wrongfully jailed prisoners. It would have come to a head when President Woodrow Wilson—a Virginia-born Scots-Irishman who was educated at Princeton and became governor of New Jersey—decided to enter World War I, a war many Southerners would have opposed for interventionist reasons. The Espionage Act of 1917 and Sedition Act of 1918, leading up to the American entrance into the war, would have outlawed anti-British sentiment—to great southern protest.

New Britain would have been invaded at last, not by the United States but by a coalition of nearby Southern states led by Virginia.

ANOTHER VIEW Victory

What if the United States had won the war? What would winning the war even entail?

Beating Britain in this case would mean subduing Canada; the United States had no ability to invade Britain itself or attack it in any force, and with the Napoleonic Wars occupying Europe, no ally could have been found there to attack on America's behalf. But what if Canada had been conquered as easily as so many Americans expected it to be? The war would likely have lasted at least another year or two, because of the additional campaigns to fight; the abolition of impressment would have been granted because of its sheer irrelevance at that point.

With Britain removed from North America and France having already sold its territories, only the United States, Spain, and Mexico would have remained. Texas would have declared its independence from Mexico in the 1830s, and Russia controlled Alaska in the far northwest. Canada, especially western Canada, was more sparsely settled than the United States, and it would have provided a greater supply of frontier, so to speak. In actual history, the frontier was closed in 1890, when population density grew to the point that nothing was left empty. In an alternate history, however, all this added land would mean another two or three decades before the land became saturated. American imperialism and Pacific acquisitions—a reaction to the loss of the frontier at the end of the nineteenth century—would have had no chance to thrive, as First World imperialism all but ended in the aftermath of the Great War.

Much of the city would have been burned before American federal troops could come to New Britain's aid, and Wilson would have been faced with the possibility of a Second Civil War on the eve of the Great War. Out of anxiety, he might have overreacted. The leaders of the attack would have been arrested and held without trial on behalf of the British, outraging even Southerners who opposed the attack.

Four Southern states might have seceded in protest, and several non-Southern states would have offered their support in Congress. Wilson would not have been able to fight a second civil war and a world war at the same time. The first years of World War I had demonstrated how severe and devastating war had become in the twentieth century; rather than subject his native soil to war, Wilson would have permitted the secession, charging Secretary of State Robert Lansing—a famed advocate of neutrality and responsible noninterference in foreign affairs—with the task of easing the transition and setting up mutually beneficial trade agreements with the seceding states. The Southern States of America—no Confederacy this time, but a looser union than the United States—would have practiced a policy of extreme isolationism through the next decades, avoiding even World War II, though they would permit men to enlist in the U.S. or Canadian military for the purpose of fighting the Axis powers, and would encourage the establishment of factories in their states, first to manufacture armaments and other necessities for the Allied forces, and later to help with the industrialization of the South. In the immediate aftermath of World War I, the dismantling of European empires would have led Great Britain to cede New Britain to the Southern States.

It is during the prosperous, prohibitionist 1920s, then, that America would feel its imperialist stirrings, but it could not do much about them until after World War II: the Cold War, with its lines drawn between capitalism and communism, would take a more frenetic pace, as the United States set up puppet governments throughout Latin America and Africa in response to the communist movement through Eastern Europe. "Border" skirmishes in Alaska—where only a thin strip of water separates the contiguous United States from the Soviet Union—would have become common, though they would nearly always be disavowed and sometimes denied outright. In the 1980s, a U.S./Soviet war in Afghanistan would have lasted for seven tense months: many would be convinced that because the war transpires on neither country's native soil, one or the other would have employed nuclear weapons. The war, however, would end in a series of complicated compromises; the threat of nuclear retaliation would be enough to keep either leader from drawing first blood.

The Soviet Union eventually would dissolve, and economic malaise would settle in across the United States as its sparring partner struggled to stay afloat. Japan and the European Economic Union fill the void in the world economy, leading to nearly a decade of promising health, a new era of good feelings—which, in the early twenty-first century, would be threatened by unrest in the Middle East, a region filled with countries resentful of being used as pawns in the prolonged U.S./Soviet conflicts.

Alabama, a holdout in the Southern States' initial secession, would have joined them in the years after World War II in response to federal sword-waving over the segregation issue, and George Wallace would have become the first memorable president of the Southern States. Jimmy Carter would have become mayor of Washington, D.C.— taking its name back once the New British had been chased out—and later president of the Southern States during Ronald Reagan's first term as president of the United States. The energy crisis would have hit the United States more severely than in actual history, and while Reagan's America might have gone to war in the Middle East over oil, Carter's South would have brokered an economic treaty leading to a span of southern prosperity through the 1980s and a resulting land boom. The treaty would have been short-lived, though: Arab nations would have withdrawn in response to the born-again Christian Carter's refusal to disavow Israel.

The Southern States would have abstained from the Cold War in the Reagan-Thatcher years, out of a continued distaste for Britain and perception of Reagan's America as overly Anglophilic. The primary issue in Southern foreign policy through the 1980s and into the twenty-first century would have been involvement in the United Nations—though recognized in the 1920s, the Southerners would have had little voice. In the 2000s, relations with the United States and Britain would have still been tense; though war would have remained unlikely, future violent incidents would not have been out of the question.

Bill Kte'pi

Discussion Questions

1. If Britain had held the District of Columbia and renamed it New Britain, the fact that the British abolished slavery in their overseas holdings in two steps in 1833 and 1838 would have also impacted New Britain. How do you think the presence of such an enclave of freedom on the Potomac River would have affected slavery in neighboring Maryland and Virginia in the period 1838–1860?

2. If the British had held Washington, D.C., at the end of the War of 1812, would that have emboldened other European powers to try to reestablish enclaves and colonies in the New World in the following decades? Would Spain or France have been likely or unlikely to attempt to regain territory in the Caribbean, Latin America, or the United States itself?

3. If the United States had been divided a second time with southern secession of several states in World War II, would such a development have encouraged or discouraged the tendency of other states or regions to secede? What causes might have led regions such as the West Coast or New England to consider their own secession?

4. If several Southern states had seceded from the United States during World War I, as suggested in this chapter's alternate history, would they have been more dominated by a fundamentalist Christian political orientation than the remaining United States? Consider issues such as prohibition of alcohol, female suffrage, and civil liberties.

5. In the twentieth and twenty-first centuries, southern states have represented some of the most conservative political sections of the country. If several states in the section had seceded from the Union in World War I, how would that have affected the politics of the remaining nonseceding parts of the United States? Would the Republican Party have reverted to its earlier roots as the liberal/radical party?

Bibliography and Further Reading

Allen, Robert S. "His Majesty's Indian Allies: Native Peoples, the British Crown, and the War of 1812." *Michigan Historical Review* 14, no. 2 (Fall 1988): 1–24.

Benn, Carl. *The War of 1812*. London: Osprey, 2002.

Borneman, Walter R. *1812: The War That Forged a Nation*. New York: HarperCollins, 2004.

Brown, Roger H. *The Republic in Peril: 1812*. New York: W.W. Norton, 1971.

Carter-Edwards, Dennis. "The War of 1812 along the Detroit Frontier: A Canadian Perspective." *The Michigan Historical Review* 13, no. 2 (Fall, 1987): 25–50.

Coles, Harry L. *The War of 1812*. Chicago: University of Chicago Press, 1965.

Goodman, Warren H. "The Origins of the War of 1812: A Survey of Changing Interpretations." *Mississippi Valley Historical Review* 28 (September, 1941): 171–186.

Hickey, Donald R. *The War of 1812: A Forgotten Conflict*. Chicago: University of Illinois Press, 1995.

Horsman, Reginald. *War of 1812*. New York: Random House, 1969.

Mahon, John K. *War of 1812*. London: Da Capo, 1991.

Owsley, Frank. *Struggle for the Gulf Borderlands: The Creek War and the Battle of New Orleans 1812–1815*. Tuscaloosa: University of Alabama Press, 1981.

Risjord, Norman K. "1812: Conservatives, War Hawks, and the Nation's Honor." *William and Mary Quarterly* 3d ser., 18 (April, 1961): 196–210.

Stagg, J. C. A. *Mr. Madison's War: Politics, Diplomacy, and Warfare in the Early American Republic 1783–1830*. Princeton: Princeton University Press, 1983.

Taylor, George Rogers, ed. *The War of 1812: Past Justifications and Present Interpretations*. Boston: D.C. Heath, 1963.

TURNING POINT

The Monroe Doctrine declared European powers should stay out of the Americas. What if James Monroe had allowed continued European influence in North and South America?

INTRODUCTION

American leaders from Presidents James Monroe and Theodore Roosevelt to Franklin Delano Roosevelt have grappled with the problem of European intervention in American affairs and American intervention in the affairs of its Western Hemisphere neighbors. These leaders approached the problem from very different perspectives. In 1823, Monroe and his advisers established the important nineteenth-century American foreign policy of opposing European intervention in American affairs. In 1904 and 1905, Theodore Roosevelt used his Corollary to the Monroe Doctrine to justify U.S. intervention in the affairs of its neighbors in the hemisphere. In the 1930s, Franklin D. Roosevelt circumvented the Monroe Doctrine by establishing his "Good Neighbor" policy toward South and Central American nations. Indirectly, the United States invoked the Monroe Doctrine during the Civil War and during the expansion and annexation eras of the 1890s and invoked the Roosevelt Corollary during both the Cold War and as part of the Iran-Contra scandal of the Ronald Reagan administration.

When he delivered his annual message to the U.S. Congress on December 2, 1823, Monroe did not intend to set a U.S. foreign policy precedent for the remainder of the nineteenth century. In his address he did, however, propose a definitive foreign policy that called for European countries to cease their interference in both North and South America. Still, this policy was not the primary focus of his speech. Although the Monroe Doctrine, as the policy came to be called, would apply to only independent countries in North and South America (and not to colonies), it was essentially a second declaration of American independence from European interference into what the United States considered its territories and spheres of influence. As Monroe expressed the concept:

> The American continents, by the free and independent condition which they have assumed and maintain, are henceforth not to be considered as subjects for future colonization by any European

powers. . . . Of events in that [European] quarter of the globe, with which we have so much intercourse and from which we derive our origin, we have always been anxious and interested spectators. The citizens of the United States cherish sentiments the most friendly in favor of the liberty and happiness of their fellowmen on that side of the Atlantic. In the wars of the European powers in matters relating to themselves we have never taken any part, nor does it comport with our policy so to do. (Monroe 1995, 26–29)

As an expression of growing and expanding American nationalism that kept pace with the expansion of the still-new country, the Monroe Doctrine articulated four main foreign and domestic policy propositions for the United States. The first proposition in the Monroe Doctrine asserted that the North and South American continents were free and independent and that European powers could not consider them subjects for future colonization. The second point said that Western Hemisphere nations were republics rather monarchies. The third proposition stated that the United States would regard any European effort to interfere in governments of the Western Hemisphere nations as a threat to its own peace and safety, by implication, placing the United States in the role of protector of the independent nations in the Americas. The fourth proposition reinforced the concept of the unique Americas by pledging that the United States would not interfere in European affairs.

The issues that motivated the Monroe administration to formulate the Monroe Doctrine were older than the United States itself. The central issue revolved around the position of the United States: Did it belong with the old European political system, or had it created a distinctive new political system across the Atlantic? This question of territorial and political integrity was one of the root causes of the American Revolution. Seventeenth-century civil wars in England and continental Europe did not necessarily settle sovereignty questions or the question of whether the British North American colonists should be neutral or engaged in European wars. Some Englishmen in the Americas believed that the colonies should be involved; others thought that the colonies should be politically autonomous. When Britain and France fought a series of wars, including the Seven Years' War from 1756 to 1763, the differences of opinion about the involvement of the colonies deepened.

As the decades of British rule continued, many colonists began to feel that the British in America had developed interests that were radically different from those of the British in England. The colonists protested that most statesmen in London could not understand or appreciate the differences between the colonies and the mother country, essentially the same argument

James Monroe, president of the United States from 1817 to 1825, worked against European influence in the Americas. (Library of Congress)

that the Monroe administration would articulate nearly a century later as reasons why Europe should stay out of Western Hemispheric affairs. This isolationist idea contributed to the American Revolution, and although France and America forged a formal alliance to fight the Revolution, majorities in the Continental Congress declared that the United States should remain detached from European politics. George Washington, the first American president, firmly stated in his Farewell Address of 1796 that the United States should avoid "entangling alliances."

The two European principals in the American Revolutionary War, France and Britain, also drove the new United States of America to the Monroe Doctrine. In many respects, the United States and Great Britain fought the War of 1812 to definitively answer the pre-Revolutionary War question of whether the United States was part of the European political system or the creator of its own political and territorial destiny. From the signing of the Treaty of Paris in 1783 to the end the American Revolution, the British had remained a strong and disruptive presence in the continental United States. They did not withdraw from the American territory along the Great Lakes, they incited the Native Americans on the American frontiers, and they refused to sign commercial agreements favorable to the United States. In the meantime, France and Britain fought each other during the French Revolutionary Wars of 1782 to 1892 and the Napoleonic Wars of 1803 to 1815.

French and British maritime polices during the 1790s conflicted with American interests, and the differences accelerated after 1803. In 1807 Great Britain passed Orders in Council that proposed channeling all neutral trade from the colonies to continental Europe through Great Britain, and in 1806 and 1807 France issued Berlin and Milan decrees that declared Britain to be in a state of blockade and condemned neutral shipping that obeyed British regulations. The United States believed that both Britain and France were violating its rights as a neutral nation, but most Americans were particularly resentful of British maritime policies. Because Britain dominated the seas, it claimed the right to remove any British sailors serving aboard American merchant ships, and British officials frequently took Americans as well. British impressments policy became a major grievance.

When America's diplomatic attempts to avoid war with Britain met with failure, some Americans decided that only a declaration of war could preserve American integrity and autonomy. The 1810–1811 congress contained a group known as the War Hawks, mostly Democratic-Republicans from the West and South, who demanded war against Great Britain. Their leaders included John C. Calhoun of South Carolina, Henry Clay of Kentucky, and Felix Grundy of Tennessee. The War Hawks argued that the United States could save its honor and change British policies by invading Canada. The Federalist Party, which represented

John C. Calhoun was among those who demanded war against Great Britain. (Library of Congress)

KEY CONCEPT   Does Canada Need a Monroe Doctrine?

Canadian Prime Minister Pierre Trudeau once quipped that the United States-Canada relationship was like sleeping next to an elephant; every minor movement affected its neighbor.

The American Revolutionaries considered the presence of the British in the Canadian provinces a strategic threat and they invited French Canadians to send representatives to the Continental Congress. The Americans invaded Canada during the Revolution because they wanted to expel Britain from North America and they still hoped for an American–French Canadian alliance. Because American efforts did not produce a merger with Canada, American envoy Benjamin Franklin unsuccessfully tried to convince British diplomats to cede Canada to the United States. The British presence in Canada after the Revolutionary War soured British-American relations, especially when thousands of Loyalist refugees from British North America settled in Canada at the war's end. The Articles of the Confederation included provisions for acquiring and governing Canada.

When tensions again mounted between the United States and Great Britain after the turn of the nineteenth century, America once more turned its covetous gaze on Canada. The War of 1812 ended in American victory without the annexation of Canada, but it did not end skirmishes along the American-Canadian border. The Caroline incident of 1837 developed when Canadian authorities in U.S. waters near Buffalo, New York, destroyed an American ship called the *Caroline*, which supporters of William Lyon Mackenzie, the leader of a rebellion against British authority in Canada, used against the British. An American citizen was killed, and law enforcement officers in New York State arrested and tried a Canadian deputy marshal for his role in the attack, but he was acquitted.

The American Civil War provoked rifts between the United States and Canada. When the war began in 1861, Confederate sympathizers and spies used Canada as a base of operations against the Union. The most notorious plan, the Northwest Conspiracy of 1864, involved Confederate agents plotting to capture the USS *Michigan* and releasing the Confederate prisoners held on Johnson's Island in Lake Erie. Union sympathizers foiled the plot, but the conspirators managed to sink an

New England shippers and feared the collapse of trade, opposed war with Britain. President James Madison signed a declaration of war against Great Britain on June 18, 1812, and despite substantial opposition, Congress passed the declaration.

The United States was unprepared for war, and by 1814 it faced losing the war because, after defeating Napoleon, the British began transferring ships and experienced soldiers to America. Despite more British advances, the American victory at the Battle of New Orleans in January 1815 proved to be the decisive factor, and the British invasion was checked. The Treaty of Ghent, which ended the War of 1812, had been signed in Europe before the Battle of New Orleans, but it resolved none of the issues that had started the war. By winning the War of 1812, the fledgling United States proved that it could back up its independence with force, but the war also accentuated some inconsistencies in American policy. The United States unsuccessfully invaded Canada during the War of 1812, and throughout the nineteenth century, many Americans harbored "manifest destiny" ideas of Canadian annexation. Several of the Congressmen who had voted for the War of 1812 remained in Congress to influence the creation of the Monroe Doctrine.

American steamship. In 1864, a group of about thirty Confederate raiders entered Vermont through Quebec and robbed several banks in the town of St. Albans. After returning to Quebec, local authorities arrested the raiders, but they were soon released.

The Fenian incidents posed far more serious threats to U.S. and Canadian relations. The Fenians were militant Irish nationalists from the United States who formed the Fenian Brotherhood with the goal of conquering Canada. They staged several raids, including one on Quebec, during the 1860s and 1870s. To end this episode, Hamilton Fish, secretary of state under President Ulysses S. Grant, negotiated the Treaty of Washington between the United States and Great Britain on May 8, 1871. The treaty dealt with the Fenian Raids and other cross-border issues with the new Dominion of Canada and helped avert a war between the two countries. Canadian Prime Minister Sir John A. Macdonald served as one of the negotiators for the British and although the negotiators settled the treaty for the British Empire, Macdonald's participation set the precedent for Canada to negotiate directly with the United States.

During the 1920s and 1930s, as a theoretical exercise, the U.S. military developed a plan to invade Canada. Documents declassified in 1974 reveal that War Plan Red called for seizing the key port of Halifax, cutting communication between eastern and western Canada by capturing Winnipeg, securing bridgeheads near Buffalo, Detroit, and Sault Ste. Marie, and attacking Quebec overland from New England. After this the U.S. military would take the Great Lakes region and St. Lawrence valley before moving on the prairies and British Columbia. Later when the U.S. naval forces were built up, they might be able to take Bermuda and Britain's Caribbean possessions on the road toward victory.

Canada and the United States closely cooperated in fighting the two world wars, and they were allies during the Cold War. The Canadian military supported the United States in the Korean War, the Gulf War, the Kosovo war, and the War on Terror. The Canadian government opposed the Vietnam War and the 2003 invasion of Iraq, causing some diplomatic tensions between the two countries. A U.S. proposal requiring mandatory passports for travel between the two countries has steered U.S. and Canada diplomatic relations in a new and unexplored direction.

Events in South America also influenced American foreign policy. An 1820 revolution in Spain hastened many South American countries moves toward independence. Between 1815 and 1822, Jose de San Martín led Argentina, Chile, and Peru to independence, and Simón Bolívar guided Colombia out of colonialism. In 1822, Dom Pedro, the Portuguese regent, declared Brazil independent from Portugal, and Ecuador declared its independence after defeating the Spanish at the battle of Mount Pichincha (near Quito).

In 1823, the French intervened in the Spanish revolution. They invaded Spain, forcing the rebel forces to hand over Ferdinand VII and restoring him to power. Ferdinand ruled Spain with an iron fist for the next ten years. The United States and Great Britain also reacted to the Spanish revolution and the new republics in the Americas. Monroe and John Quincy Adams, the U.S. secretary of state, reacted ambiguously to the new republics in the New World. On one hand, they acknowledged the wars between Spain and its former colonies and declared the neutrality of the United States. On the other hand, they were not willing to go beyond implicitly recognizing the legitimacy of the new nations and declaring war against Spain and France in support of new nations whose survival was uncertain. Yet the United States sold naval vessels to the rebel armies, and in 1822—after the United States had ratified the Treaty with Spain for the purchase of Florida—the Monroe administration acknowledged Argentina, Chile, Peru, Colombia, and Mexico.

Great Britain was caught in a vise between monarchical principles and the desire for new markets. At this time, South America represented a larger market for British goods than did the United States, and when Russia and France proposed that Britain help Spain regain her New World colonies, Britain vetoed the idea. In 1823, France urged Spain to restore the Bourbons to power, and France considered joining with Spain to war on the new republics with the backing of the "holy alliance" composed of Russia, Prussia, and Austria. If this alliance were to come about, the work of the eighteenth-century British statesmen James Wolfe, William Pitt, and others to eject France from the New World would be undone, and France would once again be a power in the Americas.

British Foreign Minister George Canning proposed that Britain and the United States form an alliance to divert France and Spain from intervention. Thomas Jefferson and James Madison urged Monroe to accept the British offer, but John Quincy Adams questioned the wisdom of the alliance. Adams also worried about efforts by Russia and Mexico to gain influence over the joint British-American–claimed Oregon Country, and Alexander I of Russia was making ominous noises about Alaska. Many American citizens were urging diplomatic recognition of Greece, which had just declared its independence from the Ottoman Empire, and the Monroe administration had to decide whether to act on this entirely European matter.

The Monroe administration faced a major complicating factor in deciding whether to join Great Britain in an alliance against Spanish and French interests in South America. The year 1824 was a presidential election year, and Monroe planned to retire. Secretary of State John Quincy Adams was one of the leading candidates to succeed him.

TURNING POINT

The presidential cabinet meeting of November 7, 1823, marked a turning point in American foreign policy and the implementation of what came to be known as the Monroe Doctrine. The meeting's atmosphere reverberated with the clash of political parties and expansionists and conservative philosophies, but the complex personalities and political ambitions of John Quincy Adams and the other 1824 presidential candidates set the meeting's tone.

Thomas Jefferson and James Madison had founded the Republican Party, which dominated the political scene in 1823, and Adams was running for president as a Republican. The Republican Party in several of the large states had to nominate him before he had a chance of being elected. His political rivals set to work reminding voters that his father, John Adams, had been a Federalist and had opposed Jefferson. His opponents also reminded voters that John Quincy Adams himself had been a member of the Federalist Party until 1808, when he broke with the Federalists to become a Republican.

Republicans and Federalists were sharply divided over relations with Great Britain. The Federalists generally favored friendly relations with the British while the Republicans were more anti-British. Presidential candidate Adams knew that if outgoing President Monroe agreed to British foreign minister Canning's proposal for an alliance between the United States and Britain to thwart Spanish and French ambitions in the Western Hemisphere, Adams's opponents would blame him for the alliance. They would allege that he was an unrepentant Federalist. If the Monroe administration extended diplomatic recognition to Greece, this would also embarrass Adams because the New England Federalists avidly supported this action.

Secretary of War John C. Calhoun, also a presidential candidate, advocated accepting the alliance with Britain. He contended that the French and Spanish peril to South America was real and immediate and only an alliance with the British could deflect it. He also advocated recognizing Greece, arguing that the United States should support liberalism against despotism whenever it had the opportunity. Former presidents Jefferson and Madison were both opposed to the nomination of Adams and advised Monroe to enter the alliance with Great Britain. Madison also advocated the recognition of Greece.

Adams garnered his considerable intelligence, learning, and skill to convince Monroe to reject the recommendations of Calhoun, Jefferson, and Madison. He downplayed the danger of European intervention in Latin America and predicted that if Great Britain did decide to intervene in Latin America it would be out of British national interest and not because of a partnership with the United States.

Adams advised Monroe not to recognize Greece. He felt that the United States should adhere to the position that the European and American systems were distinct. Both Monroe and Adams wanted to ensure that countries such as Britain did not reintroduce European mercantilism in Latin America, which was assuming increasing economic and ideological importance to the United States.

Monroe gradually yielded to the power and force of the Adams arguments. The president allowed Adams to send carefully worded documents to the Russian minister in Washington, D.C., protesting any extension of the Russian domain in the Americas and any effort by the members of the holy alliance to restore Spanish dominion in Latin America. In his annual message to Congress, Monroe made a speech, mainly drafted by Adams, that spelled out the terms of the new American foreign policy. During the early weeks of the congressional session of 1823–1824, Monroe used his influence to defeat a resolution recommending recognition of Greece.

Many historians assert that Adams formulated most of the Monroe Doctrine, but a closer examination of the expansionist principles of Monroe reveals that he and Adams were both ideological partners and skilled diplomats. John Adams had taken John Quincy Adams to Europe at an early age, and the young man had acquired a broad view of the world. After returning to America and graduating from Harvard University, John Quincy Adams began a law practice in Boston. George

Washington appointed him minister to the Netherlands and Portugal and his father appointed him minister to Prussia from 1797 to 1801. He also served as minister to Russia from 1809 to 1814, chief negotiator of the United States Commission for the Treaty of Ghent in 1814, and minister to the Court of St. James in Britain from 1815 to 1817. He served as secretary of state in Monroe's cabinet from 1817 to 1825, and during his term he spearheaded the acquisition of Florida and steered the United States away from becoming dependent on Britain.

Under President Jefferson, Monroe had played a key role in the Louisiana Purchase, which doubled the size of the United States by the stroke of a pen. Monroe was elected as a hero of the War of 1812, in which he negotiated an end to a trade embargo with France and Britain. In the White House, Monroe pushed American's frontier fifteen hundred miles to the west and superintended the purchase of Florida. While many of the Federalists and conservative old guard maintained a policy of protecting America from foreign invasion, Monroe had big dreams for the American republic and wrote that "an overcautious policy often risks more than a bold one."

When Monroe's cabinet met during the 1823–1824 political season, Adams convinced Monroe to endorse his foreign policy principles, and the president articulated both of their foreign policy ideas in his annual message to Congress on December 2, 1823. From this point on, the United States would take an independent stand, one in which it informed the Old World that the Americas could no longer be colonized and that the United States would consider any European effort to extend its political influence over the New World "as dangerous to our peace and safety." In return, the United States would not interfere in European internal affairs or wars. Some twenty years after James Monroe died in 1831, this policy became known as the Monroe Doctrine.

ACTUAL HISTORY

The Monroe Doctrine was not an instant success. European editorial writers and political leaders declared the Monroe-Adams policies presumptuous. Americans generally praised Monroe's policy, but interpreted it as responses to current issues. In the first decades after the president's speech, American policy makers did not use the doctrine against European powers. The term "Monroe Doctrine" did not even come into general use until the 1850s.

The Policy of Indian Removal was a logical extension of the Monroe Doctrine. It increased Americans' belief that their expansion was divinely and historically ordained and allowed economic considerations and greed to shape and harden the attitudes of Monroe and the American people toward the Native Americans (who still occupied the continent in great numbers). Cherokee, Choctaw, Chickasaw, and Creek tribes held millions of acres in what later would become the states of Georgia, Alabama, and Mississippi. Native Americans traded furs and hunted and fished in the Great Lakes region and the tribes and nations of the Great Plains pursued their lifestyles relatively undisturbed by white settlements. Monroe faced the key political issue of handling white expansion and treaty enforcement. His 1825 message to Congress reveals the influence of Manifest Destiny, stating that it would be impossible to incorporate masses of Native Americans into American society.

Slavery also was an important factor in implementing the Monroe Doctrine. As expansionism and Manifest Destiny principles dominated American culture and the United States acquired more territory, slavery became a more divisive issue. Some Americans felt that Manifest Destiny did not include enslaving peoples, while others believed that African Americans and Native Americans had either to be assimilated or marginalized. The Monroe administration itself did not consistently apply the doctrine's domestic or foreign policy principles. For example, Colombia and Brazil unsuccessfully petitioned Secretary of State Adams to enter into a defensive alliance against Europe. In 1826, Simón Bolívar called a conference of Western Hemisphere nations, but American President John Quincy Adams did not enthusiastically endorse the alliance.

President James K. Polk pragmatically applied the Monroe Doctrine from 1845 to 1849, when he helped the United States grow by more than one million square miles, across Texas and New Mexico to California and even Oregon. In his annual message to Congress on December 2, 1845, Polk announced that the principles of the Monroe Doctrine would be strictly enforced and that the United States would pursue a policy of westward expansion. More than any other president, Polk practiced the belief that the United States had a divine and historical mandate to rule as much of the continent as it could acquire. In 1845 Polk also cited the Monroe Doctrine as a precedent when he claimed that the United States instead of Great Britain held the rightful claim to the disputed Oregon Territory. He went on to invoke the Monroe Doctrine to warn Britain and Europe not to interfere in the controversy between the United States and Mexico that would eventually produce the Mexican War of 1846–1848.

One of Polk's most far-reaching Monroe-Adams policy applications involved the Republic of Texas, when between 1836 and 1845 the United States objected to the British alliance with Texas using the principles of the doctrine. The Republic of Texas had fought a revolution to win its independence from Mexico, and it claimed land that included all of the present-day state of Texas and parts of present-day New Mexico, Oklahoma, Kansas, Colorado, and Wyoming. The prospect of Texas being admitted as a slave state to the United States prevented its speedy admission. During the years that Texas was perched as a sovereign nation in the middle of the United States, Great Britain and France

President James Knox Polk pragmatically applied the Monroe Doctrine from 1845 to 1849. (Library of Congress)

ANOTHER VIEW Manifest Destiny and the Monroe Doctrine Are Alive and Well

The roots of Manifest Destiny grew in English soil in the Old World centuries before the British North American colonies transplanted the idea as part of the cultural baggage they brought to the New World. Ideas of military, political, and cultural dominance and the economic slave labor and indentured servant system that the British established in the New World are based on Manifest Destiny, as would be the British and later American attitudes and treatment of the Native American people.

Manifest Destiny and the Monroe Doctrine are two philosophical and political ideas that gradually became entwined with American culture and as decades of American life unfolded, part of the American psyche. The way these English precepts were implemented and transformed on the North American continent made them uniquely American.

The more pragmatic manifestations of Manifest Destiny in the United States appeared in the 1840s decade of American history when the United States added more than one million square miles of new territory to its domain. This was the largest expansion since the Louisiana Purchase forty years earlier, and by the end of the 1840s, the United States had acquired all its present territory except for Alaska, Hawaii, and some small areas gained through border adjustments. As America expanded, so did the ambitions and ideas of its citizens. This territorial expansion generated American nationalism and the American vision of social perfection and a sense of mission, the idea that God and history had earmarked the United States to expand its boundaries over a vast area not necessarily restricted to the North American continent. It also spawned the idea of cultural, religious, and racial superiority that provided the ideological underpinnings for this expansion.

involved themselves in its affairs, an intervention that alarmed Polk who had his own expansionist agenda.

As Polk and his adherents saw it, peace with Mexico and European recognition of the Republic of Texas presented a formidable obstacle to the westward expansion of the United States. If the Southern states joined the Republic of Texas, its boundaries would stretch halfway across the continent and the United States would face not only a civil war (which many people already foretold) but a world war. To some it seemed that the Republic of Texas held the balance of world power in its precarious existence. On January 12, 1845, France and England officially offered to negotiate a peace treaty between Texas and Mexico, an offer that galvanized Polk and the U.S. Congress into action. On January 25, 1845, the United States passed a joint resolution for the annexation of Texas.

During the 1850s, Great Britain continued to fuel American application of the Monroe Doctrine. Strained relations between the Americans and the English over sovereignty in several areas in Central America as well as the Republic of Texas issue intensified American use of the Doctrine's principles. In 1852, a few American politicians used the principles of the Monroe Doctrine to unsuccessfully argue for the forcible removal of the Spanish from Cuba.

The United States also applied the Monroe Doctrine during the years of its Civil War (1861–1865). Secretary of State William H. Seward said in 1861 that the United States should challenge European interventions

The adherents of Manifest Destiny argued that it was not selfish domination but rather an unselfish attempt to extend American liberty and ideas for the benefit of the world. Manifest Destiny became the ideological justification for the annexation of Texas, followed by California and Oregon. It impelled the purchase of Alaska from Russia; continued the centuries-old American fantasies about annexing Canada; and resurfaced once more in the seizure of Cuba in 1898 and the annexation of Hawaii. However, advocates of Manifest Destiny did not enjoy a consensus on how to implement their ideals. Some had limited territorial goals while others imagined a vast empire that would include Canada, Mexico, the Caribbean, and Pacific Islands. A few expanded their dream to world domination.

In modern discussions, the Monroe Doctrine is often shorthand for American colonialism in the Americas. The political meaning varies with the situation, and the perspective of the speaker. Generally the Monroe Doctrine is used as a symbol and rationalization of modern empire. Manifest Destiny, on the other hand, is used as an indicator of future imperial ambitions.

The adherents of Manifest Destiny and the Monroe Doctrine still argue that it is not selfish domination but rather an unselfish attempt to extend American liberty and ideas for the benefit of the world. President George W. Bush expressed the unchanging nature of the twenty-first-century Monroe Doctrine and Manifest Destiny in his State of the Union Message in January 2003. He declared, "Americans are a free people, who know that freedom is the right of every person and the future of every nation. The liberty we prize is not America's gift to the world; it is God's gift to humanity." Latin American nations, Mexicans, Filipinos, Hawaiians, and African Americans might have a different perspective of Manifest Destiny and the Monroe Doctrine.

in the Western Hemisphere by launching a drive to liberate Cuba and end the last vestiges of colonialism in the Americas. President Abraham Lincoln turned down the idea. When Spain reannexed the Dominican Republic, formerly Santo Domingo, the United States protested the fleeting reoccupation without quoting the Monroe Doctrine. Members of Congress and editorial writers were not as tactful as Seward, however. Over and over they reported that Seward was applying the Monroe Doctrine, and when the Dominican Republic regained its independence in 1865, Europeans acknowledged the Monroe Doctrine as an important factor.

After the Civil War, Secretary Seward applied the Monroe Doctrine more freely. In 1867 he negotiated the purchase of Alaska from Russia for $7.2 million, which anti-expansionists called "Seward's Folly" and "Seward's Ice Box." He also negotiated a treaty for the United States to buy the Virgin Islands from Denmark for $7.6 million, but the Senate refused to ratify the treaty.

Secretary of State William Seward continued the policy of the Monroe Doctrine in 1861. (Library of Congress)

IN CONTEXT   Conquering Cuba

On June 23, 1783, John Adams, the second president of the United States, articulated the U.S. attitude toward Cuba that would endure until the end of the nineteenth century. Depicting Cuba as a natural extension of the North American continent, he argued that the continuation of the United States required annexing Cuba. He calculated that Cuba should remain under Spanish rule until the United States could directly seize it and that Cuba would never be allowed its independence.

John Quincy Adams, son of John Adams and secretary of state in the James Monroe administration, and President James Monroe solidified an American foreign policy of blocking European interference with any of the newly formed Latin

American republics and called this policy the Monroe Doctrine. They and succeeding administrations believed that the United States had a special mission to implement its economic, social, cultural, religious, and political system across the Western Hemisphere and this aggressive expansionism called "Manifest Destiny" was coupled with the defensive paternalism of the Monroe Doctrine.

By the 1880s the United States had invested capital heavily in the Cuban economy and in 1895 the United States offered to buy Cuba for $100 million, but Spain refused. As a counter, the United States turned to interfering in the Cuban war against Spanish rule. When the USS *Maine* blew up on February 15, 1898, in Havana harbor, the United

The United States continued to apply the Monroe Doctrine in its dealings with Mexico. Between 1864 and 1867, Napoleon III of France attempted to establish a monarchy in Mexico by placing Emperor Maximilian on the throne. Americans charged that his actions violated the doctrine, the first time the Monroe Doctrine was popularly called "the Doctrine." In 1865 the American government used military and diplomatic pressure to support Mexican President Benito Juarez and help him lead a successful revolt against Emperor Maximilian. They used the Monroe Doctrine as a diplomatic tool.

President Ulysses S. Grant expanded the Monroe Doctrine in the 1870s, asserting that the United States would not allow European countries to transfer territories in the Western Hemisphere. Although Secretary of State Hamilton Fish did not fully endorse the idea, in 1870 Grant decided that the United States should annex the Dominican Republic and sent an agent to negotiate the agreement. His cabinet disapproved of the idea, but the president sent the proposal to the Senate, which rejected the formal treaty. Grant protested the rejection.

Grant enjoyed more success in applying the Monroe Doctrine to British and Confederate raiding during the Civil War in the 1871 case of the Alabama Claims. During the Civil War, the British built Confederate raiders that destroyed 100,000 tons of U.S. cargo. Seward negotiated the Johnson-Clarendon Convention in 1869 to judge the claims, and the Senate rejected the agreement by a margin of fifty-three to one. Grant's Secretary of State, Hamilton Fish, reopened the issue, and on May 8, 1871, Fish negotiated the Treaty of Washington between the United States and Great Britain. The treaty addressed the grievances from the American Civil War such as the Alabama claims and awarded the United States $15.5 million after stating that the British had failed to exercise due diligence.

IN CONTEXT *Conquering Cuba (Continued)*

States held the Spanish responsible and declared war. When Spain signed the Treaty of Paris on December 10, 1898, it ceded Cuba, Puerto Rico, Guam, the Philippines, and territory in the West Indies to the United States. Spain granted Cuban independence in 1902, although limited by the Platt Amendment, which granted the United States a major influence in Cuban affairs and required Cuba to grant the United States a lease for Guantánamo Bay. Using the provisions of the Platt Amendment, U.S. troops occupied Cuba a second time from 1906 to 1909. The Platt Amendment was revoked in 1934, but the lease of Guantánamo Bay was extended.

In 1940, Fulgencio Batista became official president or dictator of Cuba after spending decades as

the power behind a series of puppet governors. Fidel Castro, a young lawyer from a wealthy family, spent years waging a guerilla campaign against his regime, and Batista fled the country in January 1959. Castro took control of the government and moved to consolidate his power. Hundreds of thousands of Cubans fled as the revolution became more radical. The Castro Revolution resulted in the seizure of American property and the loss of American investments, and the United States broke diplomatic relations with Cuba on January 3, 1961. America imposed an embargo against Cuba on February 3, 1962, which was still in place in 2006. Castro's enforcement of a Marxist system in Cuba caused thousands of Cubans to flee to the United States and other countries.

The Treaty of Washington also dealt with the Fenian Raids and other cross-border issues with the new Dominion of Canada and helped avert a war between Britain and the United States. Canadian Prime Minister Sir John A. Macdonald served as one of the negotiators for the British, and although the principals negotiated the treaty for the British Empire, Macdonald's participation set the precedent for Canada to negotiate directly with the United States. This treaty was the outstanding achievement of the Grant administration.

In 1868, a rebellion known as the Ten Years' War erupted in Cuba. The rebels declared Cuban independence and set up a provisional government. When Grant took office, no one knew the status of the provisional government. A U.S. mediation plan failed, and Secretary of State Fish worked hard to keep the United States from intervening. Then, in 1873, the Spanish captured the *Virginius*, a gun runner for the Cuban rebels, and executed its crew, including some Americans. Just before the Spanish hanged him, Captain Fry, master of the *Virginius*, sent a poignant letter to his wife that she published in a New York City newspaper. War fever swept the nation, and coastal cities armed and drilled, but Fish moderated American demands. Eventually Cuba paid an $80,000 indemnity to the families of the executed Americas, but bloodshed in Cuba continued until Spain restored peace in 1878. The *Virginius* incident foretold the U.S. struggle with Spain over Cuba.

As the United States became more militarily powerful and imperialistic, Latin American countries began to associate the Monroe Doctrine not only with the exclusion of European powers from the Americas but also with the expansion of U.S. power and influence in the area. Although the United States did not formally use the Monroe Doctrine to justify

President Teddy Roosevelt extended the Monroe Doctrine with the Roosevelt Corollary. (Library of Congress)

American intervention, the Latin American nations began to distrust and dislike the American policy.

In 1895, President Grover Cleveland explicitly invoked the Monroe Doctrine when he forced Great Britain to submit to arbitration of a boundary dispute between British Guyana and Venezuela. He claimed that the British were violating the Monroe Doctrine and threatened London with war. His secretary of state, Richard Olney, asserted that the United States was practically sovereign on the continent. The British yielded to the demands of the United States, implying that the major European powers recognized the Monroe Doctrine.

In his annual messages to Congress in December 1904 and 1905, President Theodore Roosevelt announced the largest extension that had ever been added to the Monroe Doctrine, which became known as the Roosevelt Corollary. Roosevelt amended the Monroe Doctrine because he wanted to stop European powers from coming to the Western Hemisphere to collect debts or to mistreat foreign subjects. He feared that they might come as earnest creditors but remain as occupying powers. Roosevelt especially dreaded the thought of foreign powers in the Western Hemisphere because the United States had not finished building the Panama Canal, and America had to carefully guard its defensive interests in the Caribbean.

Immediately acting on his corollary, Roosevelt sent U.S. Marines into Santo Domingo in 1904, Nicaragua in 1911, and Haiti in 1915 with the rationale that the United States had to keep the Europeans out. Other Latin American nations were alarmed at the United States' assumption of international police power and relations between the United States and Latin America deteriorated. Roosevelt's predecessors also endorsed Roosevelt's idea that continued disturbances in a Latin American country justified U.S. intervention to avoid European interference. In fact, Presidents William Howard Taft and Woodrow Wilson enforced the Roosevelt Corollary more often than did Roosevelt. Even Wilson, a Democrat and arch-critic of Republican foreign policy, pursued a strategy of armed intervention in Haiti and the Dominican Republic in 1915 and 1916. In the first decades of the twentieth century, the Wilson administration and other administrations implemented arbitrary policies in Cuba, Nicaragua, and Mexico and revisited Haiti and the Dominican Republic.

By the 1920s, American policy makers began to press for a softer tone and a smaller "stick" in U.S. relations with Latin American countries, which had distrusted and even hated America for decades. J. Reuben Clark served as under secretary of state and later ambassador to Mexico under President Calvin Coolidge. Clark favored more conciliatory views toward Latin America and reinterpreted the Monroe Doctrine.

Clark stated his belief that the Roosevelt Corollary and the Monroe Doctrine were separate and that the United States acted as a sovereign nation in its intervention in Latin American affairs, not by permission of the Monroe Doctrine. He played down the Monroe Doctrine and its imperialistic aspects in an effort to foster better relations with Latin America. In the Clark memorandum of December 1928, the U.S. State Department repudiated the Roosevelt Corollary. Beginning in March 1930, during the Herbert Hoover administration, Secretary of State Henry L. Stimson guided American diplomacy toward a Good Neighbor Policy with its Latin American neighbors.

President Franklin Delano Roosevelt established the Monroe Doctrine as a redefined multilateral undertaking to be implemented by all the nations of the Western Hemisphere acting together. Roosevelt emphasized Pan-Americanism and the Good Neighbor Policy. He took office determined to improve relations with the nations of Central and South America. Under his leadership, the United States emphasized cooperation and trade rather than military force to maintain stability in the hemisphere.

Roosevelt's secretary of state, Cordell Hull, participated in the Montevideo Conference of December 1933, where he backed a declaration favored by most nations of the Western Hemisphere stating that no state had the right to interfere in the affairs of another. In 1934, at Roosevelt's direction, the 1903 treaty with Cuba (based on the Platt amendment) was abrogated; this was the treaty that gave the United States the right to intervene to preserve internal stability or independence. Although domestic economic problems and World War II diverted attention from the Western Hemisphere, Roosevelt's Good Neighbor Policy represented an attempt to distance the United States from earlier interventionist policies, such as the Roosevelt Corollary and military interventions in the region during the 1910s and 1920s.

In the 1950s and 1960s the United States again became involved in Guatemala, Cuba, and the Dominican Republic, but for the most part it continued to support hemispheric cooperation within the framework of the Organization of American States. President John Fitzgerald Kennedy symbolically invoked the Monroe Doctrine in 1962 when the Soviet Union began to build missile launching sites in Cuba. With the support of the Organization of American States, the president placed a naval and air quarantine around Cuba. After several tense days, the Soviet Union agreed to withdraw the missiles and dismantle the sites.

According to C. M. Wilson in *The Monroe Doctrine: An American Frame of Mind*, at an August 29, 1962, news conference President John F. Kennedy said:

The Monroe Doctrine means what it has meant since President Monroe and John Quincy Adams enunciated it, and that is that we would oppose a foreign power extending its power to the Western Hemisphere, and that is why we oppose what is happening in Cuba today. That is why we have cut off our trade. That is why we worked in the OAS and in other ways to isolate the Communist menace in Cuba. That is why we will continue to give a good deal of our effort and attention to it.

In the early 1970s, the United States helped overthrow the democratically elected government of Chile and took similar steps in the Dominican

Republic. The United States justified these invasions as stopping the spread of communism throughout Latin America and preventing "another Cuba." In 1984, the debate over this new version of the Monroe Doctrine focused on the Iran-Contra scandal. The scandal erupted with the revelation of the Central Intelligence Agency's (CIA) covert training of Contra guerilla soldiers in Nicaragua in an attempt to overthrow the democratically elected government and its president, Daniel Ortega. During the period of the civil war, the Contras killed an estimated forty to seventy thousand people and were responsible for the displacement of more than one hundred fifty thousand. CIA director Robert Gates vigorously defended the Contra scheme, arguing that avoiding the U.S. intervention in Nicaragua would be to give up on the Monroe Doctrine. Critics of the Reagan administration's support for Britain in the Falklands War (1982) also invoked the Monroe Doctrine, charging that the United States ignored the Monroe Doctrine even though a Latin American nation, Argentina, attacked the possession of an existing European power, Britain, that predated the doctrine.

Some have interpreted the Monroe Doctrine as isolationist, and others allege that the doctrine has functioned as a rationale for U.S. intervention in the affairs of nations of the Western Hemisphere, citing the statistics of thirty military interventions and forty-seven covert or indirect operations in Latin America since 1846.

ALTERNATE HISTORY

What if James Monroe had allowed continued European influence in the Americas, resulting in the United Nations of North America?

The breakup of the Spanish empire in the New World between 1815 and 1822 presented the fledgling United States with a diplomatic dilemma. British foreign minister George Canning implemented a policy of recognizing the independence of the Spanish colonies in America, which in turn marked a turning point in United States foreign policy.

Argentina, Chile, and Venezuela had won their independence from Spain, and as new republics they expected the United States' recognition. Many Americans agreed with this idea, but President James Monroe and his secretary of state, John Quincy Adams, were not sure that these nations would survive. They did not want to risk going to war with Spain if they recognized the new countries and then the countries reverted to Spanish control. If the other European powers did not intervene, the U.S. government could leave it to Spain and its rebellious colonies to resolve their own problems. As part of its territorial expansion, the United States was negotiating with Spain to purchase Florida and after the treaty was ratified, the Monroe administration began to recognize the new Latin American republics.

In 1823, the diplomatic situation became more tangled when France urged Spain to restore monarchical power and fight the new Latin American republics. Britain became alarmed at the idea of France reestablishing itself in the Western Hemisphere. Foreign Minister Canning argued that the United States and Great Britain should form an alliance to keep France and Spain from intervening in the new Latin American republics. Former Presidents Thomas Jefferson and James Madison urged Monroe to accept Canning's proposal, but Adams disagreed. He viewed with alarm the Russian efforts to gain a foothold along the Pacific coast from Alaska south to California, but he thought that the United States would be more credible if it dealt directly with Russia and France instead of forming an alliance with Britain to deal with them.

The cabinet meeting of November 7, 1823, marked a turning point in this foreign-policy dilemma that would shape the United States both geographically and politically. Because Canning believed so strongly that an alliance with the United States was necessary, he might have traveled to the United States on the diplomatic mission of arguing his case at the November cabinet meeting and elsewhere. Canning had a polarizing and abrasive personality. In England, he had fought a duel with his political opponent Lord Castlereagh, and he would have been prepared to argue with Adams just as forcefully.

Had Canning come, he and Adams would have confined themselves to a war of words instead of a duel, but Canning's words would have been just as fatal to Adams's arguments as a bullet would have been to Adams himself. When that November 7, 1823, cabinet meeting ended, Monroe would have sided with Canning, and Canning would have won his alliance with the United States. The victory could have been solidified with a document called the Canning Treaty of 1823 instead of a Monroe Doctrine. One of the reasons for Canning's victory might have been the fact that the United States had shrunk instead of grown from the time that it had declared its independence from Britain in 1776.

Rather than create the Monroe Doctrine, this turning point would replace the United States with a group of nations. In December 1814, twenty-six delegates from the New England States met at Hartford, Connecticut, to demand states' rights. There were twelve delegates from Massachusetts, including the district of Maine, seven from Connecticut, four from Rhode Island, two from New Hampshire, and one from Vermont. The delegates drafted proposals for constitutional amendments challenging what they called President James Madison's military despotism and calling for his resignation. The delegates hated the Jeffersonian Republicans who held power in the nation's capitol. When the Hartford delegation arrived in Washington, D.C., to propose their constitutional amendment, Madison had already signed the Treaty of Ghent that ended the war and news of Andrew Jackson's victory at New Orleans had reached Washington, D.C.

Instead of withdrawing their proposal as they did in actual history, the Hartford delegates might have presented it to Congress, despite the ridicule it had received, and if Congress had refused to consider their proposal, the New England states might have seceded from the Union. The remainder of the country might have allowed the New England states to secede "on principle." Secretary of War John C. Calhoun of South Carolina and the other states in the Southern block steadfastly maintained that any of the states in the Union had the right to nullify federal laws that they disagreed with and could secede from the Union if they desired. President Madison and the Congress might have allowed the New England states to leave the Union because the administration was more concerned with dealing with the Native American nations in America, and developing a maritime trade on the Great Lakes and the Mississippi River. After all, the New England states probably would have promptly allied themselves with British Canada, so everyone would have stayed in the same family of nations.

Canning might have inadvertently laid the foundation for another group of states to secede from the United States, causing a civil war. He agitated for the abolition of slavery along with fellow Englishman William Wilburforce, and slavery was abolished in Britain in 1833. Slavery was an entrenched political and economic system in America that Calhoun and his fellow southerners staunchly defended. Calhoun believed that slavery was a good rather than a necessary evil and he spoke out strongly in defense of it. Canning would have just as strongly defended its abolition. This belief and his equally strong belief that the French and Spanish peril to South America was real and immediate and only an alliance with the British could deflect might have made Calhoun both respect and despise Canning and England, an attitude that would have played a part in the coming civil war.

Britain would have continued to shape the map of North America, so much so that satirists in eastern newspapers might have quipped that losing the Revolutionary War and fighting the War of 1812 to a stalemate had increased, not diminished, British power and influence in North America. The Republic of Texas had fought a revolution to win its independence from Mexico and it claimed land that included all of the present-day state of Texas and parts of present-day New Mexico, Oklahoma, Kansas, Colorado, and Wyoming. Britain and France routinely involved themselves in the affairs of the Republic of Texas, and on January 12, 1845, they officially offered to negotiate a peace treaty between Texas and Mexico.

This state of affairs would have allowed President James K. Polk and the U.S. Congress to send a futile diplomatic protest because the Canning Treaty of 1823 would have made Britain an ally instead of an intruder. Even though Polk might have angrily pointed out that Britain had stabbed the United States in the back by collaborating with France in Texas, Britain would have continued to negotiate the treaty with the Republic of Texas. In March 1845, the Republic of Texas might have announced its independence from Mexico and its friendship with its neighboring states of Louisiana and the block of Mexican territory on its western boundary. Texas would have pushed its border from the Nueces to the Rio Grande and refused the offers of the United States to accept it into statehood.

In 1846 American settlers in Oregon petitioned for annexation to the United States, but the slave states voted against them, fearing that another free state would upset the delicate balance of power between free and slave states. The territory of Oregon might have been organized in August 1848 after the United States and Great Britain negotiated the

Oregon Treaty. Many senators would have refused to vote for it, claiming that Great Britain had diplomatically blackmailed the United States; however, Democratic president Polk, in a game of political chess with Britain, might have convinced his party to support the treaty because he wanted to bolster the Canning Treaty of 1823, so he could depend on British help in expelling the Spanish from the Western Hemisphere. The Oregon Territory included all of the present-day states of Idaho, Oregon, Washington, and Montana west of the continental divide, and Wyoming, west of the continental divide and north of the 42nd parallel. In a truly checkmate move, Oregon might have merged with British Columbia.

Much as they had done during the French and Indian War, the American Revolution, and the War of 1812, the British overtly and covertly used the Native American people as a weapon to spread their influence over the Western Hemisphere. The British, as well as the French and Spanish, might have sent envoys to the Indian Nations in North America. The five Indian Nations in the territory above the Republic of Texas would have been especially receptive because their northernmost boundary abutted the U.S. border. The Sioux and Dakota Nations, situated between Oregon and the Midwest might have negotiated agreements with the Metis Nation in Canada to create a formidable block of Indian Territory. Britain, France, and Spain would have frequently negotiated with this United Indian Nation as well. U.S. presidents from Madison to Lincoln would have decried the existence of Native American nations that contained more territory than the United States in the middle of the U.S. portion of the continent; but influenced by Canning's diplomatic precedents, Britain would have insisted that the United States use diplomatic means to deal with the Native Americans rather than force of removals.

In 1848 gold was discovered in California at Sutter's Mill and gold seekers invaded the territory. By now, the Mormon territories would have established the State of Deseret, and California and the State of Deseret would possibly have forged a secret alliance and declared their independence from Mexico in 1852.

Now the free state voting bloc might not be able to annex any more territory because of British, French, and Spanish interference in North America. The slave state voting bloc would have been boosted by Texas, the Louisiana Territory, and Florida. The South would have become increasingly angry at the British refusal to allow slave catchers to operate in the Oregon Territory. With the election to the presidency of Abraham Lincoln, the minority president of the Abolitionist Republican party, the South feared that slavery would be abolished. Following in the footsteps of New England, it would have seceded from the Union. Only this time, the United States would not have allowed a bloc of "rebellious" states to secede without a battle. President James Buchanan would have been aware of the conflicting interests and politics that forced the United States to fight a war to force the seceding states back into the Union.

Both geography and the need for living space would have driven the country toward civil war, as had already occurred in Europe. The

United States needed more territory. On the eve of the civil war, the continent of North America would have housed many nations, so many that it would have resembled a patchwork quilt. It would have consisted of the following groups:

- The Maritime Union: made up of the former states of Maine, New Hampshire, Vermont, Connecticut, Massachusetts, Rhode Island, and the Maritime Provinces of Canada. This unit would have dominated the Northeast

- Spanish Territory: Florida and much of the territory to the west of the Republic of Texas

- British-controlled Oregon and British Columbia

- Indian Nations

- California and the state of Deseret

- The Confederate States of America: Georgia, North Carolina, South Carolina, Virginia, Arkansas, Louisiana, Mississippi, Alabama, and Tennessee

- The Republic of Texas

- The states of New York, New Jersey, Delaware, Maryland, Pennsylvania, Kentucky, Michigan, Indiana, Ohio, Illinois, Wisconsin, Iowa, Missouri, and Minnesota—the remaining United States of America.

President James Buchanan could have ignored the issues of slavery and states' rights that many of his contemporaries thought were the reasons for the impending civil war, recognizing the real reason for the crisis: the necessity for territorial expansion on a rapidly shrinking continent. The United States would have constantly had to put its territorial expansion at the top of its agenda.

In 1861, Secretary of State William H. Seward would have advocated liberating Cuba. President Abraham Lincoln, endorsing the idea, would have sent a Union brigade to conquer the island. It could have been intercepted at sea by the Texas navy and massacred. Soon, in both actual history and alternate history, President Abraham Lincoln had to contend with the secession of the southern states and the subsequent civil war. The Republic of Texas and some of the Indian nations would have sided with the South. The Maritime Union, British Oregon, and British Columbia, and some of the Indian nations would have sided with the North. California and the state of Deseret would have remained neutral. The two groups of states might have fought to a stalemate and the Confederate States of America probably would have become a sovereign nation.

U.S. president Ulysses S. Grant and Secretary of State Hamilton Fish would have participated in delicate post–Civil War negotiations with Great Britain and Canada to preserve the United States. Canada could have wanted to annex the United States as a logical extension of the Maritime Union and the British Territory of Oregon. Canadian Prime Minister Sir John A. Macdonald could have argued that a United States-Canadian merger would provide a powerful buffer against the Metis

Nation and the Sioux and Dakota and Five Nations that flanked the United States on its western boundaries. Grant and Fish would have managed to prevent outright annexation, but Canada would have continued to heavily influence U.S. affairs.

Into the twentieth century, actual world history would have paralleled this alternate history. President Franklin Delano Roosevelt and his secretary of state Cordell Hull participated in the Montevideo Conference of December 1933, where in actual history, Roosevelt backed a declaration favored by most nations of the Western Hemisphere, stating that no country had the right to intervene in the internal or external affairs of another. But then the Nazis invaded Poland and then western Europe. In alternate history, Roosevelt and British Prime Minister Winston Churchill would have negotiated a treaty with the United States of America, the Confederate States of America, the Republic of Texas, Spanish Florida, the Indian Alliance, British Oregon, and the Maritime Union as well as the rest of Canada. All the North American nations would have signed a declaration of war against Germany, calling themselves the United Nations of North America.

After the end of World War II the United Nations of North America would have continued their alliance. None of the other countries would have intervened when the United States unsuccessfully invaded Cuba in 1961, nor would they have assisted the United States when it faced down Russia in the Cuban missile crisis of 1962.

In one last alternate history addition to the nations of North America, in 2001, a group backed by the Catholic Church would have collected thousands of signatures on a petition requesting a referendum on Cuba's political system. Former president Jimmy Carter would have openly supported the petition during his historic 2002 visit to Cuba, in alternate history. The petition would have contained sufficient signatures, but the Fidel Castro government would have rejected it. For the second time in 200 years, the United Nations of North America would have come together as one, in this case to force Castro to allow the Cuban people a plebiscite to decide their own fate. They would have voted to become a republic and join the United Nations of North America.

Kathy Warnes

Discussion Questions

1. The sidebar titled "Conquering Cuba" notes that the United States continues to hold a lease on a base in Cuba called Guantánamo Bay. What role did this base play in George W. Bush's War on Terrorism in the early 2000s?

2. In the alternate history, the lack of a Monroe Doctrine leads to the creation of separate countries that eventually unite as the United Nations of North America. But what if such unification did not occur? How would the different entities have related to one another over the decades? Would one of the countries have become more powerful than the others?

3. The author suggests that some historians believe aspects of the Monroe Doctrine and Manifest Destiny—that is, keeping European powers out of North and South American affairs and exporting American values—are still at play in today's world. Describe some examples of this philosophy. Is the Iraq War related to some of these beliefs?

4. In the alternate history, Canada plays a much larger role in the unfolding of events than it did in actual history. Why, in actual history, is Canada not a major force in world events? How much do population and proximity to the superpower United States influence Canada's foreign policy?

5. In considering alternate histories, what would be different about the United States today if America had annexed Canada, as some early American politicians had wanted? What cultural aspects might be different? How strong would the French influence be?

6. In this alternate history, North America is divided into many different nations. What do you think the boundaries would be of the various separate nations described in this chapter?

7. Maryland, Missouri, and Kentucky were slave states in actual history, but they remained in the Union during the Civil War and did not secede to join the Confederacy. In this alternate history, do you think they would be more or less likely to remain loyal to the Union?

8. In the alternate history, the Confederate States successfully secede from the United States. Do you think that the Confederate States would have eventually abolished slavery, and if so, when do you think it might have happened?

9. One of the reasons that "Deseret" (based in Utah) would have sought its independence was that the Church of Latter Day Saints (the Mormons) endorsed polygamy. Do you think polygamy would have persisted in an independent Deseret into the twentieth century, or do you think that Deseret would have eventually outlawed the practice?

10. In the alternate history, New England seceded from the Union first and joined the Maritime provinces to the north to form the Maritime Union. One of the reasons in actual history for the growth of abolitionism in New England was that residents there (like William Lloyd Garrison) did not want to be associated in the same nation with slavery. How would the early separation of New England from the Union have affected the growth and development of abolitionism? How would it have affected the development of the Underground Railroad, by which escaped slaves were transported through a network of safe houses to freedom in Canada?

Bibliography and Further Reading

Bemis, Samuel Flagg. *John Quincy Adams and the Foundations of American Foreign Policy*. Westport, CT: Greenwood Press, 1981.

Cobbs, Elizabeth A. *The Rich Neighbor Policy: Rockefeller and Kaiser in Brazil*. New Haven, CT: Yale University Press, 1992.

Gellman, Irwin F. *Good Neighbor Diplomacy: United States Policy in Latin America, 1933–1945*. Baltimore, MD: Johns Hopkins University Press, 1979.

Holt, Thaddeus. "Joint Plan Red." *MHQ: The Quarterly Journal of Military History* 1, no. 1 (Autumn 1988).

Lafeber, Walter. *The American Search for Opportunity, 1865–1913*, vol. 2. Cambridge, UK: Cambridge University Press, 1993.

May, Ernest R. *The Making of the Monroe Doctrine*. Cambridge, MA: Harvard University Press, 1975.

Merk, Frederick. *The Monroe Doctrine and American Expansionism, 1843–1849*. New York: Knopf, 1966.

Monroe, James. "Message of President James Monroe at the Commencement of the First Session of the 28th Congress, December 2, 1823." Presidential Messages of the 18th Congress, ca. 12/02/1823–ca. 03/03/1825, Record Group 46, Records of the United States Senate, 1789–1990. Washington, DC: National Archives and Records Administration.

Monroe, James. "Milestone Documents." Washington, DC: National Archives and Records Administration, 1995.

Morgan, H. Wayne. *America's Road to Empire: The War with Spain and Overseas Expansion*. New York: McGraw-Hill, 1965.

Murphy, Gretchen. *Hemispheric Imaginings: The Monroe Doctrine and Narratives of U.S. Empire*. Durham, NC: Duke University Press, 2005.

Neidhardt, W. S. *Fenianism in North America*. University Park: Pennsylvania State University Press, 1975.

Preston, Richard A. *The Defence of the Undefended Border: Planning for War in North America 1867–1939*. Montreal, Canada: McGill-Queen's University Press, 1977.

Smith, Gaddis. *The Last Years of the Monroe Doctrine, 1945–1993*. New York: Hill & Wang, 1994.

Wilson, C. M. *The Monroe Doctrine: An American Frame of Mind*. New York: Auerbach Publishers, 1971.

> *The railroad and telegraph were the infrastructure of westward expansion. What if these crucial inventions had been developed later?*

INTRODUCTION

The spirit of Manifest Destiny required infrastructure—the mechanisms through which American influence could expand and grow to occupy areas beyond the settlements in the colonial north and south parts of the East Coast. Culture provided some of this support by creating a new American identity that could expand to include diverse peoples from throughout the world. But European observers still brought up nagging concerns that the United States was simply too large to be administered by a central authority. By the 1840s, when the United States stretched to include expansive western territories, many people doubted the nation's capacity to succeed.

However, technological innovation was on the side of the new nation. New technologies promised to connect far-flung regions of the country to create a cohesive whole in the near future. Most important, the technology of the railroad that had been used to enhance industry throughout the northeastern part of the country would be applied to greater distances, ultimately connecting the far West with the eastern cities.

By contemporary standards, a train may seem slow and inefficient. In the nineteenth century, though, its ability to move raw materials and to shrink time and space was viewed by Americans as nothing less than magic. For railroads, image has been as important as reality. In the process of knitting together the nation, railroads became an important symbol of an age of expansion in which the nation sought to solidify a social and economic foundation in national commerce. From the commuter-cities to container-hauling diesel engines of today, railroads have permeated the American being. Toy trains and nostalgia continue to perpetuate the romance of the rails.

From the beginning, the success of railroading depended on systems of scale. The basic technology was readily available in the early 1800s. George Stephenson, who conceived of the idea to use a tubular boiler, built his *Rocket* in Great Britain and entered it in trials sponsored by the Liverpool and Manchester Railway. He won 500 pounds and gained immortality as the inventor of the steam locomotive. Once the problem of

KEY CONCEPT   The City the Railroad Made: Altoona, Pennsylvania

Between 1835 and 1850, more railroad building was done in Pennsylvania than in any other state. When Charles Schlatter surveyed possible routes for a rail line from Philadelphia to Pittsburgh in the late 1830s, he recommended a route that ran along the Juniata River in the east and the Conemaugh in the west. Although the western portion of the railroad was completed by 1852, engineers remained befuddled on how to cross the Allegheny Mountains, and passengers and freight still depended on the slow and dangerous state-owned Allegheny Portage Railroad.

John Edgar Thomson, chief engineer and later president of the Pennsylvania Railroad (PRR), designed the new technology that would replace the Portage Railroad. Studying the ridges surrounding the town of Altoona, Thomson settled on a point that rose 122 feet at a practical grade of less than 2 percent, which could be managed by most locomotives.

Irish laborers from Cork, Mayo, and Antrim Counties used picks and shovels to form a ledge on which they could place the tracks. The tracks ended up in the shape of a horseshoe: they went up the eastern side of the mountain, turned left to cross the valleys to the western side where they turned left again.

When the Horseshoe Curve opened in 1854, it reduced travel time from Philadelphia to Pittsburgh by four days! In 1854, the passenger service between Philadelphia and Pittsburgh began, and the average trip took just fifteen hours and cost $8.00 a ticket. Considered an international engineering marvel, the Horseshoe Curve was modeled at the 1893 Columbian Exposition in Chicago. The Curve also solidified Altoona's growing reputation as the nation's railroad capital.

Nearby, this grand rail empire created its center, which was organized around service, maintenance,

motive power had been solved, little stood in the way of the rapid displacement of earlier forms of transportation.

In the United States, the early use of railroads was concentrated in the Northeast. In 1827, Erastus Corning chartered the Mohawk and Hudson Railroad to run along the Erie Canal. Often, railroads followed the beds of existing canals. This image created a clear representation of the old and the new: the slow, relatively unreliable canal boats pulled by animals and the fast, reliable, machine-powered steam engine. The rationale for this placement, though, was utilitarian: canal builders had already cleared passage through hills and even through mountains. Railroads could take advantage of these existing openings. This neighboring technology soon made the canal's limitations obvious. By 1850, most canal systems had been replaced by rail lines and their sponsoring companies recast as transportation companies.

Regions seeking to grow began to look at railroads as the path to success. In 1828, Baltimore residents chose this new technology as their best hope to compete with the canals of New York and Pennsylvania. The Baltimore and Ohio became the first American railroad to haul both freight and passengers by steam on a regular schedule. Most railroads continued to be short lines involved only in specific industries, such as the mining of anthracite coal in Pennsylvania. However, by 1840 there were as many miles of railroads in the United States as miles of canal. During the 1840s, this infrastructural shift gained intensity throughout the nation. By the 1850s, a period had begun of not only railroad building but also of the formal and informal consolidation of individual lines into a national system. It was becoming increasingly clear that the railroad would not merely connect navigable bodies of water; instead they would become the basic means of transportation regardless of distances and difficulty of terrain.

KEY CONCEPT *The City the Railroad Made: Altoona, Pennsylvania (Continued)*

and administration. In 1849, the PRR purchased thirty-five acres of the 220-acre Robinson farm. Robinson's former farm was then bisected by a great system of railroad tracks, which ran down the center of town with the streets running parallel to the tracks. In the center of all of this lay the Twelfth Street shops, which were the first railroad shops and opened in 1852. It was a mammoth complex, the first within the industry to be self-sufficient in manufacturing, repair, and service for its fleet of locomotives, freight, and passenger rail cars. With a population of 200, Altoona became a borough in 1854. On the strength of the rail industry, Altoona's population sky-rocketed to 8,000 by 1868, when Altoona officially became a city.

Altoona's population nearly tripled between 1860 and 1870 with the influx of immigrant laborers, particularly from eastern Europe. In addition, merchants moved to Altoona from all over the state to help make the city the region's hub for trade and industry. The PRR's acquisition of smaller lines made it the world's largest corporation by 1880, with $400 million in capital and 30,000 employees.

The physical structures of Altoona defined the state of the art for railroads throughout the world. These structures included the Juniata Locomotive Shops, which were the largest in the world at the time, and the Hollidaysburg Car Shops. These facilities soon became the world's largest producers of box, flat, hopper, gondola, tank, and steel coil cars. In addition, Altoona was once home to the two largest roundhouses in the world. Roundhouses were used to store locomotives. Turntables in roundhouses were used to point a locomotive into a specific stall or turn it around.

Although railroading remade each American city and town, Altoona was built around the railroad. Its present and future were directly tied to this single transportation technology.

Under the leadership of Corning, the New York Central opened up the first major westward corridor that would culminate in linking New York City with Chicago. As the economic power of such undertakings became evident, railroad development attracted the attention of political onlookers. Politicians became important tools for the railroad's development, and formal and informal graft was frequent when such massive amounts of capital were at stake. Most often, railroads were viewed as a common good and politicians courted their development.

The antebellum railroad was a thing of wonder to a people whose ideas of what it cost and how long it took to move goods and people had been formed in the age of wagons on turnpikes, steamboats on rivers, and the barges on man-made canals. Even though railroads required significant construction, developers were able to keep rates low—often below those of the other possible modes of transport.

The low price of rail transport relied on regimented systemization, a concept that was impossible in the early industrial era that often fell prey to the vagaries of technology, nature, and human failure. In creating the railroad system, though, communication was crucial. Previous modes of transport allowed the perpetuation of existing forms of communication (such as writing), but railroads demanded something more.

The most important development in the early railroad system was the telegraph, which was invented by Samuel F. B. Morse in 1844. From the fateful day when Congress rejected the idea that the telegraph was a logical extension of the postal service, the growth of the new technology was sporadic. How could such a system be financed and made profitable? In the mid-1850s, Hiram Sibley convinced investors that a whole telegraphy system would be more valuable than the sum of its parts. He and his

KEY CONCEPT   Small-Scale Railroading Spurs Industry

The acceleration of industrial development was nearly as much a cultural development as a technological one. Although harvesting, processing, and shipping industrial materials involved hundreds of different communities, one was specifically designed to serve as a showcase of industrial development. The town of Mauch Chunk, Pennsylvania, which is today known as Jim Thorpe, was designed to demonstrate industrial processes to others involved in industry as well as to the general public.

Mauch Chunk was owned and developed by the Lehigh Coal & Navigation Company from 1818

to 1831. The entire town focused around the mining of hard, anthracite coal, which had been discovered on Sharp Mountain by Philip Ginter in 1791. With a large supply of this important energy source, Mauch Chunk developed the additional industry of transporting coal. The Lehigh River became an integral link along this shipping corridor and roads were made to connect the primary coal mine to the river. However, the valuable coal made Mauch Chunk ripe for the use of new technologies.

In 1827, a new era in technology was ushered in when the wagon road was transformed into a

associates built Western Union, which over the next ten years became the corporate hub for the entire American telegraphic system. Focusing on the corridor between Buffalo and Chicago, Western Union became the dominant player in the settlement of the American West. Sibley and Western Union were hired by the federal government to string a wire across the vast American West just prior to the Civil War. As a defining technology of the new railroad era, the telegraph business and Western Union soon became a most attractive investment. The famous financier Jay Gould soon made Sibley's company one of his most valuable properties.

Samuel F. B. Morse invented the telegraph in 1844. (Library of Congress)

Ultimately, the railroad and telegraph technologies developed symbiotically. Railroads followed the easiest route across the landscape. Therefore, it was sensible for telegraph lines to follow these same passages. More important, telegraphy soon became essential to longer distance railroading. When the transcontinental railroad was completed in Utah in 1869, it also connected the first transcontinental telegraph line. By the 1870s, telegraphic dispatching was almost entirely responsible for systematizing railways and making them run with regularity. This reliability transformed railroads into a transportation technology on which Americans could depend. Ultimately, commerce could structure itself around railroading and telegraphy offices could be found in every train station.

As the railroad and telegraph became part of everyday living, each technology significantly impacted American life. Due to the timing of these technologies, railroading easily became one of the most critical elements of

KEY CONCEPT *Small-Scale Railroading Spurs Industry (Continued)*

gravity railroad. One of the nation's first small-scale rail lines, Mauch Chunk's railroad became known as the Switchback Gravity Railroad. From the mine's location at higher elevation, the coal could then travel down the mountain by means of this railroad system utilizing gravity. The empty cars were then hauled up the mountain by mules.

All the coal from Summit Hill and Panther Valley arrived at the canal landing in this fashion. Then, in 1872, a large tunnel opened that ended the need for the gravity railroad. At approximately the same time, the gravity railroad was replaced for coal hauling by the steam-locomotive-powered Panther Creek Railroad. This, however, did not end the gravity line's history. In 1874, developers purchased the switchback gravity railroad and made it the centerpiece attraction in Mauch Chunk, the tourist attraction of the industrial era. Eventually, the switchback railroad inspired roller coasters.

Visitors to Mauch Chunk altered expectations of industry throughout the country. Although the town's railroads carried materials only short distances, they were a vision of a future of long-distance railroading that was just around the nation's corner.

American development after the American Civil War. In particular, the integral role of railroading in American life stimulated American expansion into the western territories of North America. In fact, without railroads in the late–nineteenth century, the American West of today would look quite different.

An 1864 photograph of Manassas Junction railroad and telegraph station. (Library of Congress)

KEY CONCEPT   Spurring Ethnic Diversity in the West

The settlement of the West was made more compli-cated by a basic characteristic of the needs of the growing railroad enterprise: ethnic diversity. Even before the railroad, the American West was a meet-ing place of diverse peoples. Managing and living with such diversity was an ongoing difficulty along the frontier; however, the varied peoples eventually became a defining characteristic of the American West.

Some early groups of settlers, such as the Mormons, sought distance from most Americans in hopes of developing a distinct and insulated soci-ety. Traveling west to construct the Deseret king-dom in 1847, Brigham Young and the Mormon faithful constructed an irrigation society in the

deserts of Utah. While other utopian communities would find success in the open expanse of the West, tolerance of native groups dwindled as American settlement increased.

Initially, reservation policies allowed native tra-ditions to endure, albeit in difficult circumstances. As settlement pressures increased, the U.S. Army for-mally and informally made independent life impos-sible for native communities. Native groups reacted differently. Some fought these American influences: the most famous example is the Lakota Sioux band-ing with other tribes to defeat General George Armstrong Custer at Little Big Horn in 1876. Violent resistance, however, helped to solidify racist policies of the federal government, including the Dawes

TURNING POINT

Most early settlers traveled over land trails in covered wagons that served as equivalents of modern-day U-Haul trucks. These trails quickly became institutionalized, with trading posts and forts along the way to aid settlers in their movement westward. The Oregon and Sante Fe Trails are the best known. The slow wagon travel along these trails would continue for set-tlers, but Asian, Irish, and other immigrants worked through the 1860s to complete the Transcontinental Railroad at Promontory Point, Utah, in 1869. From this spine, the rest of the West would rapidly be entwined in a national system of commerce. Seen as a civilizing force, the railroad also brokered political and economic power in the West.

In 1865, after thirty-five years of steady, cautious development in the Northeast and Midwest, the American railroad system was far from com-plete. From 35,000 miles in 1865 the network had grown to embrace nearly 200,000 miles by 1897. As a unit, the trunk-line railroads of the Northeast may rank among the most impressive concentrations of eco-nomic capital in human history. This infrastructure, then, allowed late-nineteenth-century American society to achieve unrivaled industrial and commercial development. From the start, the New York Central and the Pennsylvania railroads were successes; the Baltimore and Ohio and the Erie railroads played significant roles in this development, but they were secondary to the two former rail lines. All lines pointed westward for expansion.

The growth westward moved from trunk lines and through Chicago and secondarily St. Louis. These lines included the Chicago, Burlington, and Quincy; the Chicago and North Western; and the Chicago, Rock Island, and Pacific. This was the first line to cross the Mississippi, which

KEY CONCEPT *Spurring Ethnic Diversity in the West (Continued)*

Severalty Act of 1887, which sought to undermine tribal authority and group ownership of land.

Additional diversity came from the influx of people to work in the California gold fields after 1849. Following an initial rush of American miners and prospectors, additional fortune seekers arrived from all over the world, particularly coming from Asia where California was being advertised as "the Golden Mountain." Many prospectors would remain, creating significant Asian populations in San Francisco and other urban areas. They also offered a ready labor force for building the enterprise that would shape the West so dramatically: the railroad.

In California, many Chinese immigrants had worked to construct a central railroad in the 1860s.

When the Central Pacific Railroad Company looked for a workforce to lay its track eastward, the Chinese were a natural fit. By 1868, 4,000 workers manned the railroad project. Approximately two-thirds of those workers were Chinese. From the other direction, a largely Irish labor force laid the track. The completion of the transcontinental railroad was a symbol of a new beginning for the United States, but it also heralded the ethnic diversity of the West.

The corridor brought immigrants straight from ports such as New York City to western states, including Minnesota, Idaho, and Kansas. Often, ethnic groups such as Norwegians, Germans, and Swedes controlled land in a specific area in order to create ethnic enclaves. Many of these have endured into the twenty-first century.

was a watershed achievement for the development of railroads. Then the Burlington set out to control the route to the Pacific coast. This same strategy inspired James J. Hill as he created a new rail empire out of small but strategically important lines in Minnesota. Soon he dominated the region, which meant that he was a significant player in any railroad's effort to reach the Pacific.

The race to finish the nation's first transcontinental railroad culminated with its completion at Promontory Point. Although the crews coming west from main lines near Chicago covered a great expanse, those coming east had miraculously brought the line of rails through the snow-capped Sierra-Nevada Mountains. The completion of the railroad was a turning point in the history of the western United States; however, it also defined the future of the entire country. When the golden spike was driven to complete the railroad at Promontory Point, it marked a great psychological boost for the nation. But the nation's rail network would not function well for years.

The continued development of the network of rails was largely carried out by Hill's Great Northern Railroad Company. By 1901 he controlled the Northern Pacific, the Burlington, and the Great Northern, constituting one of the best-conceived regional consolidations of transportation in American history. It was through these efforts that America used the railroad better than any other nation to minimize the constraints of space and time. From its wise use of this technology, the United States surpassed every other nation in the world in industrial production by the early 1900s.

For the nation, the railroad became an important symbol of success. In the case of the West, the railroad's symbolic role is clear in visual images such as William S. Jewett's *The Promised Land*. The painting depicts Lady Liberty and the civilizing abilities of Americans with their supporting tools, including the railroads. These tools of expansion brought a region and its resources under the control of the U.S. government. While

---

IN CONTEXT   An Excerpt from *The Octopus* by Frank Norris

The symbolic imagery of the railroad usually emphasized the economic development that was possible with this new technology. The frustrated Norris, however, believed that the railroad had great destructive capabilities as well. He worried that the corrupt politics that governed railroad pricing and development would squeeze out Western farmers.

But suddenly there was an interruption. Presley had climbed the fence at the limit of the Quien Sabe ranch. Beyond was Los Muertos, but between the two ran the railroad. He had only time to jump back upon the embankment when, with a quivering of all the earth, a locomotive, single, unattached, shot by him with a roar, filling the air with the reek of hot oil, vomiting smoke and sparks; its enormous eye, cyclopean, red, throwing a glare far in advance, shooting by in a sudden crash of confused thunder; filling the night with the terrific clamor of its iron hoofs....

Before Presley could recover from the shock of the eruption, while the earth was still vibrating, the rails still humming, the engine was far away, flinging the echo of its frantic gallop over all the valley. For a brief instant it roared with a hollow diapason on the Long Trestle over Broderson Creek, then plunged into a cutting farther on, the quivering glare of its fires losing itself in the night, its thunder abruptly diminishing to a subdued and distant humming. All at once this ceased. The engine was gone.

But the moment the noise of the engine lapsed, Presley—about to start forward again—was conscious of a confusion of lamentable sounds that rose into the night from out the engine's wake. Prolonged cries of agony, sobbing wails of infinite pain, heart-rending, pitiful." (Norris, 12–15)

---

such development would have been extremely difficult without the railroad, its influence on western development was not entirely progressive. The railroad certainly marked the demise of Native Americans in the West as well as that of the buffalo, which played an important role in the natives' spiritual lives. Additionally, the railroad pulled the distant lands into the American commercial network. Farming in distant places and shipping produce to urban centers suddenly became conceivable and profitable.

By the end of the nineteenth century, many critics would claim that the power of the railroad in the West had become too great. In such a commercial environment, the railroad's power was supreme. Dispersing lands and controlling rates were simply a few ways that railroads controlled western development. In the 1890s, farmers' frustration with the bullying role of the railroad fed the populist political movement. This exploitive relationship also fed the literary imagination of Frank Norris in his 1901 classic *The Octopus*. In the novel, the octopus is the railroad that has come to manipulate all life in the American West.

Although the transcontinental railroad provided barons of industry and politics with excessive power, it also provided the mechanism for Americans to take control of the West. By the end of the nineteenth century, it was clear to many Americans that the areas to the west of the Mississippi River differed from others in basic ways. One of the primary distinctions is climate. Many observers have presented readers with visions of the American West, yet possibly none seems as authentic as that portrayed by Wallace Stegner. In *The American West as Living Space,* Stegner wrote:

> The West has had a way of warping well-carpentered habits, and raising the grain on exposed dreams. . . . The fact is, it has been as notable for mirages as for the realization of dreams. . . . Aridity and aridity alone, makes the various Wests one. The distinctive western plants and animals, the hard clarity . . . of western air, the look and location of western towns, the empty spaces that separate them, the way farms and ranches are either densely concentrated where water is plentiful or widely scattered where it is scarce.

Facing up to the nature of the West required a grit and determination bordering on stubbornness. It was exactly this spirit that President James K. Polk would parlay into a rationale for the 1848 war with Mexico. In the 1840s, this spirit found expression in the policies of Franklin Pierce, and Polk wrested control of the Pacific Northwest from Native American tribes and Europeans. Thanks to the 1848 expansionist war and other negotiations, by 1850 the United States stretched from sea to sea. But what truly connected this area with the rest of the country was the system of railroading in the late nineteenth century.

The iron horse made trade possible in even the most remote stretches of the West. The railroad made it profitable for farmers to establish wheat farms in far-off areas of Idaho because they could still get their crop to market easily. Similarly, areas such as Texas could be used to profitably raise cattle that would ultimately be sold as beef in Chicago, Illinois, or Omaha, Nebraska. By linking these stretches of the West into profitable trade networks, railroads forced developers to figure out ways to make inhospitable regions more livable.

ACTUAL HISTORY

The planning and construction of railroads in the United States progressed rapidly after 1840. Some historians say it occurred too rapidly. With little direction and supervision from the state governments that were granting charters for construction, railroad companies constructed lines at sites in which they were able to take possession of land or on ground that required the least amount of alteration. If done properly, though, the first step in constructing a rail line was to survey possible passages. Such surveys allowed planners to establish the most sensible route in terms of grade, elevation, and terrain.

Before 1840, most surveys were made for short passenger lines that proved to be financially unprofitable. Under stiff competition from canal companies, many lines were started and abandoned before they were completed. The first real success came when the Boston and Lowell Railroad diverted traffic from the Middlesex Canal in the 1830s. After the first few successful companies demonstrated the economic feasibility of transporting commodities via rail, others followed throughout the northeastern United States.

The process of constructing railroads began with revising humans' view of the landscape. Issues such as grade, elevation, and passages between mountains became part of a new way of mapping the United States. Typically, early railroad surveys and their subsequent construction were financed by private investors. When shorter lines proved successful, investors began talking about grander schemes.

The possibility of railroads connecting the Atlantic and Pacific coasts was soon discussed in Congress, and this initiated federal efforts to map and survey the western United States. A series of surveys showed that a railroad could follow any one of a number of different routes. The least expensive, though, appeared to be the route following the 32nd parallel. The Southern Pacific Railroad was subsequently built along this parallel. Even though it offered the best route, the decision was highly political: Southern routes were objectionable to Northern politicians (and vice versa).

Although the issue continued to be openly debated, the Railroad Act of 1862 put the support of the federal government behind the transcontinental railroad. With federal support, the Union Pacific Railroad eventually joined with the Central Pacific. They met in Utah on May 10, 1869, and signaled the linking of the continent. News of this great national accomplishment spread across the continent, using the technology that ran parallel with the tracks—the telegraph.

An 1868 photograph shows construction of a railroad bridge in the Green River Valley, Wyoming, and Citadel Rock, a prominent rock formation rising above the plateau. (Library of Congress)

Very quickly, the telegraph made itself indispensable to the railroad system. By the 1870s telegraphic dispatching had organized the railways into a regimented endeavor on which Americans could depend, and around which commerce could structure itself—including the use of train stations as telegraph offices. The telegraph and railroad became a marriage of related technologies. As they passed endless hours crossing the nation, train crews were required to keep a sharp eye out for breaks in either the rail or telegraph system.

Running in synchronicity, the wires and poles extended across the nation, typically taking advantage of the railroad's right-of-way and running directly next to the tracks. This complement to the rail technology shrank time and space further by facilitating communication between stations. This communication, which was considered to be essential to the scheduling and safety of rail travel, also allowed Americans their first long-distance communication network. In fact, railroading left little on the American landscape unchanged after 1850.

Following 1880, the railroad industry reshaped the American environment and reoriented American thinking away from a horse-drawn past and toward a future of rails. Throughout the nation, the luxury passenger expresses blew through crossings and passed small-town depots as they pursued urban destinations. In industrial zones, the slow freight trains took materials to their destinations steadily and consistently. Finally, morning and evening commuters shuttled back and forth between suburban stations and underground urban terminals, creating new types of communities as well as the landscapes to support them.

In order for this system to function, each American needed to learn to live with the needs of the railroad. This ubiquitous infrastructure included the actual railroad right-of-way of roadbed and tracks; signals and depots; bridges and junctions; and the omnipresent wail of the passing locomotive. Trains and the "right-of-way" that cleared a path for them transformed adjacent built environments in novel, sometimes startling ways. The railroad also influenced many related patterns of land use. For instance, they nurtured factory complexes and electricity generating stations in accessible locations, and they contributed to the development of commuter suburbs, while initiating the decline of main streets and many urban centers. It should be pointed out, however, that although trains initiated suburbanization, their transportation centers in the hearts of urban areas also helped revitalize many cities.

The suburban trend, though, was the railroad's greatest effect on the living patterns of most Americans. In the years between 1880 and 1930, hundreds of thousands of Americans declared their dependence on railroads and moved to suburbs. Magazines presented the railroad suburbs as perfect living environments in which wives and children were liberated from the unhealthful aspects of urban life. Most towns created railroad stations, and railroad suburbs entirely laid themselves out around them. Terminals and rail yards became sprawling centers of commercial activity, inspiring awe in their scale and scope.

Many train stations included central clock towers that made the first public display of the time in many American communities. The typical small-town depot existed to serve several purposes, each of which was clearly defined by its builders. It provided accommodation for passengers

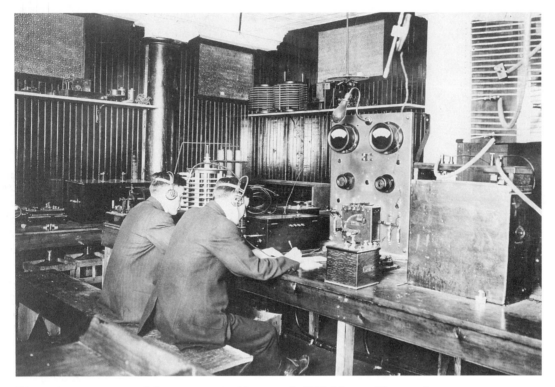

Telegraph operators transmitting messages to ships at sea in 1912. (Library of Congress)

Cornelius Vanderbilt developed his railroad line into the first rapid transit system in the nation. (Library of Congress)

waiting to board, sheltered people waiting for arrivals, and received people having business in the telegraph office. With the imposition of standard time in 1886, the railroad made itself time keeper for the nation. While the public enjoyed chiming church-steeple clocks, the station clocks provided perfect accuracy. Once a week the telegraph flashed the exact time, and clocks would be adjusted.

The railroad's dominance in the late 1800s did not derive only from moving goods. With the completion of the transcontinental connection, railroading eventually adjusted the nature of trade and travel to an entirely new scale. Systematic routes were constructed so that passengers could reliably use rails for transportation between cities in vastly different portions of the nation. From the beginning, passengers were a primary customer of railroads.

Even on shorter lines, railroads initiated the first stages of a commuter society. In the 1870s, Cornelius Vanderbilt developed the New York and Harlem line as a model—the first rapid transit line in the nation. Grand Central Terminal

A photograph taken between 1870 and 1890 of an early train wreck. (Library of Congress)

became the bustling symbol of a new, metropolitan era growing out of rails. Vanderbilt's son, William, developed limited passenger service throughout the nation that did not stop at each station and therefore could make passenger travel quicker and more reliable. Eventually, the plush Pullman car made traveling accommodations as luxurious as those of the nation's leading hotels.

This era brought the nation together in a period of integration and unification that created one great national economy. As railroads consolidated in the late nineteenth century, the limited trains were further systematized as through routes. Unlike airline hubs, writes historian Albro Martin in *Railroads Trumphant*, the through routes were like "mighty steel clotheslines, along which were pinned the dozens of intermediate points, including good-size cities as well as towns that were so important in the America of that day." Furthermore, the Pullman sleeping car saved businessmen's entire days for work. As the trunk lines took shape, American life was becoming standardized around the railroads.

The golden age for railroading lasted from 1897 to 1920. In 1890, 492 million people boarded American trains and rode a total of 11.8 billion passenger miles. The average trip was only twenty-four miles long. The record for passengers, however, was set in 1920 when a billion and a quarter passengers boarded trains and rode 47.4 million passenger miles. From 1920 forward, rail passengers began to opt for auto and air travel in increasing numbers. The shift from steam to diesel power kept railroading the greatest option for moving cargo; however, the automobile and the airplane offered passengers conveniences that railroads could not match.

The centrality of the railroad was physically obvious from railroad crossings on highways to distant whistle calls echoing over the countryside. More subtle artifacts, though, showed just how deeply Americans appreciated railroads in their past and present. By 1900, one of the most desired toys of American boys, for instance, was the toy train. The Lionel Company began making toy trains in 1900, but by 1930 the toy train was firmly ensconced as the most-desired toy by boys across the nation. Powered by electricity, toy trains remain a rallying point for hobbyists. As the economic influence of railroads lessened in the late twentieth century, toy trains still grew in popularity.

Could the train, though, truly be responsible for the development of an entire portion of the nation? In 1893, historian Frederick Jackson Turner studied the impact of the railroad in the American West in *The United States, 1830–1850*. Census data demonstrated to him that in the Western United States there remained no areas that he would consider to be "unsettled." The frontier, as Turner referred to it, had aided the nation in recovering its unity after Civil War, but now the nation needed to move on. He told Americans that the frontier was "closed."

In theory, Turner had made an important observation. However, the impact of the railroad did not allow development of the West to falter. In fact, throughout the twentieth century, the American West urbanized and developed to hold some of the nation's most populous cities. Although many details of life and culture aided this growth, possibly none was as intrinsic to the West as the synchronized technologies of the railroad and telegraph. It makes one wonder how the nation would differ today if the golden spike had not been driven at Promontory Point in 1869.

ALTERNATE HISTORY

Without the completion of the transcontinental railroad in the 1860s, the effort to achieve national recovery after the Civil War would likely have lost one of its most important engines of change. Although this would have slowed American expansion into Western areas, the most pronounced effect would likely have been most obvious on the ground level. Very likely, the West as a region would appear very different today.

Without the influence of the railroad, original patterns of human and animal life in the region might have endured longer. The railroad disrupted many of the basic patterns of native and animal life. For instance, if the American bison had been allowed to endure—even in a large expanse of the central Plains—it is very likely that native peoples who placed importance on the animal could have persisted. Possibly, this persistence would have resulted in increased tribal continuity and allowed these nations to negotiate with the American government from a stronger position.

As it was, of course, the railroad helped to commodify Western lands. Remote areas were now accessible, whether they would serve as a source for energy or mineral resources, an attraction for tourists to national parks, or as the raw material for expansive crops of wheat, corn, or cattle. In almost every case, native populations needed to be displaced to make way for the American view of progress and development. Reservations served as a solution in many areas of the West, but would these have been necessary without the commercial possibilities brought with the railroad and telegraph? Most likely the very definition of "remote" and "accessible" would have evolved quite differently. Even if native groups had still been placed on reservations, their locations might have been considered differently.

The access brought by railroad technology also gave Americans a remarkable ability to connect with and see the wonders of the Western lands. By the end of the nineteenth century, the earliest designated parks formed a symbiotic relationship with the railroad. The ability of travelers to come to Yellowstone, Yosemite, or other areas had a clear impact on Americans' definition of what a national park should be. Without this accessibility, would Americans have expanded their national parks in the early twentieth century? Very likely not. In addition, Congress would not have felt the same compulsion to establish the National Park Service in 1916 to coordinate and protect America's most special natural resources. By bringing settlement to the West, the railroad, in a back-handed way, forced preservationists to line up and protect areas they thought were most unique and important.

Finally, by bringing American patterns of settlement to the Western lands, the railroad tied the federal government into an undertaking that has defined the region's story: water management. The call for federal involvement occurred on the heels of decades of disinformation from land speculators, railroads, and government officials that depicted the West as a great garden in which anyone could grow anything. When some settlers began to complain about the region's aridity, railroad companies helped to spread a new motto: "Rain follows the plow," in which quasi-scientific proof was used to argue that increased agriculture created moisture that resulted in increased rainfall.

The understanding that the Western United States was dry or arid was accepted slowly. However, the timing of the railroad stimulated population settlement throughout the West at the end of the nineteenth century. It is no coincidence that once communities had been established, it became imperative to help them manage their region's aridity in the early 1900s. Therefore, one can assume that without the railroad's arrival at this time, efforts to manage Western water would have also very likely been delayed. This would have dramatically altered the development of major cities such as Las Vegas and, more importantly, entire agricultural regions such as the Central or Great Valleys of California.

In the case of California, the scale of the implications related to water development made it the next great political and social mechanism for wielding power after the railroad had been constructed. Los Angeles, for instance, became a great opportunity for developers seeking to use hydraulic planning to enhance the value of cheap real estate. To the north in California, massive orange groves were developed and

KEY CONCEPT   National Parks and Railroads in the West

The railroad was a vital mechanism for overcoming the natural constraints of the West. In addition, though, it provided crucial access to the West's awesome natural features. Many of these peaks, waterfalls, forests, and rock formations ultimately became part of America's revolutionary National Parks system. This system very likely would not have been created without the railroad, which helped to unlock an important and productive resource for the western states: tourism.

Advertising and camping lodges constructed by railroad companies brought tourists to see the beauties and oddities of the western regions as early as the 1870s. This flow of visitors contributed to the first efforts at preservation of natural resources, focusing on Yosemite and Yellowstone National Parks.

Yellowstone, established as the first national park in 1872, developed closely with railroad interests who hoped it would attract tourists to the American West. Its features—geysers, waterfalls—proved more important to observers than its unspoiled wilderness. Such features also made questionable the area's utility for settlement, which allowed its sponsors to dub the area "worthless for development." Such a designation made lawmakers more willing to sponsor legislation setting it aside for altruistic reasons.

fed by manipulated water supplies. The scale of these undertakings was gargantuan. Without the railroad already in place, such development might not have occurred. Very likely, though, the scale would have been minimal. It is possible that without the railroad's presence in the late 1800s, out of necessity Americans still would have sought to fashion sustainable ways of living in arid areas such as California; however, these settlements, disconnected from central systems of communication and trade, would most likely have resembled those of the Pueblos or Mormons. Such settlements would have been slower to evolve into the major cities that compose the West today.

The people living in the urban West would also likely be different if the railroad and telegraph system had not developed in the late 1800s. The ethnic diversity of the West was fed by the opportunities brought by the railroad. The most specific example is likely Asians, particularly Chinese-Americans. Brought by opportunities in the gold fields or supporting the miners from urban areas such as San Francisco, Chinese immigrants often intended to return to their homeland once they had accrued financial stability. For many, though, new opportunities intervened: just when the opportunities in gold lessened, the call went out for laborers to help build the railroad to the east during the 1860s. Instrumental in this construction process, Chinese immigrants became even more likely to remain in the United States. Without the occurrence of railroad expansion directly after the first decade of the gold rush, this labor pool might have moved elsewhere.

More than anything else, the railroad brought access to the interior West. It seems very likely that without its presence in the late nineteenth century, Western settlement would have come from the

KEY CONCEPT *National Parks and Railroads in the West (Continued)*

One of the most important figures in the preservation of Yellowstone was the Philadelphia financier Jay Cooke. He orchestrated Yellowstone's special treatment as a service to the Northern Pacific Railroad. If Yellowstone were made a federal reservation, railroads would not be able to pass through it. This would provide the Northern Pacific a monopoly on transport across the southern part of the Montana Territory. The Northern Pacific adopted Yellowstone's cause with an eye toward establishing a resort in the region.

Cooke's responsibility was to create the publicity that would make Americans want to visit the park. Stories about the region had circulated in the East for years. Now, when the park bill was signed, interest in Yellowstone as the first national park would increase as newspapers and magazines published the news of the bill's passage. In June 1972, Cooke planned a grand public event complete with the dramatic unveiling of the famed artist Thomas Moran's mammoth painting of Yellowstone. Ultimately, this canvas, which was conceived by Moran on the Hayden Expedition, was hung in the U.S. Capitol.

In the wake of the great success and appeal of Yellowstone, the railroads remained in the National Park business well into the twentieth century. Particularly in the late nineteenth century, Americans perceived no conflict of interest when railroads constructed great lodges and other facilities to make these parks more tourist friendly.

coast and moved inward after the discovery of gold in California in 1849. This approach to settlement would have radically altered the centrality and importance of locations in the Midwest, such as Chicago, Illinois.

In addition, one must question whether the United States would have been able to retain control over the stretches of the West so distant from the nation's political and financial capitals. Could Americans have fended off a potential invading force from another nation if it had attacked in Oregon or California? Or through Mexico to the Southwest? The railroad spread economic development throughout the continent; however, it also acted as a statement of ownership and control over a geographically far-flung nation.

Brian Black, Ph.D.

Discussion Questions

1. If railroad development had not gone beyond the Midwest by the end of the nineteenth century, how would that have affected the economic development of states west of Kansas and Nebraska?

2. Some have argued that railroad development tended to stifle local industries and types of agriculture by developing an early price and market system in which cheaper and more efficient producers could squeeze out less efficient producers. Would the nation be stronger or weaker with more diverse centers of steel, oil, lumber, and other producers if less efficient producers could have survived without competition brought by the railroads?

3. The growth of railroads was key to the development of the great trusts and monopolies (such as those in steel, oil, and other basic commodities) of the late nineteenth and early twentieth century. Was this a good or a bad development?

Bibliography and Further Reading

Conzen, Michael, ed. *The Making of the American Landscape*. Boston: Unwin Hyman, 1990.

Cronon, William. *Nature's Metropolis*. New York: W.W. Norton, 1991.

Hughes, Thomas P. *American Genesis: A Century of Invention and Technological Enthusiasm*. New York: Penguin Books, 1989.

Jackson, Kenneth T. *Crabgrass Frontier*. New York: Oxford University Press, 1985.

Kern, Stephen. *The Culture of Time and Space, 1880–1918*. Cambridge: Harvard University Press, 1983.

Martin, Albro. *Railroads Trumphant: The Growth, Rejection & Rebirth of a Vital American Force*. New York: Oxford University Press, 1992.

Nash, Roderick. *Wilderness and the American Mind*. New Haven, CT: Yale University Press, 1986.

Norris, Frank. *The Octopus*. New York: Penguin Group, 1994.

Reisner, Marc. *Cadillac Desert*. New York: Penguin Group, 1986.

Robbins, William G. *Colony and Empire: The Capitalist Transformation of the American West*. Lawrence: University Press of Kansas, 1995.

Runte, Alfred. *National Parks: The American Experience*. Lincoln: University of Nebraska Press, 1997.

Schlebecker, John T. *Whereby We Thrive: A History of American Farming, 1607–1972*. Ames: Iowa State University Press, 1975.

Sellars, Richard West. *Preserving Nature in the National Parks: A History*. New Haven, CT: Yale University Press, 1997.

Smith, Henry Nash. *Virgin Land: The American West as Symbol and Myth*. Cambridge, MA: Harvard University Press, 1978.

Spence, Mark D. *Dispossessing the Wilderness: Indian Removal and the Making of the National Parks*. New York: Oxford University Press, 2000.

Stegner, Wallace. *The American West as Living Space*. Ann Arbor: University of Michigan Press, 1987.

Stephanson, Anders. *Manifest Destiny: American Expansionism and the Empire of Right*. New York: Hill and Wang, 1995.

Stilgoe, John R. *Borderland*. New Haven, CT: Yale University Press, 1990.

Stilgoe, John R. *Metropolitan Corridor: Railroads and the American Scene*. New Haven, CT: Yale University Press, 1983.

Trachtenberg, Alan. *The Incorporation of America: Culture and Society in the Gilded Age*. New York: Hill and Wang, 1982.

Turner, Frederick Jackson. *The United States, 1830–1850*. New York: Henry Holt, 1934.

Ward, James A. *Railroads and the Character of America.* Knoxville: University of Tennessee Press, 1986.

West, Elliot. *The Contested Plains: Indians, Goldseekers, & the Rush to Colorado.* Lawrence: University of Kansas Press, 2000.

White, Richard. *"It's Your Misfortune and None of My Own."* Norman: University of Oklahoma Press, 1991.

Worster, Donald. *Dust Bowl: The Southern Plains in the 1930s.* New York: Oxford University Press, 1979.

TURNING POINT

Texas was annexed in 1845 after the 1844 presidential election. What if that election had turned out differently and Texas remained an independent country?

INTRODUCTION

For hundreds of years Texas was a land inhabited by a few small Native American tribes living in the shadow of the Comanches. With the European, namely Spanish, invasion of North and South America, the land that would become Texas became part of the Spanish empire. Three centuries passed between the time a Spaniard first viewed the Texas shoreline in 1519 and the day the Spanish flag of Castile and León was lowered for the final time in 1819. But Spain did not effectively colonize the region. The missions that the Spanish created in Texas never encouraged mass immigration to Texas. At the beginning of the 1800s, about 4,000 people had settled in Texas and half of them were located in San Antonio de Bexar.

Spanish Texas became a hotbed for cultural absorption. Texas natives began to acquire Hispanic cultural elements that came from native intermediaries at first, and then the Spanish themselves. There are many Spanish legacies in Texas. The Spanish gave names to numerous towns, cities, counties, and geographic features. They introduced many crops and European irrigation systems, livestock, and livestock-handling techniques at their mission sites. Spanish missionaries and settlers improved area farming. The Franciscans came to Spanish Texas and Christianized the Texas natives. They built some of the finest examples of Spanish mission architecture in places like San Antonio and Goliad. In addition, the Spanish lent their ideas about law to Texas, including judicial procedure.

There were many external and internal threats to the Spanish occupation of Texas. Spain was one of the most powerful countries in the world in the 1500s and a major player on the international stage up until the 1800s. Its rivals were the up-and-coming European countries of Britain and France. In its three-century reign, Spain probably experienced only slightly more than 100 years of uninterrupted rule. By the beginning of the 1800s, Spanish rule in Texas began to wane as a result of the American threat to Texas after the Louisiana Purchase in 1803 and

KEY CONCEPT   The Franciscans

The Franciscans who led the movement to bring Christianity to the natives in Texas were followers of St. Francis of Assisi (1182–1226) who dedicated his life to spreading the Gospel and helping the poor. St. Francis, who was baptized Giovanni after John the Baptist, was the son of Italian importer, Pietro Bernadone, and Lady Pica, a French woman of noble birth. The child soon became known as Franciscan ("the Frenchman"), later shortened to "Francis."

As a young man, Francis developed a strong desire to help the poor. After unsuccessfully attempting to sell some of his father's textiles to raise money to rebuild St. Damian's church, he was forced to return the money. Undaunted, he and a growing group of friends began rebuilding the church themselves, frequently begging on the streets for money to continue their project. St. Francis allowed his pity to overcome his lifelong fear of lepers and began

tending the "unclean," which made him an outcast among people of his own class. Thereafter, he dedicated his life to ministering to the spiritual and physical needs of the sick and poor.

St. Francis and his followers began calling themselves "Little Brown Brothers" after their rough, brown tunics. Under pressure, St. Francis and eleven followers sought an audience with Pope Innocent III who gave them permission to found the Order of the Friars Minor, "Little Brothers," after the pope dreamed that St. Francis was the one individual who could prevent the Catholic Church from crumbling into disarray. Members of the order, which was founded in 1210, were required to take oaths of poverty, chastity, and obedience. The legend of St. Francis grew. Stories were told about his taming a wolf in one town. A remarkable tale was also told about his preaching to a flock of birds,

the rise in France of Napoleon Bonaparte, who waged war on all of Europe, including Spain.

Spain was determined not to let American intruders into Texas, fearing that the Anglo-Americans would bring political discord and illicit trade into the region. In 1806 it made an agreement with the United States that the Sabine Pass would be the boundary between the two lands, but that was not enough to keep out the American settlers. They were lured to Texas because of its potential wealth coupled with Spain's tenuous hold on the relatively unpopulated land.

While Spain was immersed with the threat that the French dictator Napoleon posed in Europe, its colonies in the Americas, including Mexico, revolted against the Crown. By 1810, revolution had broken out in Mexico. The Royalists, or those who were pro-Spain, fought to maintain the status quo, while the revolutionaries fought for the ideals of the European Enlightenment, which stressed new political, social, and economic opportunities for those who had not had them before. In Mexico that would be the native, *mestizo*, and *criollo* populations. *Mestizos* were people with mixed European and native ancestry. *Criollos* were Mexican-born people of pure European blood. The Spanish-born in Mexico were called *peninsulares*, and they were at the top of Mexican colonial society. Spanish colonial society was marked by a very rigid social hierarchy that allowed little or no movement within it. The *peninsulares* held the most important political and economic posts, while the *criollos* and *mestizos* held the rest. The war in Mexico between the Royalists and revolutionaries was horrifying. Brutalities occurred in many places as both sides massacred prisoners.

KEY CONCEPT *The Franciscans (Continued)*

after which they formed the shape of the Cross in the air. St. Francis's name became synonymous with Christian love for all living things.

In 1219 at the age of 37, St. Francis and two followers traveled to Syria to attempt conversion of the Muslims. He believed that he had an obligation to end the bloody Crusades, which began around 1096 and continued to 1270 as Christians fought Muslims for control of Jerusalem. This controversy has continued to divide the Middle East into the twenty-first century. After failing to convince Saladin, the Muslim leader, to join him in his endeavors, St. Francis offered to throw himself into the fire as a sacrifice to his beliefs. His offer was rejected, but the Muslims became convinced that he had unique powers. St. Francis contracted malaria and died at the age of forty-three; he was buried in the Basilica of St. Francis in Assisi. He was canonized by Pope Gregory IX in 1228.

In July 1629, a group of Jumanos from Texas arrived at a mission in San Antonio de la Isleta in New Mexico to beg the Franciscans for Christian instruction. They said they had been sent by a Franciscan nun, María de Jesús de Agreda, "the Lady in Blue." Convinced that it was God's will that they raise the natives from "the darkness of ignorance," the Franciscans made their way to Texas. Because of their vow of poverty, the Franciscans arrived in Texas wearing ragged habits and with few supplies. Nevertheless, their ardor for spreading the Gospel was undiminished as they set about converting the natives. They made Texas their home and named the first settlement San Francisco de los Tejas after their founder. Thus, the Franciscans became an inextricable part of the history of Texas as it evolved from a Mexican territory into an integral part of the United States.

Texas was at the outer periphery of the Spanish empire and what would later become the country of Mexico. Although it was a barren province, key events happened in Texas during these revolutionary times. The Mexicans sought aid from the United States. But Americans also had interests in Texas. In 1813, several hundred men invaded Texas from Louisiana. The Republican Army of the North fighting in the revolution had more Americans than Mexicans. Its leader was a former U.S. army officer. Still, the Americans involved wanted to secure Texas for Mexico, not for the United States. Eventually, the Republican Army of the North defeated the Royalist forces and occupied San Antonio in 1814, thus securing southern Texas.

The Royalists launched a counteroffensive of their own in 1814 and tried to retake South Texas. Royalists defeated the revolutionaries at the Medina River, near San Antonio. Almost two thousand rebels were killed in the battle. The Royalists massacred the rebel prisoners and attacked the citizens of San Antonio. A young Royalist lieutenant, Antonio López de Santa Anna, distinguished himself in this campaign and received recognition for his courage.

For four years Texas did not witness any rebel intrusion. Then in 1818, Dr. James Long, an American, received a commission from one rebel faction in Mexico to lead an expedition to Texas. Long and his 300 men occupied the Texan city of Nacogdoches. He then proceeded to San Antonio but was stopped by Royalist forces after a brief skirmish. He and his men were sent to Mexico City and jailed. Long was shot, but his men were released after Mexico gained its independence from Spain.

These expeditions and subsequent battles had a deep impact on Tejano (Texas) society. The settled population of four thousand had

IN CONTEXT   Napoleonic Wars

From 1791 to 1815, France and Britain were involved in a series of bitter battles for supremacy among European nations. It was a time when both countries were also building empires around the world. In 1799, Napoleon Bonaparte (1769–1821) seized control of France. By 1802, he had instituted his plan to conquer the rest of Europe. Although he was successful to a large degree, Napoleon was not able to topple Britain. After a disastrous invasion of Russia, his power declined rapidly. Napoleon was soundly defeated at the Battle of Waterloo in Belgium on June 18, 1815. Determined to return to power, he reinstalled himself on the French throne but was removed when British forces, led by the Duke of Wellington, forced him out of power. Napoleon died at the age of fifty-two on the island of St. Helena where he had been banished. The official cause of

death was stomach cancer, although rumors have persisted that he died of arsenic poisoning.

In 1808, Napoleon turned his attention to Spain, where his involvement served to bring down the Spanish monarchy. Appalled at the atrocities committed by the Spanish around the world, many Spanish Liberals and intellectuals saw Napoleon's involvement in Spain as a way to advance nineteenth-century Enlightenment thought and as a means of establishing rational government to replace a heritage of tyranny and corruption. Most members of the Spanish Enlightenment were, therefore, sympathetic to France. In fact, the French did abolish the hated Spanish Inquisition, which had allowed the Spanish government to conduct a campaign of blood-cleansing that was intended to eradicate all

declined to half that number. By the end of the 1810s, it was clear that the Royalist forces in Mexico were defeating the opposition. Spain was concerned about the population of its northern province. But by 1821, a successful Mexican independence movement brought Texas under the sway of Mexico. Texas passed from Spanish to Mexican control without any protest by its inhabitants. Now it was up to Mexico to maintain the population and guard its northernmost province from foreign intruders.

It would soon be evident that Mexico lacked the population numbers to effectively populate Texas. Mexico took an action that would ultimately lead to independence for Texas—it allowed European and American immigrants into Texas to act as defense forces against natives and foreign powers. At first, Mexico's immigration policies were very lenient. In 1821, a man from Connecticut named Moses Austin contracted with Mexico to bring three hundred American families to an area near San Antonio. Austin died shortly afterward, but his son Stephen took over the enterprise and led the settlers there in 1823.

Right before the revolution began, Austin's colony had twenty thousand white colonists and two thousand black slaves. It had four times the number of Mexicans in Texas. Mexico abolished slavery in 1831, but Austin ignored the law. He also ignored the law requiring the settlers to convert to Roman Catholicism. More and more the settlers thought of themselves less as Mexican subjects and more of a cross between Mexicans and Texans—or "Texians," as they called themselves.

There were plenty of people who wanted Texas to be part of the Union. President John Quincy Adams offered Mexico $1 million for Texas; Andrew Jackson offered $5 million. Mexico did not sell but did

---

descendents of converted Jews and Muslims from Spain.

No one in Spain was more susceptible to Napoleon's charisma and promises of a dazzling future than the Spanish royal family. Carlos IV, a weak and vacillating ruler, saw Napoleon's presence in Spain as a way to overcome the challenges to his power directed by members of his own family. His son, Ferdinand, was determined to topple his father; and Godoy, the queen's lover, was acting as a virtual dictator when Napoleon arrived in France. A master manipulator, Napoleon offered to serve as a mediator in the family quarrel and managed to convince Carlos IV to abdicate the throne. Forthwith, Napoleon imprisoned the royal family under strict military guard and installed his brother Joseph on the Spanish throne.

While Napoleon was successful in destroying the Spanish monarchy, he overlooked two impor-

tant factors. First, his presence in Spain would ultimately expose his forces to the British, a strong presence in neighboring Portugal. Second, the Spanish people as a whole were not ready to cede their sovereignty to the French invaders. Despite Napoleon's visions of smooth sailing, the population of Madrid revolted on May 1808, and the new king was forced to flee for his life. Total deaths in the Madrid Revolt have been estimated to be as high as 25,000. Even though the revolt was overturned by Napoleon's military might and Joseph was reinstalled in Madrid, fierce guerilla warfare continued to plague the French troops. The revolutionaries, composed of peasants, shepherds, and booty-seekers, received the full support of the Spanish clergy who were convinced that the French were heretics sent by the devil. They were also outraged that the hated French had sold property belonging to the church.

---

allow more and more Americans to come into the area and settle. The areas began to attract restless and sometimes lawless Americans such as Jim Bowie; Sam Houston, a soldier and good friend of Andrew Jackson; and David Crockett, a Tennessee ex-congressman and backwoodsman who was an expert at self-promotion.

In the mid-1820s, Mexico reevaluated its immigration policy. Mexican officials alleged that Americans squatted on lands without going through the proper procedures and did not make a serious commitment to obey the laws of the Mexican Constitution. In 1826, there was a short-lived episode to declare the Nacogdoches area of Texas an independent republic (the so-called Fredonian Republic). It failed, but the movement was a wake-up call to Mexican authorities that something had to be done about these immigrants or new secessionist sentiments would arise. The new settlers soon raised political issues that affected the entire region's relationship with the Mexican federal government.

In 1830, the Mexican government passed laws that prohibited further immigration into Texas with the exception of two colonies, established military bases to police immigration, and forbade the further importation of slaves to Texas. This was the hated Law of April 6, 1830. Many of the people who settled in Texas were from the slaveholding states of the American South. This law, if obeyed, would hinder the potential wealth of these people in Texas. The Anglo-American settlers in Texas had numerous grievances with the Mexican government by the beginning of the 1830s. They wanted local self-government in Texas; resented Mexican laws suspending land contracts, imposing self-duties on imported goods, and forbidding foreigners to enter the province; and feared that the Mexican government would force them to convert to Catholicism and take steps to free their slaves. Eventually, Mexico lifted the law prohibiting foreign immigrants, but Santa Anna reduced Texas to the status of a military district in the province of Coahuila.

Anglo-Americans attacked the military post at Anahuac in the summer of 1832. The following year, Antonio López de Santa Anna entered Mexico City and removed the ruling party from power. He allowed American immigration back into Texas, but that was only until he changed his political stance from a Federalist to a Centralist. He sought to centralize power under his leadership and abandoned the Federalist Constitution of 1824. There were anti-Santa Anna uprisings in other Mexican provinces like Zacatecas, but these were not independence movements and were quickly put down.

The Texas Revolution began with the battle of Gonzales in October 1835 and ended with the battle of San Jacinto in April 1836. In 1835, the Texas army was divided and not organized. Santa Anna took advantage of this disorganization and crossed the Rio Grande into Texas at the beginning of 1836. He thought the Texans were pirates and he was out to show them a lesson or two about rising up against authority. His target was San Antonio and the Texans who were stationed there. The Texas defense forces were split up and positioned like a triangle. On the west was San Antonio, on the south was San Patricio, and on the northeast was La Bahía (Goliad). Texas formally voted for independence on March 2, 1836, at a convention meeting at Washington-on-the-Brazos. This convention also appointed Sam Houston major general of the Texas army and commander of the forces at Gonzales.

In hindsight, San Antonio was not important to the success of Santa Anna's campaign. The garrison at Goliad was more important because it held about five hundred Texans under the command of James Fannin. Conversely, the Alamo mission in San Antonio had about 180 men under the divided command of William B. Travis and James Bowie. Santa Anna, however, had a score to settle with the garrison at San Antonio. They had embarrassed his family by defeating his son-in-law, General Martín Perfecto de Cos several months earlier in the city. After a thirteen-day siege, Santa Anna defeated the Alamo combatants on March 6, 1836. Santa Anna was also dealt a harsh blow as he lost many men in the battle.

Another, smaller Mexican force had crossed the Rio Grande and captured San Patricio. Fannin and his men faced an inevitable defeat at Goliad and asked for terms of surrender. Fannin was told that his men would be treated honorably and as prisoners of war. The Texans were imprisoned in Goliad and assured of their release. Santa Anna, however, ordered the execution of the Texan prisoners, an order that was carried out on March 27,

Sam Houston was in charge of American forces in Texas. (Library of Congress)

1836. With the San Antonio and Goliad garrisons soundly defeated and General Houston, with his 800 to 900 men, on a full retreat from Gonzales into East Texas, the insurrection appeared over. But Houston surprise-attacked Santa Anna's 1,300-man army near the San Jacinto River on April 21, 1836, killing, capturing, or scattering virtually the entire Mexican army. The battle took only eighteen minutes as the Texans cried for vengeance by shouting, "Remember the Alamo!" and "Remember Goliad!" The Texans captured Santa Anna the following day and forced him to order all Mexican troops out of Texas and recognize its independence. Later, Santa Anna would recant everything he said while he was a captive of the Texans.

The Mexican government itself had been partly to blame for the Texas uprising. Federalist Mexicans encouraged American immigration to Texas but Centralists, such as Santa Anna in the 1830s, feared the Americanization of Texas. After Texas won its independence, the region had some unique characteristics. The Anglos had implemented a republican form of government, established a different language, and created a social order in which minorities, such as the Mexican Texans who helped the Anglos gain independence, were subordinated. All these things gave Texas unique Anglo-American aspects. Still, Texas remained a largely underdeveloped frontier and its settlers still depended on an agrarian economy. Texas slaves were not given their freedom.

The fate of Texas was still to be determined even after independence was achieved. Texas claimed much of the land east along the Rio Grande to its source. This included areas belonging to the modern-day states of New Mexico, Oklahoma, Colorado, and Wyoming. While the Texans were busy establishing a government, there was talk of Mexico invading Texas once again to try to recover its former recalcitrant province. But Mexico became caught up in similar Texas-like revolts against its centralist government in other provinces and separatist revolts in northern Mexico and the Yucatan peninsula. These revolts were not successful but they kept the Mexican government and army bogged down, diverting attention from Texas and allowing it to remain independent.

Texas independence did not mean the new country and its inhabitants had a stable political and social life. The native Texans, or Tejanos, were shoved aside by waves of immigrants from the United States who sought to preside over the Texan political scene. Even the original American settlers were pushed aside by this newer wave of immigrants seeking to buy land and start a new life. Immigrants had been coming in during the revolution as well. The early 1840s also saw considerable border skirmishing between Texas and Mexico. In 1842, Mexican armies had occupied San Antonio. Texas had to reestablish a regular army to keep the Mexican threat at bay. Texas tried unsuccessfully to annex the Mexican provinces of Santa Fe (New Mexico) and Coahuila.

Texas ratified a constitution, which included slavery, and waited to be annexed into the United States. But Andrew Jackson was in no hurry. He did not want war with Mexico over Texas and risk the election of his handpicked successor Martin Van Buren. Texas was pro-slavery. If Texas entered the Union it would come in as a slave state and upset the delicate balance between free and slave states in the U.S. Congress. Jackson did formally recognize Texas on his last day in office in March 1841, after Van Buren had been safely elected.

IN CONTEXT   Davy Crockett and the Alamo

Davy Crockett was the best-known and the most charismatic American killed at the Alamo when Mexican forces overran the Texas garrison on March 6, 1836. Crockett, who was born in Tennessee in 1786, loved an audience and was expert at elaborating and embellishing on his experiences to entertain his fans. After losing his congressional seat in 1835, Crockett struck out for Texas, where he believed he would find economic success and possibly a new political career. Although the Texas territory was officially owned by Mexico, Anglo- Americans made up 75 percent of the population.

On November 1, 1835, Davy Crockett left Tennessee with Abner Burgin, William Patton, and Lindsey K. Tinkle, gathering other followers along the way. Crockett was feted in towns from Tennessee to Texas, delighting in his fame and relishing the opportunity to give speeches. To Crockett, Texas was a land of plentiful resources.

Davy Crockett, killed at the Alamo, had struck out for Texas to find his fortune and fame. (Library of Congress)

Crockett and Patton pledged their allegiance to the defense of Texas in exchange for 4,605 acres of land, but Burgin and Tinkle returned to Tennessee.

Sam Houston, chief of the American military forces in Texas, ordered Jim Bowie to blow up the Alamo on January 17, 1836, because it was considered indefensible. Also, Houston was afraid that, if captured, the Alamo would place the Mexicans in an ideal position to attack Texas. However, Houston told Bowie in private that he could defend the force if he deemed it best to do so. William Barrett Travis, the acting commander at the garrison after Bowie became ill, repeatedly attempted to negotiate a surrender with Santa Anna but was repulsed. Until the end, Travis remained convinced that help would arrive in response to his pleas.

In the view of Santa Anna, the Texas settlers were usurpers, and he was determined to drive them out at all costs. Santa Anna was a ruthless tyrant who showed no mercy to those who opposed him. When he attacked the American garrison at the Alamo, there were 183 defenders. Santa Anna, on the other hand, commanded 1,800 men with another 2,400 in reserve. He also had ten cannons. During the battle, cavalry cut down fleeing men. Bowie was likely murdered as he lay in his quarters too ill to fight back. Within ninety minutes after the attack by Santa Anna began, all 183 defenders were dead; 200 Mexicans lost their lives and another 400 were wounded.

Davy Crockett's death was as mythical as his life. By some accounts, he died early in the battle; in other descriptions he was one of the last to die. One of the most colorful versions of his death has Crockett being taken prisoner by Santa Anna's men at the end of the battle. According to adherents of this story, Crockett died lunging for Santa Anna's throat after being tortured. The legend of Davy Crockett has lived on for close to two centuries—in large part because of the success of the television series, starring Fess Parker, introduced by the Walt Disney Company in 1954. In response, little boys around the country donned "coonskin" caps and pretended to be Crockett. Located in San Antonio, the Alamo is now preserved as a shrine to those who died there on March 6, 1836.

⟳ TURNING POINT

Many U.S. citizens in Texas favored annexation to the United States. To these people, the Texan revolt became a symbol of national greatness, a continuation of the "spirit of 1776." The French visitor Frederic Gaillardet compared the Texans to the mythic heroes of ancient Greece, according to Stephen L. Hardin in *Texian Iliad: A Military History of the Texas Revolution, 1835–1836*. Gaillardet described the revolution as a "Texian Iliad," in which all Americans could take pride. Still, there were people who vocally opposed the annexation of Texas into the United States. One such individual, Theodore Sedgwick, mistakenly emphasized the Mexicans' pathetic fighting capabilities and questioned the Texan victory over these troops. He reported on the "infamous" significance of the Alamo and viewed the conflict as very "burlesque," according to Hardin.

Mexico had admired the U.S. Constitution, using it as a model for its own constitution after it won its independence from Spain. After 1836, Mexico felt betrayed by the Americans who came into Texas and initiated and sustained this revolt. Mexico believed that U.S. citizens fomented and encouraged this rebellion and there was overwhelming Mexican sentiment for another war to retake the province from these rebels. Consequently, many in the United States saw Texas as a de facto (if not de jure) state of Mexico. The Mexican government had refused to accept many of the terms ending the war. There were many politicians who voiced their objections against the annexation of Texas. Despite a prevailing sense of Manifest Destiny, the U.S. government viewed Texas with much trepidation. The issue consumed U.S. politics. Northern politicians wanted no part of Texas's admission into the Union because it was another slave state. The Southern politicians felt the opposite. People in the United States felt that the turning point for whether Texas was to enter the Union would be the 1844 presidential election.

An earlier 1838 request for annexation led by Sam Houston had died down and nothing serious came out of it. Houston had also sought European recognition of the Republic of Texas. After the initial annexation proposal was removed, Houston sent delegates to England and France. France recognized Texas as a country in 1839, and England did likewise the following year. In the 1840s, President John Tyler reopened negotiations regarding the annexation of Texas. Many were still concerned over the Mexican-Texas difficulties on the diplomatic and political front. Whoever meddled in Texan affairs had to deal with Mexico as well. Still, there was much U.S. sympathy for the Texas cause. When Tyler reopened annexation negotiations, Mexico suddenly became friendly toward the United States but warned of the threat of war if Texas entered the Union. The United States also became increasingly concerned over a strong British influence looming in Texas, as the British were very interested in mediating Texas-Mexican difficulties.

At the 1844 Democratic national convention, many expected that former president Van Buren would get the nomination. But he did not

A cartoon depicts the 1844 presidential election as a cockfight between candidates Henry Clay, left, and James Polk. (Library of Congress)

receive the required two-thirds vote. Instead, a dark-horse candidate, James Polk, received the votes needed to win the nomination on the ninth ballot. The Democratic Party's platform centered on the annexation of both Texas and Oregon. The other major party, the Whigs, nominated Henry Clay. Clay was not a pro-Texas man.

During the 1844 presidential election, opposition mounted against the Texas annexation. Pro-Texas democrats pushed for the election of Polk, who in turn pushed for the annexation of Texas and the nation's expansion. Clay, the Whig nominee, took a firm stance against the annexation of Texas. James G. Birney of the Liberty Party was also in the running. Van Buren, the other Democratic candidate, did not take a firm stance on the Texas issue.

Support for the admission of Texas came from Manifest Destiny expansionists; those who feared the potential of an independent Texas and the designs of Great Britain; those eager for new lands, intending to expand the cash crop agriculture model of the South; and a small group of speculators in Texas land and depreciated Texas bonds.

When the annexation of Texas was being considered many organized workingmen in the north of the United States opposed the annexation. A newspaper in Manchester, New Hampshire, wrote: "We have heretofore held our peace in regard to the annexation of Texas, for the purpose of seeing whether our Nation would attempt so base an action. We call it base, because it would be giving men that live upon the blood of others, an opportunity of dipping their hand still deeper in the sin of slavery. . . . Have we not slaves enough now?" There were anti-annexation demonstrations by Irish workers in New York, Boston, and Lowell, Massachusetts. When the Mexican-American war broke out in 1846 there was much opposition to the war in New England.

Just before he left office, President John Tyler sponsored a joint resolution in Congress for the annexation of Texas. Tyler saw the election of James K. Polk as an indication that there was a consensus to admit Texas into the Union. Polk was from Tennessee and an ardent expansionist. The resolution, which required only a majority vote in Congress, passed just three days before the end of Tyler's term and Polk's ascension to the presidency. Texas accepted the terms.

President John Tyler sponsored a joint resolution in Congress for the annexation of Texas. (Library of Congress)

ACTUAL HISTORY

The Mexican government saw the U.S. annexation of Texas as an illegal acquisition. Because Mexico had never really acknowledged the independence of Texas and its subsequent republic status, the U.S. acquisition of Texas was seen as a sign of war. The Mexican-American War of 1846–1848 was a political plot to extend the boundaries of the United States, and for Southerners, a way to extend slavery. The war was very successful for the United States as it allowed the capture of lands that had once been part of Mexico. Before and after the war, the dominant Texan view of the Union was that it was composed of sovereign states (the doctrine of states' rights). Texans resented all national interference in state affairs in matters relating to finances, boundaries, or internal politics.

Texas was Southern in its cultural patterns and a slave state in the nineteenth century. Between 1835 and 1861, 90 percent of the immigration into Texas was by native-born people from the Old South. About half of them came from the upper South. The rest of them came from the plantation economies and the black belts of the deep Gulf of Mexico bend. Both the government of the Republic of Texas and the later Texas state government used every means possible to lure people into the region. The great bait had always been open lands. The republic freely gave its lands away, and the state (which owned all of the public lands) continued the same policy. The slave plantation economy had enjoyed a large expansion between 1835 and 1860.

However, Texas had one major difference from the Southern states: it still possessed a long and savage internal Native American frontier. Between 1845 and 1879, the federal government attempted to make peace with Native Americans and Mexicans. But it failed to act along the Texas frontier, where war between the natives, Texans, and Mexicans was already endemic. The U.S. Army kept only a few thousand soldiers in the state and these men were heavy infantry, occasionally mounted on mules. They provided no defense against the wide-ranging Comanches. Washington, D.C., remained reluctant to act, and the state government increasingly had to order state troops, the Texas Rangers, to act against the natives.

By the beginning of the 1860s, two societies had emerged in the United States. The Northern industrial society feared Southern political power, and the expansion of slavery and states' rights. The Southern "slavocracy" feared a Northern industrialism that threatened to uproot the foundations of the South's agricultural economy. The South seceded from the Union, and Texas went with it, joining the newly created Confederate States of America (Confederacy). Sam Houston appealed to the people to reconsider their decision. He supported slavery and the U.S. Constitution, but he had pledged allegiance to the Union and he could not believe that Texans were prepared to forsake the greater nation he had done so much to build. Houston ran for governor but was defeated badly by wealthy states' rightist and planter Hardin Runnels. It was the first time that Texans had repudiated Houston at the polls.

Texas's greatest contribution to the Southern cause was manpower. There are no exact accounts of the troops Texas gave the Confederacy because records were poorly kept. The last battle of the Civil War was fought at Palmetto Hill, Texas, in 1865. The Confederate army and state government melted away as the Union emerged victorious. Texas, along with the other states of the Confederacy, was placed under military rule and army tribunals replaced the civil courts. It was also the legal end of slavery. Texas entered one of its most disastrous periods.

Texas was massively in debt and economically ruined. In addition, the state had sustained political and social damage that few could repair. State expenditures were stopped, salaries were cut, and school funds dried up. The Texas legislature had to restore law and order. The Texas Rangers were brought back and were more successful than in the antebellum years. Both Native American and internal anarchy disappeared as order and then law was restored. The new state constitution gave the government many responsibilities but few powers. The lieutenant governor was far more politically powerful than the governor.

As Texas entered the twentieth century, its industry was underdeveloped relative to the American mainstream. During the previous century of explosive conquest and settlement, the land and the people had changed very little. In the twentieth century, however, Texas witnessed explosive economic change, as agriculture and ranching were continuously improved, more lands were developed, and the mineral resources of the state, such as oil, were discovered and extracted. Oil, cattle, and cotton became the staples of the Texas economic machine. As in the rest of the nation, all public services and administration were regularly improved. Texas spent enormous amounts of money on roads, both urban and rural, and the automobile accelerated the process of urbanization.

By the second half of the twentieth century, Texas was full of gleaming, growing cities that became some of the nation's largest, including Houston, Dallas-Fort Worth, and San Antonio. The economy also continued to grow and diversify, allowing the state to absorb the inevitable changes of time. When the cotton kingdom crashed, Texas had depended upon cattle. When its cattle empire faded into the past, there was the monumental discovery of gas and oil. Amid all these booms and busts, entrepreneurial Texas diversified. By the 1990s, the computer and electronic industries created as much employment and wealth as the oil industry. Still, the border areas between Texas and Mexico suffered from increasing violence, both from the huge narcotics-smuggling trade and a lively business in crossing illegal aliens, not just from Mexico but from around the world. But bad times seem to strengthen, not weaken, the Texas resolve and mystique.

ALTERNATE HISTORY

Texan history would have been vastly different, however, if pro-Texas Democrats had been unable to engineer the nomination of dark-horse candidate James K. Polk in 1844. Henry Clay would then have been elected president in a close contest, polling 49.6 percent of the total vote to Polk's 48.1 percent. The shift of a few thousand voters in the state of New York would have enabled Clay to win narrowly there, giving him the margin of victory in the electoral college. The newly elected president would have had nothing to do with the Texas issue or the possible occupation of Oregon. At best, he would have wrested Oregon from European interests, which included Russia and Great Britain.

Suppose, before Tyler left office he had sponsored a joint resolution in Congress for the annexation of Texas (as he did in actual history). But in alternate history, riots would have broken out in New York and Boston against the resolution and possible annexation. These riots would have continued for weeks. President Tyler would have had to declare martial law in New York and some areas of New England. Texas would have thus remained an independent country in 1845. With no immediate dispute with the United States, Mexico would then have been free to "recapture" its former wayward province. In the spring of 1846, Mexico might have sent an army of around six thousand men from Mexico City to begin marching toward the Rio Grande and points northward. Texas president David G. Burnet would have called for an army once he received word of the Mexican advance, and the Second War for Texas Independence would have been ready to begin.

Great Britain would have seen the Texas-Mexican struggle as an opportunity to advance its own interests. Britain wanted to keep Mexico and, especially the United States, in check to make sure those countries would not infringe on British interests in western North America. Texas, Britain believed, would be a great buffer zone between British western North America and the United States. Britain and Texas would have agreed to an alliance. Britain would have agreed to help Texas militarily against Mexico if Texas had agreed to support British interests in the west once its war with Mexico was concluded. Texas would have agreed and promised not to interfere with British claims west of the Rocky Mountains. British ships would have been sent from bases in the Caribbean loaded with much-needed supplies and men. They would have docked near Corpus Christi and Galveston and lingered offshore to secure those ports as Texas-British supply centers.

The Texan army and militia would have numbered anywhere from five to eight thousand men. The British would have sent about two thousand troops. Most of the Texas army would have been centered in San Antonio, with the rest of the troops scattered along the southeast coast of the country. As the Mexican army crossed the Rio Grande, they would have met little resistance. It was at this time that the Mexican general could have committed a grave error. He might have split his army of six thousand men in two to launch a two-pronged attack against the Texas-British stronghold near Corpus Christi as well as the city of San Antonio. He would have realized that the war could not be won without the capture of the Texas ports that secured British aid. The Mexican army would have been victorious at San Antonio but would have suffered a miserable defeat at Corpus Christi. Three-fourths of the Mexican army there would have been killed or captured. The rest of the army would have retreated to San Antonio to meet up with the other army. But the Texas-British army would have paralleled the Mexican army's movement and eventually launched an attack between San Antonio and Corpus Christi, marking another defeat for the Mexicans.

The only significant Mexican force in Texas would have been in San Antonio. It would have stayed there during the winter of 1846–1847. By the spring of 1847, acquiring supplies would have become hard for the Mexican army, and the threat of a new Texas-British offensive would have loomed on the horizon. The Mexican army would have been crushed in May 1847, and Texas would have been freed from the Mexican threat once and for all.

The British would then have been able to pursue their territorial interests west of the Rocky Mountains. The British would have fought Mexico in California and defeated them in 1848. Several thousand Texans would have volunteered to fight for the British in Mexico to repay the debt incurred during the Texas-Mexican war. The British would have discovered gold in California in 1849 and hired foreigners like Asians, Texans, Americans, and Mexicans to work for them in the gold mines. The profits to be gained there would have benefited only Great Britain. With no American territorial threat, the British also would have controlled the Oregon territory by the end of 1849. They now would have had the entire North American west coast in their hands.

American slavery would have had nowhere to expand. The Southern states of the United States would have urged the federal government to contemplate war with Texas in order to expand the institution, but the government would have not given in, realizing that it would have to go to war with Britain as well. In our alternate history, Texas is a slave country and war with it would have had to be a war of conquest. Texans, though slaveholders, would have had no desire to join the United States at this time. By the mid-1860s, Britain would have purchased the Alaska territory from Russia.

In 1868, war would have broken out in the United States over slavery. Because Texas would have been sympathetic to slavery, it would have joined with the Southern Confederate States of America. Britain would have jumped at the chance to split apart the United States so it too would have sided with the Confederate States of America. Even though Texas and Britain might not have sent men to fight for the Confederacy, they would have committed much needed supplies like food, clothes, and munitions. The British also would have harassed Union shipping along the Confederate Gulf and Atlantic coasts. The Confederates would have continued the war into the mid-1870s. Union sentiment for peace would have begun to gain momentum by then, and by May 1875, the United States would have wanted to sue for peace. The Confederate States of America would have gained its independence and slavery would have been allowed to continue. In the 1880s, Texas and the Confederacy might have entered a military alliance. They could have gone to war with Spain in the 1890s to acquire territory in the Caribbean for the expansion of slavery. They would have been victorious, creating a vast "slavocracy" from the North American Gulf Coast to the Caribbean to Brazil in South America.

By the beginning of the 1900s there would have been new forces at work, like industrialization and manufacturing, spreading into Texas and the Confederacy. Those countries, however, would have lagged behind Britain and the United States in those areas. Then, just as gold might have been discovered in British California, oil would have been discovered in the country of Texas. The economic status of Texas would have doubled, even tripled, overnight. Oil reserves at Spindletop would have been phenomenal. Slaves now would work in the oil fields and the countryside, and many Texans would have become wealthy.

In the mid-1910s, in actual and in our alternate history, war broke out in Europe (World War I). And Texas would have done its best to stay out of the fighting. Its old ally, Britain, was heavily involved in its war with Germany and would have pressured Texas into committing to the conflict in some capacity. Texas would have sent Britain oil and some of its financial reserves. Germany, in turn, attempted to coerce Mexico (in both actual and alternate history) into entering the war on its side and promised to reward Mexico by giving Texas and California back to Mexico once the war was over. Texans would have been outraged and would have declared war on Germany. The Confederate States of America, Texas's ally, also would have committed to the war. Both countries would have sent troops (many of them black) and supplies to Europe. These would have tipped the scale of the war against Germany and it would have had to sue for peace. In our alternate history, the United States never entered the war and was a passive observer.

Many black slaves would have asked to become citizens because of their involvement in the conflict. The international community also would have put pressure on Texas and the Confederacy to emancipate their slaves and make them respectful and responsible citizens of their countries. A civil rights movement could have occurred in Texas in 1919, which would have spilled over into the Confederate States of America by the early 1920s. Texas and Confederate legislators, under intense pressure from foreign politicians and their own citizens, would have passed legislation that freed the slaves in both countries in 1923. Coupled with the civil rights legislation might have been a document giving women the right to vote in Texas. In the past, women only could have voted in select Texas regions (small regions at that), not on a nationwide basis. Texan and Confederate blacks would have become citizens and now would have had to be paid for their services. Still, they would have been second-class citizens. In Texas, many blacks would have continued working in the oil industry for their rich, white former owners. They also would have worked in the service industries and performed odd jobs. As expected, they would not have been paid very well.

In the early 1920s, Texas would have experienced a wave of progressive legislative measures. Many of those measures would have been taken from one of the most progressive countries in the world at that time—the United States. The United States, in actual and alternate history, had been instrumental in improving the working conditions for factory employees, and had passed strict laws against the use of child labor, drinking, gambling, prostitution, and other vices that its politicians saw fit to address. By 1923, Texas would have also addressed many of these issues and changed laws for the better, including those that dealt with women and blacks.

Many people would have immigrated to Texas to seek jobs in the oil industry. Houston would have become a boomtown during the first half of the 1900s. The country of Texas would have become financially wealthy, but would have suffered a setback as the world plunged into a depression in the early 1930s. By the late 1930s, the world was at war again (in actual and alternate history) against the imperialist countries of Germany, Japan, and Italy. Texas would have tried its best to adhere to an isolationist policy but would not have been successful. Germany would have attacked Texas shipping along the Gulf of Mexico and Atlantic Ocean. Then, in 1941, Britain would have been attacked in the Pacific Ocean by Japan. In actual and alternate history, Britain fought a two-front war. The Confederate States of America and the United States would have entered the war on the side of the Allies: Britain, France, Russia, and Texas. Texas, the Confederacy, and the United States would have helped turn the tide of the war in favor of the Allies, and Germany would have been defeated in 1945, as it was in actual history.

During the early part of the war, some European scientists had been fleeing war-ravaged Europe and heading to the Americas. These were among the most brilliant scientific minds in the world. All throughout the early 1940s, they had been working on trying to split the atom to make a more potent weapon to be used against Germany. Many of them had no idea of just how potent this weapon would be. The Allies would have tested the atom bomb in the Pacific and would have decided to use two of them on Japan. Japan would have surrendered in the spring of 1946. The war would have been over.

The Allies would have ruled the post–World War II world. The Republic of Texas, the Confederacy, and the United States would have been closer diplomatically and politically than they would ever have been in their histories. These three countries would have continued on a path of self-dependence as well as reliance on one another throughout the twentieth century. The three nations would have formed the North American Treaty Organization (NATO) in order to safeguard one another's interests and ambitions for many years.

David Treviño

Discussion Questions

1. In the alternate history presented in this chapter, westward expansion of the United States is blocked by both Texas and British holdings west of the Rockies. Where would the western boundary of the United States have been established, and what states that are in fact in the United States today do you think would have been under British or Texas jurisdiction?

2. If the votes for James Birney had shifted to Clay, the election of 1844 might indeed have gone as suggested in this alternate history. What could Clay have done to attract the Birney vote?

3. If the alternate history presented in this chapter had worked out, what states do you believe would be members of the Confederate States of America? What Caribbean territories might have been acquired by the Confederacy or Texas from Spain?

4. If the Confederacy had won its independence in the mid-1870s, as presented in this alternate history, what factors would have led to emancipation of slaves? Do you think those factors would have ended slavery before 1910, or during the World War as suggested in this alternate?

5. In actual history, one factor that tied Texas economically to the rest of the United States after the Civil War was the practice of driving cattle northward to railroad points in Kansas, such as Abilene, for shipment to the markets of Chicago and the eastern states. If Texas had been independent, would the forces of geography and economics have led to the same sort of trade, or would national boundaries and the history of national rivalry between Texas and the United States have prevented such commerce?

6. If the British had held Canada, Alaska, and the West Coast of North America, do you think that Britain and the United States would have become traditional allies or enemies in the twentieth century? What factors would have worked to keep their relationship like that of the United States and Canada in actual history, and what factors would have worked against such a friendly relationship?

Bibliography and Further Reading

Binkley, William Campbell. *The Texas Revolution*. Baton Rouge: Louisiana State University Press, 1952.

Campbell, Randolph B. *Gone to Texas: A History of the Lone Star State*. New York: Oxford University Press, 2003.

Chipman, Donald E. *Spanish Texas: 1519–1821*. Austin: University of Texas Press, 1992.

Davis, William C. *Lone Star Rising: The Revolutionary Birth of the Texas Republic*. New York: Free Press, 2004.

Edmondson, J. R. *The Alamo Story: From Early History to Current Conflicts*. Plano: Republic of Texas Press, 2000.

Esdaile, Charles. *The French Wars, 1792–1815*. New York: Routledge, 2001.

Fehrenbach, T. R. *Lone Star: A History of Texas and the Texans*. New York: Da Capo Press, 2000.

Ford, John Salmon. *Origin and Fall of the Alamo, March 6, 1836*. San Antonio, TX: Johnson Bros., 1895.

Hardin, Stephen L. *Texian Iliad: A Military History of the Texas Revolution, 1835–1836*. Austin: University of Texas Press, 1994.

Lyons, Martyn. *Napoleon Bonaparte and the Legacy of the French Revolution*. New York: St. Martin's Press, 1994.

"Mexican Texas" http://www.tsha.utexas.edu (cited September 25, 2005).

Nofi, Albert A. *The Alamo and the Texas War for Independence: September 30, 1835, to April 21, 1836; Heroes, Myths, and History*. New York: Da Capo Press, 1994.

"Presidential Elections: 1844." www.multied.com (accessed September 29, 2005).

Raat, W. Dirk. *Mexico and the United States: Ambivalent Vistas*. Athens: University of Georgia Press, 2004.

Reichstein, Andreas. *Rise of the Lone Star: The Making of Texas*. College Station: Texas A&M University Press, 1989.

"Spanish Texas." www.tsha.utexas.edu (accessed September 26, 2005).

"Texas Revolution." www.tsha.utexas.edu (accessed September 26, 2005).

Thonoff, Robert H. *The Texas Connection with the American Revolution*. New York: Eakin Press, 1981.

Todish, Timothy J. *Alamo Sourcebook, 1836: A Comprehensive Guide to the Alamo and the Texas Revolution*. New York: Eakin Press, 1998.

TURNING POINT

The United States acquired territory from Mexico in the Mexican-American War (1846–1848). What if Mexico had held onto California and Arizona?

INTRODUCTION

In the first half of the nineteenth century, Mexico and the United States seemed to be on a collision course. After achieving independence from Spain, Mexico experienced much infighting among its elite. For much of the nineteenth century, the country was marked by an inability to fill the power vacuum left by the break with Spain, leading to an almost constant state of civil war in Mexico. This lack of political unity made Mexico vulnerable to foreign invasion—especially in Mexico's northern frontier region, which had been sparsely populated under Spanish rule. Spain had never had enough resources to settle northern Mexico beyond establishing a string of missions.

The United States, on the other hand, was advancing westward. A sense of Manifest Destiny led many in the United States to look toward expansion from the Atlantic Ocean to the Pacific Ocean as a God-given right. Many expansionists used the idea of Manifest Destiny to justify territorial acquisition and conquest. In 1803, the United States acquired the Louisiana Purchase from France, greatly increasing the size of the country. The next logical step for U.S. expansionists was into Mexican territory. In 1818, the Adams-Onís Treaty defined the boundary between Spain and the United States. When the United States acquired the Louisiana Purchase, Spain attempted to populate the northern frontier to protect against possible intrusion by the United States. Such attempts were largely unsuccessful. Mexico inherited this boundary upon gaining independence from Spain. However, the United States soon sought to modify the border. Expansionists in the United States looked to Texas and California as areas that should come under U.S. control. Smaller, weaker, and divided Mexico began to worry about possible U.S. intervention.

An initial dispute between the North American neighbors arose over Texas. Starting in the 1820s, the Mexican government encouraged immigrants from the United States to settle there. In 1821, a group of U.S. settlers led by Stephen Austin arrived in Texas, marking the beginning of a

IN CONTEXT   The Alamo

Originally named Misión San Antonio de Valero, the Alamo served as home to missionaries and their Indian converts for nearly seventy years. Construction began on the present site in 1724. In 1793, Spanish officials secularized San Antonio's five missions and distributed their lands to the remaining Indian residents. These men and women continued to farm the fields, once the mission's but now their own, and participated in the growing community of San Antonio.

In the early 1800s, the Spanish military stationed a cavalry unit at the former mission. The soldiers referred to the old mission as the Alamo (the Spanish word for "cottonwood") in honor of their hometown Alamo de Parras, Coahuila. The post's commander established the first recorded hospital in Texas in the Long Barrack. The Alamo was home to both Revolutionaries and Royalists during Mexico's

ten-year struggle for independence. The military— Spanish, Rebel, and then Mexican—continued to occupy the Alamo until the Texas Revolution.

San Antonio and the Alamo played a critical role in the Texas Revolution. In December 1835, Ben Milam led Texian and Tejano volunteers against Mexican troops quartered in the city. After five days of house-to-house fighting, they forced General Martín Perfecto de Cos and his soldiers to surrender. The victorious volunteers then occupied the Alamo—already fortified prior to the battle by Cós's men—and strengthened its defenses.

On February 23, 1836, the arrival of General Antonio López de Santa Anna's army outside San Antonio nearly caught them by surprise. Undaunted, the Texians and Tejanos prepared to defend the Alamo together. The defenders held out for thirteen days against Santa Anna's army. William B. Travis, the

large wave of U.S. immigrants. However, by the 1830s, Mexico saw that the Americans were not assimilating into Mexican society; also, Mexico wanted to limit the spread of slavery. For these reasons it began attempting to limit the entrance of these immigrants into Texas. At the same time, many of the settlers hoped that Texas might one day become part of the United States. In 1835, Texans revolted and declared their independence from Mexico. Mexican leader General Antonio López de Santa Anna sent the Mexican army to put down the Texas rebellion and dealt the rebels a number of defeats, including the famous massacre at the Alamo in 1836. However, in April 1836, the Texas Army captured Santa Anna, forcing the Mexican leader to surrender and accept the independence of Texas.

Texas then became an independent republic. Many Texans, however, called for the United States to annex Texas as a state. The issue of slavery in Texas made annexation an important political issue in the United States in the 1840s. In 1845, the U.S. Congress passed a resolution calling for the annexation of Texas as a state. With this formal takeover of Texas, relations with Mexico quickly deteriorated and the two countries prepared for war. Mexico authorized a civilian militia to reinforce the regular army units. U.S. President James K. Polk sent troops to the border region and navy ships to the Mexican coast.

The United States made one last attempt to negotiate a settlement when Polk sent special envoy John Slidell to meet with Mexican president José Joaquín Herrera to negotiate the Texas boundary. Historically, the Texas border had been at the Nueces River. However, in 1836, the Republic of Texas claimed that the Rio Grande was the border, which would give Texas another 150-mile-wide swath of Mexican territory. Furthermore, Texas claimed the land all the way to the source of the Rio

IN CONTEXT   *The Alamo (Continued)*

commander of the Alamo, sent out couriers carrying pleas for help to communities in Texas. On the eighth day of the siege, a band of thirty-two volunteers from Gonzales arrived, bringing the number of defenders to nearly two hundred. Legend holds that with the possibility of additional help fading, Colonel Travis drew a line on the ground and asked any man willing to stay and fight to step over—all except one did. As the defenders saw it, the Alamo was the key to the defense of Texas, and they were ready to give their lives rather than surrender their position to General Santa Anna. Among the Alamo's garrison were Jim Bowie, renowned knife fighter, and David Crockett, famed frontiersman and former congressman from Tennessee.

The final assault came before daybreak on the morning of March 6, 1836, as columns of Mexican soldiers emerged from the predawn darkness and headed for the Alamo's walls. Cannon and small arms fire from inside the Alamo beat back several attacks. Regrouping, the Mexicans scaled the walls and rushed into the compound. Once inside, they turned a captured cannon on the Long Barrack and church, blasting open the barricaded doors. The desperate struggle continued until the defenders were overwhelmed. By sunrise, the battle had ended and Santa Anna entered the Alamo compound to survey the scene of his victory.

While the facts surrounding the siege of the Alamo continue to be debated, there is no doubt about what the battle has come to symbolize. People worldwide continue to remember the Alamo as a heroic struggle against overwhelming odds—a place where men made the ultimate sacrifice for freedom. For this reason the Alamo remains hallowed ground and the Shrine of Texas Liberty. (Dr. Richard B. Winders, www.thealamo.org) [reprint permission on file]

Grande, which would allow it claim territory in New Mexico and Colorado. Slidell also had secret instructions to purchase the rest of New Mexico and California. However, word of these instructions leaked out. The Mexican press reacted strongly and appealed to the Mexican people's sense of nationalism. The Mexican government informed the United States that there was nothing left to discuss.

At this time, the elite of Mexico were far from unified. General Manuel Paredes used the army to overthrow the government and install himself as the new president. This lack of unity made Mexico a tempting target for the United States. Polk clearly favored going to war. However, some members of his cabinet—including Secretary of the Navy George Bancroft and Secretary of State James Buchanan—would support a declaration of war only if Mexico attacked first. On May 9, 1846, Polk was able to gain the support of the more reluctant members of his cabinet when hostilities broke out. General Zachary Taylor led U.S. troops into the disputed area between the rivers. Mexico ordered them out, but Taylor refused and the two sides skirmished. This confrontation gave Polk the excuse he needed and the United States quickly declared war.

General Zachary Taylor, hero of the Mexican War. (Library of Congress)

Meanwhile, in Mexico, the military stepped into politics once again, this time overthrowing General Paredes. Mexico now brought back Santa Anna to face the United States on the battlefield.

The United States went on the offensive with a three-pronged attack against Mexico. The Army of the West fought in New Mexico and California. The Army of the Center would operate in northern Mexico. The Army of Occupation would be responsible for taking Mexico City. The Army of the West under General Stephen W. Kearny acted first. Kearny left Fort Leavenworth, Kansas, for Santa Fe, New Mexico, in June 1846. The Mexican population in Santa Fe evacuated without resistance and no shots were fired. California also fell easily. By 1847, U.S. forces also had taken Chihuahua in northern Mexico.

The Army of the Center under Zachary Taylor had a more difficult time. Taylor moved on Monterrey in August 1846. By mid-September, the city had fallen, but the United States suffered heavy losses. The American troops then fought Santa Anna to a stalemate in northern Mexico. However, Santa Anna decided to withdraw to Mexico City, leaving the north to the United States. Despite his country's setbacks, Santa Anna would fight on.

TURNING POINT

While the early part of the Mexican War took place in northern Mexico, it soon became evident that the United States needed to capture Mexico City in order to force the Mexicans to the bargaining table. By October 1846, General Winfield Scott began to convince Polk of this necessity. As

The landing of American forces under General Winfield Scott. (Library of Congress)

general-in-chief of the Army, Scott devised a plan for winning the war, but Polk worried about the possibility that the general, a key political rival, would win the military glory and prestige. Finally, once it became clear that the United States was not going to attain a quick victory and under pressure from Secretary of War William Marcy and others, Polk gave in and permitted Scott to implement his plan for a strike at Mexico City.

Scott had several key beliefs regarding winning the war. He felt that Mexico City should be taken from the eastern port of Veracruz rather than from the north. He also emphasized that speed was essential to avoid the ravages of the yellow fever season in Mexico, and that only Veracruz could be used as a base for the invasion. Scott believed that Fort San Juan de Ulloa, which protected Veracruz, could not be assaulted directly. Rather, the general was of the opinion that his forces should land at a distance from Veracruz, and then proceed with an attack or siege. Finally, Scott insisted that special boats be constructed to serve as landing craft so his troops could go ashore outside of enemy range. After hearing Scott's plans, Polk reluctantly agreed to land 20,000 men at Veracruz and then march inland to the Mexican capital.

In February 1847, Scott arrived at a staging area at Lobos Island, fifty miles south of Tampico, Mexico. Scott planned to use 150 specially constructed landing vessels to secure a beachhead at Veracruz. However, the War Department did not hold up its end of the bargain, as it provided Scott with only 12,000 men and 65 craft.

On March 2, Scott began the trip south to Veracruz with 80 ships. By March 5, those aboard the U.S. ships saw the imposing fortifications at Veracruz, including the San Juan Fort that guarded the approach to the city. At this point, Scott knew that he needed to make his way inland by April or his troops would be decimated by yellow fever.

Flight of the Mexican Army at the Battle of Buena Vista, February 23, 1847. (Library of Congress)

A group of people on the porch of a hotel in Washington, D.C., reading news of the Mexican War. (Library of Congress)

In preparation for the attack, Commodore David Conner, commander of the U.S. naval squadron, took Scott and his staff in a small patrol boat to survey landing sites. The passengers on board included such key military figures as George Meade and Robert E. Lee. This reconnaissance mission got too close to San Juan Fort and the Mexican forces shelled the boat, almost sinking it. This potential disaster could have greatly affected future events.

Scott decided to land at Collada, a small beach that would make a good staging area for constructing siege batteries. The attack on Veracruz began on March 9. By midnight, the United States had landed some ten thousand men without suffering a single loss. The Mexicans offered little resistance at this early stage.

Scott's division commanders urged him to attack the fort and city immediately. However, Scott wanted to keep his losses low and instead began the siege. The U.S. soldiers dragged their siege artillery to the sandy hills behind the city, often working in ankle-deep sand. They established an eight-mile-long investing line with four batteries of cannon. However, the War Department never delivered the promised heavy siege guns. The guns available to Scott were not big enough to destroy the walls of Fort San Juan de Ulloa.

Scott decided to avoid a direct attack on the fort. Instead, the U.S. troops surrounded the city and attacked it from the rear. This strategy neutralized the fort, cut off supplies to the city, and left no exit for those in Veracruz. The attack continued for forty-eight hours, leading to numerous civilian casualties despite the pleas of foreign consuls to allow women, children, and other noncombatants to leave. Finally, on March 27, Veracruz formally surrendered. Sixty-seven Americans died in the attack. Some 1,000 to 1,500 Mexicans died in the assault, a majority of them civilians.

ACTUAL HISTORY

The U.S. victory at Veracruz allowed Scott to attack Mexico City. Santa Anna, upon hearing of the Mexican defeat at Veracruz, tried to make a stand at Cerro Gordo, near the city of Jalapa. This strategy failed and Santa Anna sought to stop the U.S. advance at the city of Puebla. However, the city's residents refused to cooperate and the U.S. forces took the city. Mexico made its final stand in the capital of Mexico City. The government placed the city under martial law and conscripted civilians to fight.

After some intense fighting on the outskirts of the capital, Scott demanded a surrender on August 20. A brief armistice followed before the fighting continued. September 7 was the bloodiest day of the attack on Mexico City, when 2,000 Mexicans died and some 700 U.S. troops lost their lives. The last encounter took place at Chapultepec Castle, which housed 1,000 troops and the young cadets of the Military Academy. On September 13, U.S. forces stormed the castle and engaged the Mexicans in hand-to-hand combat. Many of the so-called boy-heroes died defending the castle. The fall of Chapultepec Castle brought the hostilities to an end.

The Mexican-American War formally closed with the signing of the treaty of Guadalupe Hidalgo in February 1848. The United States paid Mexico $15 million. In exchange, the United States took the entire region stretching from Texas to California. This area represented about half of all of Mexico's territory. Such territorial loss became a painful memory for most Mexicans and contributed to a negative feeling toward the United States. Indeed, the conflict was known in Mexico as the War of the North American Invasion.

The devastating loss contributed to even more political conflict among the Mexican elite. The Liberal Party had dominated Mexico since independence. The Conservatives now went on the offensive, blaming the Liberals for the loss on the battlefield, accusing them of having adopted the Anglo-Saxon values of the United States. The Conservatives called for a return to Hispanic traditions, emphasizing aristocratic ideals, the military, and the Catholic Church. Some even toyed with the idea of creating a monarchy in Mexico.

The 1848 landing of the naval expedition against Tabasco, Mexico. Commodore M. C. Perry in command. (Library of Congress)

KEY CONCEPT   Treaty of Guadalupe Hidalgo

The Treaty of Guadalupe Hidalgo, which brought an official end to the Mexican-American War (1846–1848), was signed on February 2, 1848, at Guadalupe Hidalgo, a city to which the Mexican government had fled with the advance of U.S. forces.

With the defeat of its army and the fall of the capital, Mexico City, in September 1847, the Mexican government surrendered to the United States and entered negotiations to end the war. The peace talks were negotiated by Nicholas Trist, chief clerk of the State Department, who had accompanied General Winfield Scott as a diplomat and President Polk's representative. Trist and General Scott, after two previous unsuccessful attempts to negotiate a

At the same time, the Liberals in Mexico called for a series of reforms. In a period known simply as *La Reforma*, the Liberal leaders instituted a new constitution and revoked many of the privileges of the military and the church. At first, the conflict was a war of words between the two parties. However, in 1858, the two sides began a military conflict and Mexico would witness nearly two decades of civil war.

This period was also marked by yet another foreign invasion. The French installed Maximilian von Hapsburg as the monarch of Mexico from 1863 to 1867. However, this foreign presence inspired Mexican nationalists to fight back. In May 1867, Maximilian surrendered to Mexican republican troops and was executed in June.

The successful overthrow of Maximilian led to a rise in Mexican nationalism. However, the country's economy was in poor shape and Mexico was still politically unsettled. Mexicans chose Benito Juarez as their president after Maximilian's death. Juarez won reelection in a hotly contested race in 1871. However, he died in 1872, leaving a political vacuum.

This unstable period in Mexican history came to an end with the dictatorship of Porfirio Díaz from 1876 to 1911. On the one hand, Diaz succeeded in ending the decades-long power struggle in Mexico, bringing a period of relative political stability. The economy also grew under Diaz, in large part because of significant foreign investment. On the other hand, there was a cost to the Díaz dictatorship. Mexico during the so-called Porfiriato was very undemocratic, as only a small elite participated in politics. Also, despite the overall economic growth, there was extreme economic inequality as foreigners and a handful of elite Mexicans prospered while most of the country's citizens remained poor.

The Díaz era was followed by the chaotic Mexican Revolution. In 1910, Francisco Madero, a member of a wealthy Mexican family, ran against Díaz in the presidential elections, posing the greatest threat to date for Díaz. In response to the growing popularity of Madero, Diaz jailed him and thousands of his followers. In his Plan of San Luis Potosí following his release from jail, Madero called for an armed response to the repression of the Mexican government. Madero and his followers took Ciudad Juarez (across the border from El Paso, Texas). Under growing pressure from Madero's forces, Díaz fled the country in May 1911.

In 1912, Madero assumed the presidency of Mexico. However, he soon lost control of the revolution that he had started. In the south, Emiliano Zapata led landless peasants in their own revolution once they

---

KEY CONCEPT   *Treaty of Guadalupe Hidalgo (Continued)*

treaty with President Santa Anna, determined that the only way to deal with Mexico was as a conquered enemy. Nicholas Trist negotiated with a special commission representing the collapsed government led by Don Bernardo Couto, Don Miguel Atristain, and Don Luis Gonzaga Cuevas.

President Polk had recalled Trist under the belief that negotiations would be carried out with a

Mexican delegation in Washington, D.C. In the six weeks it took to deliver Polk's message, Trist had received word that the Mexican government had named its special commission to negotiate. Trist determined that Washington, D.C., did not understand the situation in Mexico and negotiated the peace treaty in defiance of the president's instructions.

---

realized that Madero was not sympathetic to their demands for land. At the same time, the Mexican military, led by General Victoriano Huerta, longed to reestablish the Díaz system. Aided by U.S. Ambassador Henry Lane Wilson, Huerta had Madero killed. Huerta proceeded to attempt to impose a Díaz-like regime. Along with Zapata, Pancho Villa in northern Mexico opposed the Huerta government. Villa led an army of jobless ranch hands, obtaining supplies and weapons from across the border in the United States. Finally, a third faction led by Venustiano Carranza battled Huerta's forces. Known as the Constitutionalists, Carranza's forces posed the main threat to Huerta.

Once again, the United States became involved in Mexican affairs. The administration of Woodrow Wilson did not recognize the Huerta government as it had not been elected by the Mexican people. Then, when Mexican authorities arrested a number of U.S. soldiers in Veracruz, the United States sent marines to occupy the port city that had been so crucial in the Mexican-American War. The United States' attack on Veracruz played an important role in the Mexican Revolution. Huerta had to divert troops to Veracruz to resist the U.S. invasion and this action greatly weakened his military position elsewhere in the country. Thus, in July 1914, Huerta resigned, blaming the United States for his downfall.

Control of the revolution was now up for grabs, with Carranza, Villa, and Zapata competing for power. Carranza eventually won out, assuming the presidency in 1917. In the same year, Mexico got a new constitution. In 1919, Zapata was murdered, eliminating a key Carranza rival. Then in 1920, Alvaro Obregón, one of Carranza's generals led an uprising. Carranza attempted to flee but was killed. Obregón then took control of the country. A number of important developments took place during the Obregón administration. In 1923, Villa was killed. Obregón then succeeded in stabilizing relations with the United States. Finally, Obregón passed power peacefully to his successor, Plutarco Elias Calles in 1924. This was the first time there had been a peaceful transfer of power in Mexico since 1880.

After a series of lesser-known presidents ruled Mexico, Lázaro Cárdenas was elected in 1934. Cárdenas sought to carry out the promise of the revolution. Cárdenas's two main contributions to the revolution were land reform and the nationalization of the oil industry. He redistributed tens of millions of acres of land to poor and landless Mexicans, solidifying his place in Mexican history. Cárdenas also expropriated the holding of foreign, including American, oil companies operating in

Mexico. Oil companies in the United States demanded that President Franklin Roosevelt take a stand against this action. However, Roosevelt's Good Neighbor Policy, the Great Depression, and the growing potential for war in Europe, meant that Roosevelt took no hostile action. Instead, Mexico paid the foreign companies for their property and nationalized the oil industry in Mexico.

The Mexican-American War would also have a profound effect on the history of the United States. Even though at first it seemed that the annexation of new territory might benefit the South, this was not necessarily the case. In July 1847, just before Scott entered Mexico City, Mormons arrived at the Great Salt Lake in present-day Utah. While the Mormons were looking for a place to practice their religion, the location turned out to be a good one on the route to the newly acquired California.

One of the great benefits of conquest for the United States was the discovery of gold in California. James Marshall first found the precious metal in a stream at Sutter's Mill in January 1848. Soon, settlers from the eastern United States and all over the world poured into California seeking their fortune. By the end of 1849, the population of California had grown from around 15,000 to more than 150,000. While many struck it rich in California and miners extracted $550 million worth of gold, most newcomers did not actually prosper. However, the massive influx of settlers to California sped up the process of making California a state. In September 1850, Congress admitted California into the United States.

Soon it seemed that the North had gained an advantage in these new developments, as California, Utah, Minnesota, and Oregon all seemed poised to ask for admission to the union as slave-free states. This situation alarmed many Southerners and contributed to a growing sectional conflict that undid the success of the Mexican War.

Sectional differences over the issue of slavery played an important role in the presidential election of 1848. The Democratic Party nominated Michigan Senator Lewis Cass, a proponent of popular sovereignty. The Whigs nominated General Zachary Taylor, hero of the Mexican War. Taylor was a slaveholder himself but was vague on the issues and refused to take a stand on slavery. Many people were unhappy with both parties, a situation that led to the formation of the Free Soil Party. The new party nominated former president Martin Van Buren. The Free Soil Party diverted enough votes from the Democrats to give the election to Taylor. Taylor, however, died after sixteen months in office.

After Taylor's death, Vice President Millard Fillmore became president. Along with Daniel Webster and Henry Clay, Fillmore sought a compromise in the growing sectional conflict. The resulting Compromise of 1850 admitted California as a free state and enforced a strict fugitive-slave law. There was much debate over the compromise and many were unhappy about it. However, it was finally pushed through Congress as five separate bills. Even so, the Compromise of 1850 marked the end of an era, as the government soon fell into the hands of more ideologically oriented men who were less willing to compromise.

One aspect of the Compromise of 1850 that particularly bothered many in the North was a harsh new Fugitive Slave Law. The new law made it easy to turn over suspected runaway slaves to their owners, leading to the possibility that some long-free ex-slaves would once again be enslaved. The backlash against the Fugitive Slave Law led to heightened sectional conflict. Abolitionists in the North increased the activity on the Underground Railroad that helped move slaves from the South to freedom in the North and Canada. The growing tension grew even more intense after the serialization of *Uncle Tom's Cabin*, which took an abolitionist stance.

The slavery issue played a role once again in the election of 1852. The Democrats nominated Franklin Pierce, a former congressman from New Hampshire, who supported the compromise and expansion. The Whigs nominated Winfield Scott, the former Mexican War hero. Scott took a vaguely antislavery stance, although he rarely articulated a strong position on any issue. Furthermore, the Whigs were deeply split into Northern and Southern factions. Many members of the party left for the Free Soil Party. Pierce won the election easily, giving the Democrats a mandate to govern the country. Soon, Southern Democrats led by Jefferson Davis came to dominate the government.

A number of important developments took place during the Pierce administration. The United States began to take more of a global stance, pursuing trade with Japan and attempting to purchase Cuba from Spain. In 1853, the United States made the Gadsden Purchase, buying some 45,000 square miles from Mexico in what is now Arizona and New Mexico. The United States used this new territory to help connect the East and West by railroad. The 1854 Kansas Nebraska Act contributed even more to the growing sectional conflict. The idea of popular sovereignty in the territories led to much violence in Kansas, including the well-known raids carried out by John Brown. In 1856 alone, more than 200 people were killed in "Bleeding Kansas."

In the 1856 election, the Democrats nominated the pro-South James Buchanan. The new Republican Party nominated John C. Frémont, yet another Mexican War hero. With solid Southern support and the presence of the Know-Nothing Party, which siphoned off Republican votes, Buchanan won the election.

During the Buchanan administration, sectional conflict came to a head. In the 1857 *Dred Scott v. Sandford case*, the slave Scott sued for his freedom, but the Supreme Court ruled that he could not do so because he was considered property. More important was the Court's ruling that abolishing slavery through legislation was unconstitutional. Talk of Southern secession soon followed. Some in the South had doubts that they could defeat the North in a war. However, there was a potential for European support for the South. Many European leaders had grown fearful of an increasingly powerful United States since the Mexican War. Any chance to break up North America into smaller, less powerful countries appealed to some in Europe. Then, with the 1859 Harpers Ferry incident (in which John Brown raided an arsenal) the situation became more ominous. When authorities captured, convicted, and hanged Brown, a conflict between North and South seemed imminent.

In 1860, the Republican nominee Abraham Lincoln won the presidential election. Lincoln, clearly with pro-North sympathies, won a long, difficult campaign that included four candidates. Soon after the Lincoln victory, South Carolina seceded from the Union on December 20, 1860. Other Southern states followed, creating the Confederate States of America, with Jefferson Davis as president. Military hostilities between

IN CONTEXT "Bleeding Kansas"

The years from 1854 to 1861 were a turbulent time in Kansas territory. The Kansas Nebraska Act of 1854 established the territorial boundaries of Kansas and Nebraska and opened the land to legal settlement. It allowed the residents of these territories to decide by popular vote whether their state would be free or slave. This concept of self-determination was called popular sovereignty. In Kansas, people on all sides of this controversial issue flooded the territory, trying to influence the vote in their favor.

Rival territorial governments, election fraud, and squabbles over land claims all contributed to

North and South began at Fort Sumter on April 12, 1861. The United States was now involved in a Civil War that lasted until 1865.

After the Union victory in the Civil War, the United States quickly grew as a world power. In the Spanish-American War of 1898, the United States expanded its empire by gaining control of the Philippines, Cuba, and Puerto Rico. By the early twentieth century, along with Germany and Japan, the United States had become a major new player on the world stage. This power was seen in the role of the United States in World War I. Although America stayed out of the early part of the war, in 1917 the country entered the conflict and played a decisive role in its outcome. During the war, Mexican-U.S. relations again played an important role. The British intercepted a note from German Foreign Minister Arthur Zimmermann to the Mexican government. He proposed an alliance in which Mexico would support the German side in the war in exchange for the restoration of the territory lost to the United States in the nineteenth century. Fortunately for the United States, Carranza refused the German offer and Mexico remained neutral in the war.

For the rest of the century, the power of the United States continued to grow. The country played a key role in the Allied victory in World War II. After the close of WWII in 1945, the United States took on the role of world superpower. This position would continually cast a shadow over Mexico. Mexicans would often look to the United States for jobs and opportunities for economic success, making immigration a contentious issue between the two countries. Economic relations would also favor the United States through the North America Free Trade Agreement (NAFTA). The United States would take advantage of cheap labor in Mexico while Mexicans often complained that their northern neighbor was exploiting the resources of their country.

ALTERNATE HISTORY

What would have happened had Mexico defeated the American attack at Veracruz and held onto its northern territory? In an alternate history, after repelling the U.S. invasion, Mexico likely would have made a conscious effort to populate the northern frontier in hopes of preventing future American incursions. At first, the cost of such a policy might

IN CONTEXT   *"Bleeding Kansas" (Continued)*

the violence of this era. Three distinct political groups occupied Kansas: pro-slavers, free-staters, and abolitionists. Violence was constant among these opposing factions and continued until 1861 when Kansas entered the Union as a free state on January 29. This era became forever known as "Bleeding Kansas."

During the time of "Bleeding Kansas," murder, mayhem, destruction, and psychological warfare became a code of conduct in Eastern Kansas and Western Missouri. Well-known examples of this violence include the massacre in May 1856 at Pottawatomie Creek where John Brown and his sons killed five pro-slavery advocates.

have seemed too expensive for the cash-strapped Mexican government. However, Santa Anna and the Mexican government could have succeeded in convincing Great Britain to make them a substantial loan. The British had already provided economic assistance to Latin American countries in the past. Despite previous problems in collecting debts from Mexico, the British would have hoped that by providing economic aid to the Mexicans, they might have further stymied the expansion of the United States to the west.

Building on the already existing system of missions in California, Mexico could have begun sending settlers to places such as Los Angeles and San Francisco in California. Then in early 1848, Mexican miners might have been the ones to discover vast deposits of gold in California. The discovery of gold could have led to a large-scale shift in population from central Mexico to California. Many residents of the once-prosperous colonial silver mining areas such as Guanajuato and Zacatecas would make the trek northward, bringing their mining knowledge and skills with them. Large urban areas would have grown up around the once-sleepy missions. San Francisco in particular might have become a major Mexican boomtown on the Pacific coast of California. The city would likely have quickly become the second largest city in Mexico, behind Mexico City. Just as the city attracted many immigrants in actual history, a Mexican San Francisco would have pulled immigrants from around the world intent on getting rich.

In an alternate history, the economic boom along the Pacific coast in northern Mexico would have led the country's government to consider building a canal that would have allowed for transportation between the Atlantic and Pacific. Mexico, however, would not have been alone in the desire to build a canal somewhere in Central America. Great Britain desired a shorter route between its Caribbean possessions and its empire in Asia. The United States, although foiled in its attempt to acquire California, would still have sought to connect the Oregon territory with the East Coast. This three-way race to build a canal might have led to an agreement in which the three countries would have agreed that none of them would build a canal alone during the next ten years. Such an agreement would have reflected the actual Clayton-Bulwer Treaty between the United States and Great Britain, in which the two countries agreed that neither would exclusively construct a canal across Central America.

When the treaty expired in 1860, tensions might have mounted as both the United States and Mexico sought to be the first to build a canal. U.S. plans would have focused on Panama, at that time a part of Colombia, as they did in actual history. Mexico would have looked to a possible route through Nicaragua. Many in the Mexican government would have begun to call for the annexation of much of Central America. At the time of independence from Spain, much of Central America had actually formed part of Mexico, so there was a historical precedent. Furthermore, many Central American leaders would have felt that joining Mexico and its now booming economy might have been advantageous, especially given the growing U.S. interest in expanding in the Caribbean basin. Thus, in the second half of the nineteenth century, Guatemala, Honduras, El Salvador, and Nicaragua all might have voted to become states of Mexico for economic and political reasons.

In an alternate history in which Mexico had the economic power and political drive to connect the far ends of its large country, in the later–1800s, the government would have gone to work on constructing a canal across Nicaragua while the United States might have been bogged down in negotiations with Colombia over a possible Panama route. With its historical, cultural, and linguistic links to Central America, Mexico would likely have found it easier to build a canal than the United States did in actual history. Furthermore, as in actual history, French interests might have become involved in the construction of an isthmian canal. Mexico could have taken advantage of France's desire to increase its presence in Latin America and utilized French technical and engineering skills to build the canal. France would have been involved through its desire to exploit its southern European "Latin" culture in order to make inroads in Spanish America. A canal across Central America would have been a perfect project for both Mexico and France.

In an alternate history, the United States likely would have resolved the issue of slavery in a very different manner. In actual history, the acquisition of territory in the Mexican War set off a series of events that led to dramatically increased sectional conflict and to the Civil War. If the United States had not had to deal with the question of slavery in the territories, compromise might have been possible and the Civil War might have been avoided. Perhaps the United States would have abolished slavery in a gradual manner, as happened in Brazil. Congress could have passed laws that would have slowly ended slavery through some sort of free birth law, allowing the institution to gradually die out.

Another possibility in an alternate history is that Mexico might have taken on the role of an expanding power in the Western Hemisphere, as the United States did in actual history. Mexico might have been in a better position to take possession of the remaining Spanish colonies in the Caribbean. In actual history, the United States came to control both Cuba and Puerto Rico in the aftermath of the Spanish-American War. However, in alternate history, a more powerful and aggressive Mexico might have had the military power and expansionist desires to make the Caribbean its own sphere of influence.

Mexico could have taken advantage of a common cultural and linguistic heritage to dominate the former Spanish colonies. Perhaps Cubans and Puerto Ricans would have even been willing to become part of Mexico, a former Spanish colony itself.

Had Mexico been able to gain control of Cuba, it could have taken advantage of the sugar industry. In actual history, the United States came to dominate sugar in Cuba. In this alternate history, Mexico could have further strengthened its economic situation by expanding into the Caribbean. Mexico already had some experience cultivating sugar in the Yucatan Peninsula, and could have extended this experience to Cuba. In the longer term, if Mexico and not the United States had taken possession of Cuba, the later Cuban revolution—largely a response to U.S. imperialism—might never have occurred.

A larger and stronger Mexico would likely have played a role in World War I. In actual history, Mexico chose to remain neutral because of an increasingly powerful United States and the chaos of its own revolution during the 1910s. The government of Carranza did receive an offer from Germany to form an alliance against the United States in the form of the infamous Zimmermann telegram. Germany promised that Mexico would regain the territory it had lost in the nineteenth century if it would help the German government. However, Carranza declined the offer.

In an alternate history, Mexico might have been tempted to ally itself with Germany. If the United States had been smaller and less powerful than in actual history, perhaps there could have been a real possibility that with German military aid, Mexico could retake Texas from the United States. The Germans hoped to keep the United States out of the European war as long as possible. They might have been willing to lend their military expertise to Mexico in order to tie up the U.S. military in a North American conflict that would have made the Great War more of a true world war. Such a scenario could have also changed the outcome of the war in Europe. Without the aid of the United States, an emerging global power in actual history, Great Britain and its allies might not have been able to defeat the Germans.

In actual twentieth-century history, there was a large flow of Mexican immigrants to the United States. This movement of people was due to both "push" factors in Mexico and "pull" factors in the United States. However, in an alternate history in which Mexico would have been larger and more prosperous, such emigration out of the country might have been minimal. Without the widespread poverty and lack of jobs that existed in actual history, fewer Mexicans would have left their homeland. Also, a smaller and perhaps less prosperous United States would have had less appeal to Mexican workers.

A number of trends might have emerged in an alternate history. First, there would likely have been significant internal migration in Mexico. Thus, California and Texas might still have received large waves of new inhabitants. However, they would simply have been Mexicans relocating to another part of their own country rather than undocumented workers crossing an international border. Their goal would still have been economic opportunity. However, many of the actual problems that have come with large-scale immigration to the United States would have been avoided. Second, Mexico might have received large numbers of immigrants itself, especially from the countries of the Western Hemisphere. A large and prosperous Mexico would likely have attracted Spanish-speaking immigrants from the Americas. Latin American immigrants would have found it easier to settle in a country in which the inhabitants spoke their language and shared with them a general cultural background.

Another key aspect of U.S.-Mexican relations that would be very different in an alternate history is that of trade between the countries. In actual history, a key milestone was the North American Free Trade Agreement (NAFTA) that went into effect in 1994. According to its critics, NAFTA seems to have greatest benefit for U.S. corporations that exploit cheap labor and less stringent environmental laws in Mexico. In an alternate history, Mexico could have taken a stronger stand in its economic relations with the United States. The two countries would be on a more equal economic footing. They likely would still have signed some sort of free trade agreement along with Canada. However, this alternate treaty would likely have provided more benefits for Mexico than the actual NAFTA has done. A more prosperous Mexico would have wages just as high as those of the United States and probably would have also imposed stricter environmental standards. Thus, any economic agreements would have been based more on true free trade, with each country taking advantage of the products it produced well and in abundance.

Ronald Young

Discussion Questions

1. When investigating landing points, General Winfield Scott and his staff narrowly escaped being killed. How do you think American history would have been different if Scott, Meade, and Lee had died in that episode?

2. If Mexico had won the Mexican-American War, do you think the larger territory and greater resources would have tended to make Mexico a more or a less politically stable and united country?

3. If the United States had not acquired any lands to the west of the Louisiana Purchase and Texas, how would that have affected the growing sectional division in the United States? As the Missouri Compromise had resolved the issue of slavery in the territories in the Louisiana Purchase prior to 1846, what issues might have brought differences over slavery before Congress if the United States had not won the Mexican-American War?

4. In the alternate history suggested here, Mexico rather than the United States dominates Cuba. Do you think Cuba would have remained independent of Mexico? If Mexican rather than American companies had exploited Cuban sugar, do you think that a revolution like that led by Fidel Castro would have erupted in the 1950s or 1960s?

5. If Mexico had accepted an alliance with Germany in World War I and some of the battles of that war had been fought along the Texas-Mexican border, how would that have affected the outcome of the war in Europe? How might it have changed the national boundaries in North America? Do you think the United States would have been more or less likely to develop an isolationist foreign policy in the 1920s and 1930s if World War I had included such battles?

Bibliography and Further Reading

Bauer, K. Jack. *The Mexican War, 1846–1848*. New York: Macmillan, 1974.

Bauer, K. Jack. *Surfboats and Horse Marines: U.S. Naval Operations in the Mexican War*. Annapolis, MD: U.S. Naval Institute, 1969.

Eisenhower, John S. D. *So Far from God: The U.S. War with Mexico, 1846–1848*. New York: Random House, 1989.

Meyer, Michael, et al. *The Course of Mexican History*. Oxford and New York: Oxford University Press, 2003.

Ruiz, Ramon Eduardo. *Triumphs and Tragedy: A History of the Mexican People*. New York: W.W. Norton, 1992.

Skidmore, Thomas, and Peter Smith. *Modern Latin America*. Oxford and New York: Oxford University Press, 2004.

Weems, John. *To Conquer a Peace: The War between the United States and Mexico*. New York: Doubleday, 1974.

TURNING POINT

Gold was discovered in California in 1848, leading to a great migration west. What if the discovery had been later or kept secret?

INTRODUCTION

The first non–Native American exploration of portions of coastal California occurred in 1542 by Joao Rodrigues Cabrilho, captain of a Portuguese ship. The first explorer of coastal California to stake any claims of ownership was Englishman Sir Francis Drake in 1579. The Spanish were the first Westerners to establish permanent settlements on what is now California.

After Mexico won its independence from Spain, California became the property of the Mexican government, which reallocated land holdings. During this period, one Johann Augustus Sutter, born in Baden, Germany, came to the United States. At this time, California was sparsely populated, with only a few hundred residents in San Francisco and Los Angeles combined. In 1834, Sutter (who soon Anglicized Johann to John) arrived, eventually settling in the Sacramento Valley. In 1839 Mexico issued him a deed for about 49,000 acres of land; later he became a citizen of Mexico and was granted governmental responsibilities. Sutter started a settlement named Nuevo Helvetia, which is the Spanish term for New Switzerland, the country Sutter last knew before coming to America. He was joined by some Native American, Polynesian, and European workers as well as several Americans, including New Jersey–born James Wilson Marshall.

Sutter had come to America to realize a dream. Leaving behind his wife and children (whom he would not see for sixteen years), Sutter came to America to attempt to build a utopian community within an agricultural empire. He eventually employed several hundred people, owned 12,000 head of cattle, and built a fort for security. Starting this operation required more capital than Sutter had, and he was heavily in debt to creditors from all over the world, most notably to a group of Russians from who he had purchased a large parcel of land (he later refused to honor the $30,000 promissory note he had signed, but no action was taken against him).

Within a few years after Sutter had settled in the valley, California became independent of Mexico. In 1846 the citizens of the San Francisco

John Sutter, on whose land gold was discovered in 1848. (Library of Congress)

Bay area revolted against Mexico, and the California Republic was established. James Wilson Marshall had been involved in the revolt against the Mexican government and the establishment of the California Republic; in the process, he had lost his farm. Sutter himself had also supported California's revolt against the Mexican government in 1846. Shortly thereafter, the Mexican-American War began over a boundary dispute between the newly annexed Texas lands and Mexico. The southwestern part of the United States was annexed from Mexico under the Treaty of Guadalupe Hidalgo on February 2, 1848, and California became a territory of the United States.

Even before the Gold Rush, U.S. citizens were beginning to come to California, some by wagon train and others by boat. No one could have imagined in 1847 that this trickle would become such a massive migration in the next couple of years, but Sutter's discovery changed everything. Sutter hired Marshall and about twenty others to construct a sawmill near the South Fork of the American River, approximately fifty miles northeast of Sutter's Fort and at the foothills of the Sierra Nevada mountains. The sawmill's construction was undertaken mainly to provide lumber for use on Sutter's land. In the autumn of 1847, after a site was selected, Sutter hired P. L. Wimmer and his relatives as well as several laborers who formerly had belonged to a Mormon unit in the Californian war for independence from Mexico. Wimmer along with his sons had the responsibility of coordinating the workers while his wife, Elizabeth Jane "Jennie" Wimmer, did the cooking for all of the workers.

More specifically, Sutter wanted lumber for construction that was to be completed at Yerba Buena, which became the modern-day San Francisco. The construction at Sutter's Mill consisted of one large wheat-grinding mill, fences, and other buildings for the city that was now growing rapidly. Sutter's endeavors during this time were not viewed by the Californian citizenry as much of a success. He had invested a lot of money in his farming empire without seeing much return. He had been offered fully equipped and well-developed ranches already in operation in trade for some of his landholdings in the Sacramento Valley. Sutter had turned all of them down because he was intent on developing his own holdings, mostly with resources extracted from his land alone.

By December 1847, California had a population of approximately 150 Native Americans and 14,000 settlers of either European or Mexican descent. In the short time that California had been a U.S. territory, the population of European descent had grown by about 10,000 residents. Sutter proved to be very open and willing to solicit and accept residents in his colony and he had gained a reputation of paying well. By the time construction began on Sutter's Mill nearly 500 citizens were employed directly by Sutter, and this does not include all those individuals linked to the economy by providing services or commerce to his company or the workers. Sutter employed gunsmiths, blacksmiths, distillers, tanners, mill workers, carpenters, farmers, shepherds, gardeners, merchants, trappers, hunters, weavers, and other skilled workers.

The soldiers at Sutter's Fort were primarily Native Americans who were organized and structured under a German commander. In early January 1848, great opportunities seemed to await Sutter, for the crew had finished the mill project and had begun to dig the bed of the stream deeper so that the mill could operate more efficiently.

 TURNING POINT

During the afternoon of January 24, 1848, at a place known as Coloma, California, near the modern city of Sacramento, Marshall went down to inspect the progress that was being made on deepening the river when he noticed something shiny in the water. He picked it up and felt certain it was gold. Then he spotted another bit in the water. Mrs. Wimmer, who was in charge of preparing meals and cleaning laundry for the workers, knew a method by which she could use lye soap for identification of the metal's value. The next morning she had determined that the object Marshall had found, weighing approximately one-third of an ounce, was pure gold. Only a few days after this discovery, a rain-soaked Marshall showed up at Fort Sutter. Sutter was surprised to see Marshall at his office only a few days after he had left for the mill.

Marshall revealed to Sutter that he had about two ounces of what might be gold that he had found in the American River. He had kept the mineral behind locked doors and had tried to keep Mrs. Wimmer's confirmation a secret. He had told the laborers at the mill that his findings might be gold, but the workers had brushed Marshall off and hadn't taken him very seriously. He showed Sutter several pieces of gold that were worth a few dollars (which was a lot of money at that time). Sutter tested the nuggets in his laboratory with a solution known as nitric acid that dissolved the metal. This process proved the metal was gold.

The gold was almost 100 percent pure, of 23 carats or more, very rarely found in nature at that purity. Marshall was impatient and insisted that they both leave for Sutter's Mill that evening. Sutter agreed to come up to Sutter's Mill in the morning, but Marshall left in the evening in a terrible rainstorm.

Early the next morning, Sutter, accompanied by a couple of his workers, started out in heavy rain for the mill site, approximately fifty-four miles away. The next day, Sutter and Marshall found several gold pieces in the stream and also received several pieces from the workers who had collected the gold. Sutter later had a ring made from the gold pieces; the ring had his family's coat of arms engraved on the outside, and the inside contained an engraving that read, "The first gold, discovered in January 1848." After prospecting for an additional day, Sutter asked his workers if they would keep the discovery a secret for six weeks. Sutter felt unhappy about the findings and didn't think it would benefit him at all. He also

IN CONTEXT   In His Own Words

In a contemporary magazine article, John Sutter described the moment when he first learned of the gold on his property:

It was a rainy afternoon when Mr. Marshall arrived at my office in the Fort, very wet. I was somewhat surprised to see him, as he was down a few days previous; and then, I sent up to Coloma a number of teams with provisions, mill irons, etc., etc. He told me then that he had some important and interesting news which

he wished to communicate secretly to me, and wished me to go with him to a place where we should not be disturbed, and where no listeners could come and hear what we had to say. I went with him to my private rooms; he requested me to lock the door; I complied, but I told him at the same time that nobody was in the house except the clerk, who was in his office in a different part of the house; after requesting of me something which he wanted, which my servants brought and then left the

doubted that the discovery would be kept secret for six weeks until his grinding mill was built.

One of the workers in the Sacramento Valley went to San Francisco to Samuel Brannan's general store. There, he bought a bottle of brandy that he paid for with gold nuggets taken by hand from the American River. The merchant was astonished and thought the worker was trying to insult him. The driver who had come into town with the worker suggested that the merchant go and see Sutter. Sutter immediately told the merchant the truth, and the merchant in turn ran and told Brannan, the store's owner. At once, Brannan came to see Sutter, who confirmed the validation of the claim. Brannan immediately leased a large house from Sutter near Sutter's Mill, transported supplies to it, and opened up a trading post for business.

Brannan next bought up every shovel, ax, and tin pan he could find and then ran through the streets of San Francisco holding up a bottle of gold dust and yelling that there was gold in the American River that was free for the taking for anyone who wanted it. Brannan also owned a newspaper (California's first), which he used to spread the word. When prospectors arrived at Sutter's Fort, Brannan sold them supplies. Nine weeks later, he had $36,000, an immense sum for the time. Even though Brannan never spent one day prospecting for gold, in only one year's time he became the richest man in California. As soon as the secret got out in San Francisco, Sutter's workers began to leave him until all began prospecting on their own for gold in the valley. The only ones who didn't take off for prospecting immediately were the Mormons, whom Sutter had hired. Once the job was completed, however, they too went out in search of their own fortunes.

By May 1848, people were rushing in from San Francisco and other regions of California in search of gold. For the first few months after the gold discovery and initial migration, the citizens of Southern California refused to believe the gold strike news. The influx of men into the valley was very unfortunate for Sutter. His workers left to pan for gold, which eventually forced him into bankruptcy. Even Sutter's millstones were looted and sold. Even though John Sutter and James Marshall had taken extra precautions to keep the discovery a secret, by now news had

IN CONTEXT *In His Own Words (Continued)*

room, I forgot to lock the doors, and it happened that the door was opened by the clerk just at the moment when Marshall took a rag from his pocket, showing me the yellow metal: he had about two ounces of it; but how quick Mr. M. put the yellow metal in his pocket again can hardly be described. The clerk came to see me on business, and excused himself for interrupting me, and as soon as he had left I was told, "now lock the doors; didn't I tell you that we might have listeners?" I told him that he need fear nothing about that, as it was not the habit of this gentleman; but I could hardly convince him that he need not to be suspicious. Then Mr. M. began to show me this metal, which consisted of small pieces and specimens, some of them worth a few dollars; he told me that he had expressed his opinion to the laborers at the mill, that this might be gold; but some of them were laughing at him and called him a crazy man, and could not believe such a thing. *(Hutchings' California Magazine, November 1857)*

leaked out to the rest of the nation and around the world, and the California gold rush was well under way. The story of gold in California spread and reached the East Coast in the summer of 1848, when the *New York Herald* published a story on the gold findings on August 19. Throughout the autumn of 1848 more and more media attention was given to California, and on December 5, President James K. Polk gave an address before Congress in which he announced that "the accounts of the abundance of gold in [California] are of such extraordinary character as would scarcely command belief were they not corroborated by authentic reports of officers in the public service," according to H. W. Brands in *The Age of Gold: The California Gold Rush and the New American Dream*.

ACTUAL HISTORY

Brannan was only the first in a long line of wealthy merchants, artists, writers, publishers, and businessmen who accumulated wealth without digging one single day for gold. As might be expected, assorted visionaries, crackpots, and unscrupulous profiteers of all types now began to appear. Rufus Porter, inventor and noted editor, took over the Tabernacle Church on New York's Broadway to demonstrate a working model of his "flying ship," a propeller-driven blimp that when completed would be 800 feet long and carry 100 passengers from New York to California in three days (probably Samuel Brannan would have then proceeded to found the world's first airport). This in 1849! Inventors such as Samuel Peppard, and the man remembered only as "Wind-Wagon Thomas" tried to reach the West by sailing across the Great Plains in wind-powered wagons. Others sold food and water for exorbitant prices to the so-called Forty-Niners now racing to California. Most people who flocked to California during this period found it difficult just to pay for daily living expenses with the enormous inflation and cost-of-living expenses.

KEY CONCEPT   "The Rush," from the *California Star*

The excitement and enthusiasm of Gold Washing still continues—increases.

Many of our countrymen are not disposed to do us justice as regards the opinion we have at different times expressed of the employment in which over two thirds of the white population of the country are engaged. There appears to have gone abroad a belief that we should raise our voices against what some one has denominated an "infatuation." We are very far from it, and would invite a calm recapitulation of our articles touching the matter, as in themselves amply satisfactory. We shall continue to report the progress of the work, to speak within bounds, and to approve, admonish, or openly censure whatever, in our opinion, may require it at our hands.

It is quite unnecessary to remind our readers of the "prospects of California" at this time, as the effects of this gold washing enthusiasm, upon the country, through every branch of business are unmistakably apparent to every one. Suffice it that there is no abatement, and that active measures will probably be taken to prevent really serious and alarming consequences.

Every seaport as far south as San Diego, and every interior town, and nearly every rancho from the base of the mountains in which the gold has been found, to the Mission of San Luis, south, has become suddenly drained of human beings. Americans, Californians, Indians and Sandwich Islanders, men, women and children, indiscriminately. Should there be that success which has repaid the efforts of those employed for the last month, during the present and next, as many are sanguine in their expectations, and we confess to unhesitatingly believe probably, not only will witness the depopulation of every town, the desertion of every rancho, and the desolation of the once promising crops of the country, but it will also draw largely upon adjacent territories—awake

An 1849 cartoon depicts grim conditions in the goldfields of California. (Library of Congress)

Sonora, and call down upon us, despite her Indian battles, a great many of the good people of Oregon. There are at this time over one thousand souls busied in washing gold, and the yield per diem may be safely estimated at from fifteen to twenty dollars, each individual.

We have by every launch from the embarcadera of New Helvetia, returns of enthusiastic gold seekers—heads of families, to effect transportation of their households to the scene of their successful labors, or others, merely returned to more fully equip themselves for a protracted, or perhaps permanent stay.

Spades, shovels, picks, wooden bowls, Indian baskets (for washing), etc., find ready purchase, and are very frequently disposed of at extortionate prices.

The gold region, so called, thus far explored, is about one hundred miles in length and twenty in width. These imperfect explorations contribute to establish the certainty of the placera extending much further south, probably three or four hundred miles, as we have before stated, while it is believed to terminate about a league north of the point at which first discovered. The probable amount taken from these mountains since the first of May last, we are informed is $100,000, and which is at this time principally in the hands of the mechanical, agricultural and laboring classes.

There is an area explored, within which a body of 50,000 men can advantageously labor. Without maliciously interfering with each other, then, there need be no cause for contention and discord, where as yet, we are gratified to know, there is harmony and good feeling existing. We really hope no unpleasant occurrences will grow out of this enthusiasm, and that our apprehensions may be quieted by continued patience and good will among the washers. (*California Star*, Saturday, June 10, 1848. Note that the *California Star* ceased publication June 14, 1848, because the staff had rushed to the gold fields.—Gladys Hansen, the Virtual Museum of the City of San Francisco.)

News spread around the world of the gold findings in California. Emigrants from Mexico, Hawaii, China, the Mississippi Valley, and the U.S. Northeast flocked to California. This era was characterized by the greatest shift in population westward as well as the greatest foreign immigration in American history; the area became a melting pot, with emigrants migrating from every continent to take part in the extravaganza. As historian H. W. Brands points out, the discovery in the banks of the American River, in effect, redefined the American Dream. The golden discovery changed the nation in such a way that America now sought to be on the move and to seek out a faster pace of life. Americans now sought instant wealth and luxury. Many intelligent, young, and talented young men set off for California with the intention of returning home rich. The new American Dream that began in California took on the characteristics of forwardness, opportunism, entrepreneurialism, and dynamism; these prospectors were full of energy. California has ever since been a haven for pioneers of cutting-edge businesses and technologies. Historian JoAnn Levy states that many women were empowered by the realization that there was serious money to be made cooking and cleaning for the grubby male prospectors who couldn't be bothered to develop domestic skills. California at this time exemplified the stimulation of energy and the spark of intellectual thought that is so characteristic of democratic ages, which Alexis de Tocqueville described in *Democracy in America*. Among those who rose at this time were Levi Strauss, who became wealthy in 1853 by selling dry goods in California and who made heavy, sturdy pants for the miners to wear. His company eventually became world famous and was

"The Way They Go to California," a lithograph published by N. Currier in 1849. (Library of Congress)

the source of the original invention of Levi's denim jeans. In 1872, Strauss added metal rivets, which made denim jeans even stronger.

Other entrepreneurs who were characteristic of this age included a New York meat packer named Phillip Armour, who walked on foot to California. After making a fortune there, he moved to Wisconsin to set up a meat-processing plant that became one of the nation's largest. John Studebaker made wheelbarrows in California and after saving his pennies for six years moved back to his home in Indiana and opened a wagon-making business. Later, his company would go on to make automobiles as well. Henry Wells and William Fargo, founded the Wells Fargo Bank. Others, who were influenced by the gold rush and the prevailing melting pot of culture included the writer Mark Twain, President Ulysses S. Grant, best-selling author Bret Harte, Civil War general William Tecumseh Sherman, and many other notable people in American history.

The influx of migrants from around the world transformed San Francisco into a cultural center; the city eventually had more newspapers than any city in the world except London. The Gold Rush, by bringing so much energy and talent to California, would set the stage for the state to become a centerpiece of American culture. Emigrants came by traveling around the southern tip of South America, across Panama and Nicaragua, or across the plains by way of wagon train. Chinese, Mexicans, Irish, Turks, Australians, Germans, French, and others all chased the dream to California. Approximately 100,000 people migrated to California in 1848 and 1849, an influx that helped to fulfill the idea of Manifest Destiny. As the year 1849 was the peak of the Gold Rush, with most of the migration coming during this period, the name "Forty-niners" was coined to describe the gold prospectors.

Early on, the California gold region was very disorderly, with the only law most often being that of the gun and the knife. By some estimates over 10,000 people died of malnutrition, disease, and lack of clothing and shelter in the first couple of years. Many criminals on the run sought refuge in California during this period, and this added to the area's lawlessness. Eventually, a court system and sufficient law enforcement were established to bring California under control.

In 1850 construction began on the world's first transcontinental railroad, the Panama Railway, which crossed the Isthmus of Panama and connected the Atlantic and Pacific Oceans. Construction was begun in 1850 in direct response to the need for a quicker way to reach California from the East Coast. The cost of $8 million was largely financed by American companies. Bizarrely, as many of the laborers had no identification and fell easy prey to tropical disease, the Railway Company generated additional revenue by selling their unclaimed corpses to hospitals and universities for research purposes. The railroad was completed in 1855.

In the broad scope of history, those who became rich overnight were in the minority, with most of the miners never seeing any return on all of their efforts. The gold that was found was mostly placer gold (meaning that it was found in sand or gravel in streambeds) mined in the foothills of the Sierra Nevada mountains, consisting of nuggets and gold particles. Some prospectors often found gold worth $300 to $400 per day in the first couple of years. At first the gold was easily found, mostly lying on the surface or under fairly shallow water. But already by 1849, the "easy" gold had been collected and the original methods for gold prospecting were replaced with lode and placer mining. Lode mining was at that time performed by digging into the ground to find pockets of gold ores. Placer mining was also practiced by digging and panning in streams and using water power through sluices to separate the heavier ore from rock and mud.

After the "easy" gold had been extracted, sentiment against foreigners began to grow in California. As a result, California passed legislation in 1850 that placed a $20-per-month tax on all foreign miners, but this seemed to add to the increasing resentment rather than to quell it. In effect, the tax caused many foreign miners to leave the state and return home. In a notable exception, most of the Chinese remained in California. Most often, the Chinese obtained employment in other occupations, where they could escape the miners' tax. They often found new lives in which they were successful. As a result, even though California lost some of its foreigners, it still became the most culturally diverse region in the entire world.

Native Americans, as in other regions of North America, were not treated well in California. Disease killed many. Others were rooted out by force or pressure from the migratory groups who were prospecting for gold. Most Native Americans were uninterested in gold hunting and did not pursue it. The 300,000 original inhabitants were reduced to 50,000 by 1850. Many were killed because of conflicts over hunting grounds, and the influx of people disturbed their entire way of life as they were removed from the land.

Some Southerners who came to California and brought African-American slaves found that their slaves had to be freed. Most of the gold

A prospector panning for gold in the 1940s. Prospecting continued for decades after the initial discovery. (Library of Congress)

prospectors objected to African-American slaves mining gold because they didn't want to work beside slaves who were working without pay and making their owners rich. Therefore, most African Americans were freed initially and, in 1850, California was admitted to the United States as a free (nonslave) state. Questions arising over California added to tensions that led up to the Civil War. However, most white Californians who objected to slavery did so not on idealistic grounds but simply because they did not want to compete with slave labor.

The Gold Rush seemed to foster a sense of social equality in California that continued into modern times. Much of this had to do with the small socioeconomic differences that existed among the miners in California. As the resources became scarce, many felt as though each miner should have to work for the gold on an equal basis. Industrial mining, conducted by large corporations with more modern mining techniques, gradually began to replace individual miners. Most of the miners in California returned to the occupations they had had before the Gold Rush. Even though major mining operations had become predominant by 1852, over 200,000 gold prospectors were still reaching California. The influx of citizens and economic activity in California caused a tremendous increase in the gross national product of the United States. Many economists believe that the great increase in wealth in the United States during this period led to the financing of the Industrial Revolution in America and brought the country to the forefront as a major world power.

The Compromise of 1850 (the Pearce Act) brought California into the nation as a state. California's constitution of October 13, 1849, provided for it to be an antislavery state, and the territory applied for admission to the Union as a free state. The projected admission of California would disturb the longtime balance between free and slave states in the Senate, and this caused debate on whether to accept California's admission as a free state or to divide California into two states with a free state in the North and a slave state in the South. In addition, the Compromise provided for Texas to receive financial compensation for relinquishing claim to lands west of the Rio Grande; the United States' New Mexico Territory (including present-day Arizona and Utah) was organized without any specific prohibition of slavery (the status of slavery was to be determined by "popular sovereignty," meaning that the population of the territory would decide). The slave trade (but not slavery itself) was abolished in Washington, D.C., and when the stringent Fugitive Slave Law of 1850 was passed, all U.S. citizens were required to assist in the return of runaway slaves.

In the 1850s, the first interest had been expressed in building a transcontinental railroad, and after the Civil War, this interest was revived. In 1869 the railroad was completed and encouraged millions more citizens to migrate to the West. Agriculture became California's largest industry, especially after farmers discovered that the soil, when irrigated, was prime agricultural land unequalled anywhere in the United States. In the years to come, the state of California would become one of the world's ten largest economies.

From the turn of the twentieth century until the Civil Rights movement in 1964 California's population grew from less than 1 million to over 30 million people, making California the most populated state in the nation. In the latter half of the twentieth century, California became even more culturally diversified, with almost every ethnicity in the world represented in the population. California today is the world's leader in the motion picture industry as well as a major player in the areas of science and technology.

Unfortunately, John Sutter and James W. Marshall did not fare so well. Sutter's land had been settled by people without a true deed or title to the land they occupied, and no law existed to bring them to justice. This situation brought about many land disputes that eventually ended up in the Supreme Court of the United States, which found that Sutter did not have a clear title to the land. Sutter filed for bankruptcy in 1852. The state of California eventually provided Sutter a monthly stipend of $250 per month after settling his claims. Sutter was never granted restitution from the federal government. Marshall never received any recompense for his holdings. His property was destroyed and confiscated by the gold diggers. He spent the final years of his life as a farmer and received no compensation from the state of California or the federal government.

ALTERNATE HISTORY

Working from the premise that the major players had had excellent reasons for keeping the news of their discovery secret, we can speculate that the events of January 24, 1848, might have transpired quite differently. After Marshall discovered gold on John Sutter's land in the

American River, he might have ridden down to Sutter's Fort to inform Sutter about the discovery. By all accounts, Sutter was known to have reacted with dismay on learning about the discovery of gold on his land, correctly foreseeing that the news would bring a mass influx of prospectors who would destroy his property and his dreams. Still, gold was gold, and though John Sutter had been heavily influenced by the ideas of Karl Marx, it is hard to imagine him completely ignoring the presence of sudden riches on land he was trying to develop into a utopian paradise (he did in fact undertake several prospecting journeys but met with little success).

Probably the secret would have been at first confined to the circle of workers surrounding Sutter's holdings (indeed, maybe not even many of those would have known; supposedly most of the laborers whom Marshall had told about the secret had refused to believe him). In any event, once the discovery had been verified and publicized most of Sutter's employees left him to begin prospecting on their own, except for the Mormons who stayed on as Sutter men until the sawmill was completed. Possibly Sutter, Marshall, and a few leading Mormons could have formed an organization to locate and mine the gold and then transport it out of the area so that it could be sold without raising a fuss. In fact, as there appears to have been little valuable material found by individual prospectors after mid-1849, it stands to reason that Sutter might have established a very successful mining operation on his property. By engaging in some low-key judicious exploitation, Sutter might have been able to finance his agricultural empire of New Helvetia and free himself from debt. The New Helvetia community and related enterprises would have continued to grow, Sutter's philosophy possibly coming under the influence of Leo Tolstoy, whose ideas (beginning in the 1850s) on education, social relations, and agriculture were later to influence Mohandas Gandhi to embrace a pastoral socialism. The possibility does exist, however, that Sutter might have simply bought Marshall's silence on the matter and simply ignored the gold on his property.

From this point forward, history could have diverged into one of two possible directions, or even both.

Scenario One: Discovery Delayed

The California Gold Rush of 1849 was the first major discovery of valuable mineral deposits in American history, creating massive population movement and economic development. But its cause was fortuitous, based on the accidental discovery of a few specks of gold in the American River. Prior to James Wilson Marshall's discovery there had been little or no prospecting activity in the area. We can assume however that since the gold was found literally "lying around," it would have been discovered by someone eventually. The real question is whether the gold rush would have occurred in time for California to have developed into a major player during the Pearce Act debates, which led to the Compromise of 1850. Without the economic rise associated with the Gold Rush, California would have still had a minimal population and would probably have been granted popular sovereignty on the slavery question, or simply not admitted to the Union at all in 1850.

The admission of California as a free state was going to upset the balance of power between Northern and Southern states in the Senate, so the possibility exists that the Compromise might not have passed in 1850; had it not, there might have been no reason for Stephen Douglas to introduce the divisive Kansas Nebraska Act in 1854. Douglas had proposed the bill as a way to organize the territories between Missouri and the lands acquired from Mexico so that land claims could be established and a railroad right-of-way could be acquired. Douglas hoped that the prospect of a railroad from Chicago to San Francisco would draw Northern support for the bill whereas establishing popular sovereignty over the issue of slavery in the territories would attract Southern support. Although the bill passed after vigorous argument for it by Douglas, one consequence was that Northern Democrats saw the bill as opening new territories to slavery. The fight over the 1854 Kansas Nebraska Act was one of the main reasons that many Northern Democrats left the Democratic Party to form the Republican Party. However, without the incentive of a rapidly growing state on the West Coast, railroad development and the push for the Kansas Nebraska Act would have been postponed.

With Southerners outraged that the Underground Railroad provided escape routes for fugitive slaves, hotheads in the South were ready for secession in 1850, but with the Fugitive Slave Act as part of the Compromise of 1850, many Southerners agreed that secession should be postponed, as long as the compromise held, and as long as the Fugitive Slave Act was enforced. This Georgia Platform, as it was known, was widely adopted throughout the South—representing at once a threat of secession and at the same time, an acceptance of the Compromise of 1850 as a working arrangement. For these reasons, the compromise may have postponed the Civil War for as much as a decade. As a result the North was wealthier and more heavily industrialized when hostilities finally broke out.

Without the crises engendered by the admission of California as a state, and the further divisive nature of the Kansas Nebraska Act, it is quite possible that the secession of the South and the Civil War would not have occurred at all. On the other hand, if other causes for secession of Southern states had developed in the 1850s, it is quite possible that the South would have either peacefully formed a separate nation (as some Northern Democrats like James Buchanan appeared to be willing to accept) or that it might have won a Civil War if the North had not been led by Republican President Abraham Lincoln, whose political and military decisions contributed greatly to that victory in actual history.

The impact of the Civil War that might have occurred in the 1850s rather than the 1860s is difficult to fully assess. Certainly without the wealth provided by the discovery of mineral deposits in California and Nevada the North might well have taken the worst of it in an earlier war, and an alternative subsequent history based on a Southern victory is not beyond the realm of possibility. An exploration of this scenario is beyond the scope of this chapter; however, the past 150 years would have been extremely (and maybe almost unimaginably) different, as almost all social institutions and events would have been affected.

Scenario Two—Discovery Monopolized

There is another possible scenario. Imagine if, after Marshall discovered gold in the American River, he rode down to Sutter's Fort to see Sutter about his newfound discovery. Marshall then could have talked over the discovery with Sutter and they both might have devised a plan that could have transformed the United States and made both men very wealthy and world famous. The plan they might have settled on would have had Marshall run the Sacramento Valley for Sutter while both men shared the proceeds.

Sutter would have been able to get a clear title to this large tract of land through the state of California and the U.S. government. Marshall would have opened up businesses and trading posts in the valley. Towns and cities would have been built, incorporating Sutter's own ideas. Sutter would have begun to advertise all over the world of the riches to be found in California. During 1848, settlers would have begun to move to the territory in search of instant wealth. Sutter and Marshall might not have prospected for gold but, rather, run businesses that supplied everything the miners needed to exist. Throughout 1848 and 1849, many more businesses would have been erected, such as theaters, dance halls, and beer halls and gardens in the German tradition, and California itself would have become a melting pot of people. As in actual history, immigrants from all over the world would flock to California.

Some sentiment would have arisen for setting a tax on foreigners. Sutter, now very wealthy and powerful, would have been able to prevent such a tax. A person of German ancestry himself, Sutter would have opposed any such xenophobic legislation. Furthermore, he would have been in a position to develop the ideal, Swiss-style democratic state about which he had dreamed.

Sutter, by 1850, would have been one of the wealthiest men in the world. Capital raised from his trading industries and mines would have enabled Sutter to also start an agricultural empire. African Americans who had migrated westward with their Southern owners might have been freed and then paid competitive wages. All industries in California would have been booming as hundreds of thousands migrated there from almost every nation on earth.

Assuming that Sutter had amassed tremendous wealth, he might have reached for political power to implement his utopian goals. Politics might have seemed irresistible for such a social visionary, and he could conceivably have achieved the governorship of California. Whereas in the East and Midwest, utopian communities established in the 1830s and 1840s were beginning to die out or to become more conventional communities by the 1850s, the whole state of California might have become a haven for communitarian experimentation under generous funding from Sutter.

Washing gold in 1916. Twentieth-century prospectors used the same techniques as the original forty-niners. (Library of Congress)

Sutter and Marshall themselves never supported or attempted to abolish any aspect of property except for owning people as slaves. They would have, however, wanted everyone to be paid competitive wages, wanted to eliminate poverty, and would have taken care of the needy and the disabled by setting up a trust fund for them. In the 1830s Alexis de Tocqueville, in *Democracy in America*, wrote about the equality of conditions in America that were unlike conditions anywhere that he had visited in the world. Now after the California Gold Rush, conditions in America would have been more favorable than ever for the promotion of such egalitarian policies. California might have developed into a state reflecting utopian ideals of social equality. Most of the wealth and capital raised there would have come from other businesses unrelated to the gold prospecting business, except that gold would have brought many people there in the first place. Following the Civil War, migration to California would have continued, much as it did in actual history, but if California had developed a more utopian reputation, the migrants would have included even more of those discontented with the conditions in the industrializing eastern regions of the country.

Like British industrialist Robert Owen, American industrialists like Henry Ford and King Gillette, and German weapons manufacturer Alfred Krupp, Sutter and his family would have had sufficient funds to have implemented some utopian and social planning ideals. However, with control of the immense riches from the gold fields and with an ability to determine the course and nature of California's early development, the Sutter plans might have had far more influence and lasting impact.

During the Industrial Revolution of the latter part of the nineteenth century, every industry imaginable might have moved to California. California might have become the world leader in the chemical, textile, automotive, steelmaking, agricultural, and publishing industries. In reality California dominated the motion picture industry, the aircraft industry, and later, the computer industry; in this alternate scenario it might have developed dominance in these other fields as well.

Sutter's heirs also would have promoted the egalitarian policies of their forebear; possibly one of them might have become a major figure in the emerging socialist international organizations of the late nineteenth century. As a cultural melting pot, a society attracting idealists and visionaries as well as a land of great prosperity, California would have continued to produce and attract others with social plans. As towns and cities grew there, they might have gone even further than they did in reality with such progressive concepts as municipal ownership of utilities, city planning, cooperatively owned enterprises, worker's compensation insurance, disability and old-age pensions, and other social innovations. In actual history, California often led the way with such programs, but in an alternate history in which most of the profits from the gold rush and the related service industries had been poured into Sutter's vision, the progressive example of California could have been even more striking and the measures implemented might have been even more successful in ameliorating the conditions that came with the rise of industrialism.

In short, the life of John Sutter could have marked the only time in American history that a utopian visionary had possessed the means to truly construct a society that matched his vision. With his wealth, Sutter might have been able to implement aspects of his vision of an egalitarian and socially just society in the large, nation-sized state of California. Conceivably, such an experiment might have created at least a part of America built on a sort of "third way" between capitalism and communism, a socioeconomic model that might have demonstrated a desirable alternative to Marx's version of socialism achieved by revolutionary means. Such an impact on life in the twentieth century could have been immeasurable.

Steven Napier and Kevin F. Wozniak

Discussion Questions

1. If the discovery of gold in California had been delayed by twenty years, what scenarios do you believe might have developed?

2. If there had been no Compromise of 1850 and no Kansas Nebraska Act of 1854, what other issues do you believe would have surfaced

in the 1850s to bring about secession from the Union by some or all of the slave states? Without the Fugitive Slave Law (part of the Compromise of 1850), would the issue of fugitive slaves have been more or less divisive?

3. If Sutter had retained control of the gold fields and had been able to monopolize the wealth from supporting industries, what social programs besides those mentioned in the alternate scenario might he have implemented? Could socialist goals be implemented successfully by a monopolistic capitalist?

4. If the Confederate States, with or without California, had achieved independence, do you think they would have been able to remain a single country or would they have further divided by internal secession? Would Mormon territory in Utah have sought complete independence, would it have remained part of the Northern United States, or would it have allied with, or joined, the Confederacy?

5. If there had been no secession and no Civil War in the 1850s or 1860s, in what ways would the history of the United States have been different in the following decades? Would the slave-holding states have succeeded in plans for expansion by taking Cuba and other territories in and around the Caribbean?

6. Without the events of the Civil War, do you think slavery in the United States would have been eliminated state by state through local emancipation plans or would it have persisted into the twentieth century?

Bibliography and Further Reading

Axon, Gordon V. *The California Gold Rush*. New York: Mason/Charter, 1976.

Bay, Helen Valeska. *The Course of Empire: First Hand Accounts of California in the Days of the Gold Rush of '49*. New York: Coward-McCann, 1931.

Blashfield, Jean F. *The California Gold Rush*. Minneapolis: Compass Point Books, 2001.

Blodgett, Peter J. *Land of Golden Dreams: California in the Gold Rush Decade, 1848–1858*. San Marino, CA: Huntington Library, 1999.

Brands, H. W. *The Age of Gold: The California Gold Rush and the New American Dream*. New York: Doubleday, 2002.

Chidsey, Donald Barr. *The California Gold Rush: An Informal History*. New York: Crown, 1968.

Gutierrez, Ramon A., and Orsi, Richard J. *Contested Eden: California before the Gold Rush*. Berkeley: University of California Press, 1998.

Holliday, J. S. *Rush for Riches: Gold Fever and the Making of California*. Berkeley: University of California Press, 1999.

Holliday, J. S., and Swain, William. *The World Rushed In: The California Gold Rush Experience*. New York: Simon & Schuster, 1981.

Johnson, Susan Lee. *Roaring Camp: The Social World of the California Gold Rush*. New York: W.W. Norton, 2000.

Lapp, Rudolph M. *Blacks in Gold Rush California*. New Haven, CT: Yale University Press, 1977.

Owens, Kenneth N. *Riches for All: The California Gold Rush and the World*. Lincoln: University of Nebraska Press, 2002.

Roberts, Brian. *American Alchemy: The California Gold Rush and Middle-Class Culture*. Chapel Hill: University of North Carolina Press, 2000.

Rohrbough, Malcolm J. *Days of Gold: The California Gold Rush and the American Nation*. Berkeley: University of California Press, 1997.

Trafzer, Clifford E., and Hyer, Joel R. *Exterminate Them: Written Accounts of the Murder, Rape, and Slavery of Native Americans during the California Gold Rush, 1848–1868*. East Lansing: Michigan State University Press, 1999.

Umbeck, John R. *A Theory of Property Rights: With Application to the California Gold Rush*. Ames: Iowa State University Press, 1981.

Walker, Dale L. *Eldorado: The California Gold Rush*. Thousand Oaks, CA: Pine Forge, 2003.

TURNING POINT

The Compromise of 1850 attempted to settle the slavery issue between North and South. What if the compromise had succeeded?

INTRODUCTION

The most divisive issue between the free states of the North and the slave states of the South was whether slavery would be allowed into new territories acquired by the United States. Since its inception, the country had sought to expand its boundaries. The 1783 Treaty of Paris, which ended the American Revolution against Great Britain, gave the new country rights to large amounts of unsettled British land between the Appalachian Mountains and the Mississippi River. This acquisition first brought the question of slavery's expansion to the new government's attention. The Northwest Ordinance of 1787 prohibited slavery in this new territory north of the Ohio River. The Southwest Ordinance of 1790 allowed slavery in the Southern area from the Ohio River to the Mississippi River by stating that slavery was permissible in any territory where it was not barred by federal law.

Slavery remained a divisive issue between the North and South as the fledgling nation created a new government. The 1787 Constitutional Convention thus had to make several compromises on the issue of slavery in order to gain support for the new U.S. Constitution. The Constitution included guarantees of the protection of private property, including slaves. Congress would not be permitted to interfere with the slave trade for twenty years, and each slave would be counted as three-fifths of a person for the purposes of apportioning representation in the U.S. House of Representatives and in terms of direct taxes. The federal government later banned the slave trade in 1809.

In the first half of the nineteenth century, the belief in Manifest Destiny—the providentially blessed inevitability of expanding U.S. territory from coast to coast—fueled sectional tensions over the expansion of slavery. The territories would prove to be a battleground between Northern and Southern ideologies. Many Northerners viewed the South as a backward region dominated by an aristocratic minority of slaveholders who held the rest of the white population in poverty. Most Northerners were

ANOTHER VIEW What Exactly Are State's Rights?

The Articles of Confederation, the first U.S. federal government created after the American Revolution had secured independence, created a weak central government dominated by stronger state governments. When it proved a failure, the architects of the new U.S. Constitution created a stronger federal government with broader powers and rights. They also wished, however, to preserve state and local autonomy, and the states maintained individual authority in numerous areas. States' rights supporters argued that the federal government was a compact created by the states, existing under their sovereign authority. Many supporters of states' rights would emerge over the next century but would disagree as to exactly how far states' rights should extend.

The first key defense of states' rights came in the late 1700s in the controversy over passage of

not demanding abolition but wanted to protect Northern ideals and institutions from slavery's corrupting influence. They wanted slavery excluded from the territories so that slaves would not provide unfair competition and discourage free laborers from migrating westward.

Southerners increasingly couched their defenses of slavery in terms of property rights. Southern politicians warned that if slavery could not be expanded, free states would increasingly outnumber slave states and dominate the federal government, with abolition as their ultimate goal. Southern radicals known as Fire-Eaters, such as South Carolina senator John C. Calhoun, argued that Congress had no authority to exclude slaves from federal territory and that such a move would violate states' rights and the right to property as guaranteed by the Constitution. The majority of white Southerners viewed slave ownership as the route to wealth, social standing, and political power and were willing to defend the "peculiar institution."

Before 1850, the issue had been settled through a series of compromises. President Thomas Jefferson acquired the huge Louisiana Purchase from France in 1803, doubling the country's size. In 1820, the Missouri Compromise settled the question of whether slavery would be allowed in this new land. Under the terms of the Compromise, Missouri entered as a slave state, balanced by the free state of Maine. The remaining Louisiana Purchase was divided at 36 degrees 30 minutes north latitude. Everything above that line would be free territory and everything below it would allow slavery. The Missouri Compromise settled the issue until the 1830s and 1840s, when the United States again expanded its boundaries through the acquisition of Mexican lands.

In 1835, American settlers in Texas fought the Mexican government for their independence. Congress admitted Texas into the Union as a slave state a decade later. President James K. Polk, an ardent expansionist elected in 1844, sought to obtain more Mexican territory. He asked Congress for an appropriation of $2 million to peacefully settle the dispute with Mexico. Democratic congressman David Wilmot of Pennsylvania added an addendum (the Wilmot Proviso) to the request declaring that any land obtained from Mexico must prohibit slavery. The Proviso touched off years of polarizing political debates in both the U.S. Congress and the country as the diplomatic mission of John Slidell to Mexico City failed to achieve the peaceful annexation of Mexican territory through purchase.

---

the federal Alien and Sedition Acts during John Adams's presidency. The Virginia and Kentucky Resolutions authored by James Madison and Thomas Jefferson expressed the rights of states to oversee and oppose federal laws by declaring the Alien and Sedition Acts to be unconstitutional. South Carolina Senator John C. Calhoun outlined a more extreme version of states' rights in the 1832–1833 nullification crisis over Southern opposition to a series of high tariffs passed by the federal government. Calhoun argued that the states could declare federal laws "null and void" within their borders. He stated that South Carolina would not enforce the tariff and threatened secession if President Andrew Jackson challenged the state. Many states' rights supporters argued with Calhoun's position, claiming that a state could secede over disagreements with federal laws, but that a state could not remain within the Union and simply disobey federal laws.

Polk then sent U.S. troops under the command of General Zachary Taylor to the disputed border region between Texas and Mexico. Mexican troops attacked Taylor's men and Congress declared war at Polk's request. Opponents of the war included those who felt it represented an attempt by the Southern "slave power conspiracy" to gain new territory in which to extend slavery at the behest of the federal government. The Mexican-American War of 1846–1848 ended in an American victory. Under the 1848 Treaty of Guadalupe Hidalgo, the United States acquired a large amount of territory known as the Mexican Cession. The Cession included California and land in the southwest that ultimately became the states of Utah and New Mexico.

California already contained some U.S. citizens but was sparsely populated until the 1848 discovery of gold and the subsequent gold rush of 1849. When the rapidly growing territory petitioned for statehood in 1849, the sectional crisis was quickly renewed. Slavery had already been outlawed in all of the Mexican Cession under Mexican law, and California had drafted a state constitution forbidding slavery. Southerners were alarmed that California, entering the Union as a nonslave state, would disrupt the balance of power between slave and free states in the Senate. A Southern convention in Nashville, Tennessee, discussed the possibility of secession for the states in the South, but ultimately the idea did not have enough support from the Southern public to come to fruition at that time.

The fate of California was just one of the many issues that were raised by the acquisition of Mexican territory. The state of Texas was involved in a dispute with New Mexico over its boundary, claiming land all the way to Santa Fe, and had millions of dollars of unpaid public debts from its period as a republic. Southerners wanted the issue resolved in favor of Texas while Northerners objected to expanding the boundaries of the slave state. The New Mexico territory was not ready for statehood but needed a territorial government, which opened the question of who would decide its slavery policy and at what point of its development. Like California, it was already a free territory because of the Mexican law forbidding slavery.

The doctrine of popular sovereignty emerged as a compromise position between Northerners who wanted slavery banned from the entire Mexican Cession under the Wilmot Proviso, Southerners who wanted equal access

KEY CONCEPT   Popular Sovereignty

Historians generally credit Senator Lewis Cass of Michigan with popularizing the doctrine of popular sovereignty in an 1847 letter to Tennessee Senator A. O. P. Nicholson known as the "Nicholson Letter." The doctrine was based on congressional nonintervention in the internal regulation of territorial life and the people's right to determine their own laws. Illinois Senator Stephen Douglas adopted the doctrine as a practical solution to the country's sectional rift over slavery's expansion. North and South disagreed as to when in the territorial process the people would make the decision in regard to slavery.

to the territories, and moderates on both sides who wanted to extend the Missouri Compromise line or find some other way to peaceably settle the growing crisis. In 1849, the thirty-first U.S. Congress arrived in Washington, D.C., to decide these issues in a mood of national crisis.

TURNING POINT

Congressmen from both the North and the South entered the thirty-first session with pressure from constituents to ensure their section's rights. Most Northerners wanted slavery prohibited throughout the new territories, whether or not they supported its abolition in the South. If the territories Southerners had died fighting to win were closed to slavery, radical Southern leaders would demand secession. Southerners also feared that most, if not all, of the new territory would ultimately remain free, upsetting the balance of power in the Senate. Southern senators, rallied by Calhoun, met frequently to discuss the issues and their stand for states' rights.

Democratic congressmen and their constituents were split between the party's Northern wing, which largely supported popular sovereignty, and its Southern wing, which wanted the territories open to slavery. Radical Northern Whigs, Democrats, and Free Soil Party members wanted no compromise, demanding that the federal government exclude slavery from the new territories. A political compromise offered the only hope of avoiding a sectional schism and possible secession. Senator Henry Clay of Kentucky, Senator Stephen Douglas of Illinois, and Senator Daniel Webster of Massachusetts emerged as leaders in the attempt to pass what became known as the Compromise of 1850 or the Great Compromise. They had experience in gaining such compromises as the architects behind the 1820 Missouri Compromise.

Daniel Webster of Massachusetts was one of the key legislators who negotiated the Compromise of 1850. (Library of Congress)

In January 1850, Clay presented a set of eight proposals grouped together in an omnibus bill that would essentially solve all of the divisive issues facing Congress. Douglas had authored most of the underlying legislation. Under the omnibus bill, California would enter the Union as a free state and the rest of the territory acquired from Mexico under the Treaty of Guadalupe Hidalgo (the Mexican Cession) would be organized into territories with the issue of slavery to be decided by popular sovereignty. Texas would surrender its boundary claims in New Mexico, while the federal government would assume Texas's public debt in exchange. The slave trade in Washington, D.C., would end but slavery would still be allowed there and Congress would enact a more effective fugitive slave law to replace the existing law that Northerners had been widely ignoring for many years.

Clay's omnibus bill met with mixed reactions in the Senate, sparking months of debate. Calhoun argued against the bill, demanding that Northerners cease trying to prohibit slavery in the territories. Virginia Senator James M. Mason delivered the speech as the ailing Calhoun watched. Calhoun felt that because of Northern hostility, the federal government must ensure Southern rights or secession was the only safe option. Northern Senators Salmon Chase, Charles Sumner, and William Henry Seward represented Northern opposition to the bill, which failed to openly prohibit slavery in the new territories. Webster offered a voice of compromise in his famous "Seventh of March" speech, trying to appeal to moderates on both sides, a stand that gave him some Northern support.

The omnibus bill was defeated in the Senate as enemies on both sides introduced numerous amendments, stripping many of its measures and causing acrimonious debates and speeches. Douglas then took a different approach, splitting the omnibus bill into five separate measures. He knew that the odds of successfully passing separate bills were better since there were sectional blocs supporting each bill. The first bill admitted California as a free state. The second bill abolished the slave trade in the District of Columbia. The third bill organized the Mexican Cession into the New Mexico, Nevada, Arizona, and Utah territories with no mention of slavery, the issue to be decided by popular sovereignty. The fourth bill included a strengthened Fugitive Slave Act, which called for strict enforcement, established a federal commission to issue warrants for arrest after summary hearings, and specifically forbade Northerners from aiding runaway slaves. The fifth bill decided the boundary dispute between Texas and New Mexico in favor of New Mexico and stated that the U.S. government would assume the public debts Texas owed before its annexation to the Union in 1845.

All of the bills subsequently passed, many with key support from pro-compromise Northern Democrats and new President Millard Fillmore.

President Millard Fillmore was in favor of the Compromise and signed it into law. (Library of Congress)

(President Zachary Taylor, who had opposed the compromise, had died and Fillmore had become president.) Fillmore was in favor of the compromise and signed all five bills into law. The last of the bills was signed on September 20, 1850. The city of Washington, D.C., as well as cities and states throughout the United States, greeted the compromise's successful passage with relief and with joyous celebrations in the hope that sectional tensions had been resolved. Some people, however, had misgivings that the compromise had brought a temporary peace, but had not provided a long-term solution to the problem of slavery's expansion or satisfied its radical opponents in the North and South. Many leaders realized its potential to either consolidate or disrupt the Union.

ACTUAL HISTORY

The citizens and politicians who hoped that the Great Compromise would end sectional tensions over slavery's expansion would soon be disappointed. It did resolve the debates over slavery in the new territory gained from Mexico, but debates over the larger question of slavery's expansion continued. In particular, the doctrine of popular sovereignty and the strengthened Fugitive Slave Act would soon divide the country even further along sectional lines. Many Northerners viewed the compromise as another harbinger of the fact that slavery would not gradually disappear on its own. Southerners were especially concerned over the disruption of the balance of power in the Senate caused by the admission of California.

The Fugitive Slave Act proved to be the first flashpoint. It did not result in the capture of large numbers of escaped slaves, but the cases of those fugitives who were returned to slavery received great publicity. Stories such as that of Anthony Burns, who was captured and returned to slavery in Boston, humanized the slaves and roused Northern sympathies. Northern anger helped overcome the region's racism. The Underground Railroad became more active and many Northern African Americans who no longer felt safe in the United States fled to Canada.

Northerners were also outraged over the act's provisions, especially those that implicated them in the maintenance of slavery. A person could claim ownership of a runaway slave simply by submitting an affidavit to a federal commissioner, who received only $5 if he rejected the claim but $10 if he approved it. Accused runaways could be seized without due process and could not testify on their own behalf. Any Northern citizen could be deputized and forced to help pursue and capture a fugitive slave; refusal could result in stiff fines and jail sentences.

In response, a number of Northern states enacted personal liberty laws that provided defense for accused runaways. The Supreme Court declared these laws to be unconstitutional in the 1859 case of *Ableman v. Booth*. Many Northern communities continued to resist compliance, a defiance of federal law that outraged many Southerners. Militant Northern abolitionists encouraged African Americans to use violent resistance as self-defense. Harriet Beecher Stowe's 1852 novel *Uncle Tom's Cabin* fueled outrage in both sections of the country through its descriptions of the cruelties of slavery, including a harrowing wintertime escape by a fugitive slave woman and her young child being pursued by slave catchers.

Like the strengthened Fugitive Slave Act, popular sovereignty proved to be a failure in practice. The doctrine faced its first big test in the Nebraska Territory in 1854. Because this territory was north of the 1820 Missouri Compromise line, it had been designated as free. However, Stephen Douglas, chairman of the Senate Committee on Territories, introduced a bill into Congress that would divide the territory into Kansas and Nebraska and incorporate popular sovereignty. He added a specific repeal of the Missouri Compromise because he knew that without it Southerners would not support the bill, dooming it to failure. Douglas also hoped to gain consideration for Chicago as an eastern terminus for a proposed transcontinental railroad, linking California to the rest of the nation, and providing a boost to his presidential ambitions. The Kansas Nebraska Act passed Congress with the support of President Franklin Pierce, specifically repealing the old Missouri Compromise.

Harriet Beecher Stowe's novel, *Uncle Tom's Cabin*, stirred emotions in both North and South. (Library of Congress)

The more settled territory of Nebraska quickly became a free territory, but the status of sparsely populated Kansas was unclear. Northeastern settlers rushed to settle Kansas and pro-slavery Missourians known as "Border Ruffians" voted illegally in Kansas elections. An often-violent guerrilla war between anti- and pro-slavery forces then erupted in "Bleeding Kansas." The two sides formed competing governments in Shawnee Mission (pro-slavery) and Topeka (antislavery) and both sought federal recognition. An 1858 attempt to have Kansas enter the Union under the pro-slavery Lecompton Constitution failed in Congress, despite President James Buchanan's support, and Kansas would not enter the Union until 1861.

Many historians feel that Douglas made a political miscalculation, as the slave and free settlers could not live together in peace and outside states interfered because of their vested interest in the outcome. The events in Kansas also resulted in the division of the Democratic Party into Northern and Southern factions and the disintegration of the Whig Party. The Know-Nothing (American) Party would form over the issue of nativism, fear of immigrant influence in a time of rising immigration, but would also ultimately split along sectional fault lines over the issue of slavery. The end of the Whig Party marked the end of the second party system and paved the way for the creation of the Republican Party.

The Republican Party formed in 1854 in part as a response to Northern outrage over the Kansas Nebraska Act and the ensuing violence. It absorbed the Northern Democrats angry over Southern control of their party as well as former Northern Whigs and Know-Nothings. Its

KEY CONCEPT The Slave Power Conspiracy

The slave power conspiracy was an antebellum belief among many Northerners that Southern slaveholders conspired to dominate the federal government in order to protect their status and property. They claimed that the minority of white Southerners who owned the majority of slaves formed an aristocracy that they called a "slavocracy." This arrogant and tyrannical group held the remaining white Southerners in poverty and was against the country's republican values of democracy and majority rule. Their reliance on slave labor afforded them the free time to study politics and served as a unifying force. They also sought to expand territory suitable for the expansion of slavery through schemes to gain Cuba and land in Central America. Northerners who supported or failed to challenge this "slavocracy" on the federal level were termed "doughfaces."

platform included stopping the spread of slavery, repeal of the Kansas Nebraska Act, repeal of the Fugitive Slave Act, and the abolition of slavery in the nation's capital. During the next several years, the Republicans grew rapidly in strength.

By the presidential election year of 1856, the Democrats had become the dominant party in the South. The main contest in the South was between those who supported states' rights and secession and the Constitutional Unionists whose foremost goal was preservation of the Union. The Democrats held their national convention in June in Cincinnati, Ohio, adopting a platform of congressional nonintervention in the territories. Their nominee was James Buchanan of Pennsylvania, chosen because he had been out of the country during the Kansas Nebraska debacle. The Republican Party had gained ascendancy in the North, utilizing Northern anger over Kansas. Their nominee was John C. Frémont. Although they lost the election, the Republicans were able to capture most of the free states and Southern awareness of their growing strength.

Sectional tensions continued to grow in the late 1850s as a series of events increased the appeal of radicals in both sections. In 1856, Massachusetts Senator Charles Sumner delivered the "Crime against Kansas" speech decrying Southern actions in that territory and insulting a South Carolina Senator. The Senator's nephew, Preston Brooks, who represented South Carolina in the U.S. House of Representatives, severely beat Sumner with a cane a few days later. It took three years for Sumner to recover from the brutal attack and Massachusetts left his Senate seat empty, treating him as a martyr. Meanwhile, Southerners celebrated Brooks's actions and sent him replacement canes. This was only the best known of a cluster of similar violent incidents that increased Northern fears that Southerners were dangerously fanatical.

The Supreme Court's decision in the case of *Dred Scott v. Sanford* sparked Northern outcries in 1857. Scott was a Missouri slave whose master had taken him into free territory in the course of his travels. After his master died, Scott sued his widow for freedom. The Supreme Court decided that Scott was not a citizen and could not sue in state or federal court. It also decided that Scott's journeys into areas that prohibited slavery did not make him free. The court's decision then went even further by stating that Congress could not prohibit slavery from any territory without depriving people of their property, guaranteed under the Fifth Amendment of the Constitution. Southerners welcomed the guarantees of their rights while Northerners were upset that the court had included slaves in a constitutional definition of property.

In 1858, Stephen Douglas again emerged in the national spotlight in a series of debates with Abraham Lincoln, his rival for an Illinois seat in the U.S. Senate. At one point, Lincoln delivered a speech declaring that the United States was like "A House Divided" and "could not remain permanently half slave and half free," according to Eric Foner in *Politics and Ideology in the Age of the Civil War*. As a Republican, his stand was to prohibit the spread of slavery and allow it to gradually die out where it already existed. During the debates, Douglas reiterated the Freeport Doctrine that a territorial legislature could keep slavery out of its borders by not enacting a slave code. The Southern wing of the Democratic Party was upset at Douglas's stand, and this cost him support. Douglas gained the Senate seat but his presidential ambitions were damaged. Lincoln lost the Senate seat but gained national recognition.

Southern states continued to demand a federal guarantee of their rights. Senator Jefferson Davis introduced a group of resolutions that became known as the slave code. Davis and his supporters demanded that slaves be recognized as property that could be taken into the territories, that territorial governments had no sovereignty to decide the slavery issue and the federal government was obligated to intervene to protect slavery if the territorial government could not do so, that the question of slavery could be decided only when a territory applied for statehood and created a constitution, and that Northern legislatures had to repeal their personal liberty laws. Meanwhile, militant abolitionist John Brown had led a raid on the federal armory and arsenal at Harpers Ferry, Virginia (now West Virginia), in an attempt to arm slaves and create an insurrection. Although the raid failed, responses to it and Brown's execution widened the sectional gulf. It was in this crisis atmosphere of sectional division that the presidential election of 1860 was held.

When the Democratic convention met in Charleston, South Carolina, leading candidate Stephen Douglas enjoyed support from the majority of the party. Many Southern Democrats, however, demanded a platform plank guaranteeing the right of slavery in any federal territory, an idea that Douglas supporters feared would cost them the election. After failing to reach a satisfactory agreement, a number of Southern delegates deserted the convention to hold their own meeting. They nominated John C. Breckinridge of Kentucky and created a platform with a federal slave code. A few dissatisfied old Whigs created the Constitutional Union Party, nominating John Bell of Tennessee and creating a platform endorsing the Union and enforcement of the laws. The Democratic Party had now completely splintered over the weight of sectional differences.

The Republican convention met in Chicago, Illinois, and nominated Abraham Lincoln, a moderate, as their candidate. Their platform called for the exclusion of slavery from the federal territories but did not attack slavery where it already existed. Instead it stated that each state would "order and control its own domestic institutions," according to Eric

Foner in *Politics and Ideology in the Age of the Civil War*. Despite this guarantee, many Southern states were already promising secession if Lincoln were to be elected. Lincoln won the election despite receiving no electoral votes and few popular votes in the South. His election immediately touched off a secession crisis in the Deep South. South Carolina was the first to secede in December 1860 and was quickly followed by Alabama, Mississippi, Florida, Georgia, Louisiana, and Texas. These states then met in Montgomery, Alabama, in February 1861 to form the Confederate States of America (Confederacy). Jefferson Davis would serve as their first president.

The Civil War (1861–1865) eliminated the contentious question of slavery's expansion with a Northern victory. Lincoln's Emancipation Proclamation of 1863 freed the slaves in rebellious areas and the Thirteenth Amendment to the U.S. Constitution permanently abolished the institution of slavery throughout the country. The issues of racism and discrimination, however, would linger in the national consciousness well beyond the postwar period of Reconstruction. The Civil War also ended the possibility of secession, as reconstructed Southern states were obligated to recognize its illegality in their new state constitutions.

The party system of Democrats and Republicans, born out of the crises of the 1850s, would remain dominant. The issue of states' rights was decided in favor of the supremacy of the federal government, a bureaucracy expanded by the war. Attention turned once again to issues the controversy over slavery had buried, such as tariffs, banking, internal improvements, the availability of Western lands, and the building of a transcontinental railroad. The federal government's growth would continue through President Franklin Roosevelt's New Deal of the 1930s and 1940s and President Lyndon Johnson's Great Society of the 1960s.

ALTERNATE HISTORY

People throughout the country breathed a sigh of relief that the immediate sectional crisis over slavery's expansion into the Mexican Cession territory had been successfully resolved. The long-term prospects for success of the Compromise of 1850 could have seemed equally bright in the next several years after its passage. The extreme abolitionists of the North and the secessionist "Fire Eaters" of the South attempted to use aspects of the Great Compromise to gain converts to their causes, but suppose the majority of Americans had ignored their pleas in favor of the spirit of compromise, observance of the law, and preservation of the Union? The underlying question of slavery's future would have remained beneath the surface much longer and the "Little Giant" Stephen Douglas would have emerged as a political statesman in the vein of the "Great Compromiser" Henry Clay.

Northern anger over the passage of the strengthened Fugitive Slave Act proved to be the compromise's first great test. Militant abolitionists and religious figures decried many of the act's provisions, including the designation of federal commissioners to hear the cases of accused fugitives and the higher payments awarded these commissioners in the cases of returned slaves versus those found to be freemen. These objectors to slavery also spoke out against the fugitives' being denied due process and not being allowed to testify on their own behalf. They encouraged fugitives to resist and expanded the work of the Underground Railroad that helped slaves to freedom. But a successful compromise would have denied them the political traction necessary for large-scale success.

These provisions did indeed alarm a number of Northern citizens but proved to have little impact once put into effect. Although a few stories of fugitive slaves returned to slavery received widespread publicity, very few fugitive slaves were ever captured and returned to the South. Most Northerners were not personally involved in the few cases that did occur and could have been content simply to ignore Southern demands for stricter enforcement. Moderate Northerners and politicians called for citizens to obey the law, no matter how morally distasteful they found it. This view would have then found widespread support among the many Northerners who had little human interest in the slaves and felt that the abolitionists would prove too disruptive to society and politics.

In 1854, Stephen Douglas further tested the strength of the compromise when he introduced a bill to organize the Nebraska Territory, once again claiming that popular sovereignty would decide the question of slavery. Douglas was anxious to organize the territory west of Iowa to allow for a possible northern terminus in Chicago, Illinois, for the proposed transcontinental railroad linking California to the rest of the country. If Northern abolitionists had not gained strength in the years following the compromise, Southerners would not have felt the need to defend their rights so vigorously. A few Northerners demanding complete exclusion of slavery from any federal territory would have formed the Republican Party, but they would have remained a minor third party that did not seem threatening to the South. Douglas would not have faced widespread Southern pressure to add a provision to the Kansas Nebraska Act repealing the old Missouri Compromise line.

Southern "Fire-Eaters" would have tried to rally support for such a provision, but their more moderate compatriots would have failed to support a move sure to antagonize the North. Moderate Southern Democrats would have argued that the territory was not worth fighting over, as it was geographically unsuited for slavery. As historian Don E. Fehrenbacher has theorized in *Slaveholding Republic: An Account of the United States Government's Relations to Slavery*, "It is difficult to believe that a political revolution of such magnitude would have occurred if Southerners had not chosen to pursue the will-o'-the-wisp of Kansas, sacrificing the realities of power to an inner need for reassurance of their equal status and moral respectability in the face of antislavery censure." Instead, Nebraska would quickly enter the Union as a free state and small farmers from the nearby regions of both North and South would migrate to the Kansas territory over time and it

In the alternate history, Stephen A. Douglas would have become the leader of the Democratic Party in the 1856 presidential election. (Library of Congress)

would quietly enter the Union as a free state a few years later.

Douglas, architect of the Compromise of 1850, would have become the leading figure in the Democratic Party by the presidential election year of 1856. He would have easily won the party's nomination at the convention in June in Cincinnati, Ohio, and the doctrine of popular sovereignty would have become the party's national platform. Massachusetts Senator Charles Sumner would have sought to make an issue of popular sovereignty in Kansas, a territory that previously had been forever closed to slavery under the Missouri Compromise. His Senate speech, however, would have received only slight support because most politicians would not wish to disrupt the fragile sectional harmony. The Democrats would have shelved more controversial issues, such as the question of whether slaves were private property protected by the Constitution, in favor of maintaining party harmony.

The small Republican Party would have fielded John C. Fremont but would have enjoyed little support. Meanwhile, a new party, the Know-Nothing (American) Party, would have rapidly gained strength. Native-born Protestant Americans, who feared the changes to the country caused by a rising number of immigrants, primarily from southern and eastern Europe, supported the Know-Nothings. The new immigrants had triggered a widespread growth of xenophobia and anti-Catholic feelings. Their platform included calls for an extension of the naturalization process from five to fourteen years, demands that only citizens be allowed to vote, and demands that only native-born Americans could hold political offices. By 1856, sectional compromises would have preserved the Know-Nothings, allowing them to replace the defunct Whig Party, beginning the Third Party System. Ex-President Millard Fillmore was their candidate. Although they would have failed to dislodge the dominant Democratic Party and capture the presidency, they would have helped deflect attention from the controversial slavery question.

In 1857, the Supreme Court handed down its eagerly awaited decision in the case of *Dred Scott v. Sandford*. Northern abolitionists would still have helped launch the case, but this time in a desperate attempt to gain support for their minority cause. Dred Scott was a Missouri slave. Scott's master, Army surgeon John Emerson of St. Louis, had taken Scott into the free state of Illinois and the free territory of Wisconsin. After Emerson died, Scott sued his widow for freedom. The Supreme Court decided that Scott was not a citizen and could not sue in state or federal court. It also decided that Scott's journeys into areas that prohibited slavery did not make him free. The Court's decision then went even further by stating that Congress could not prohibit slavery from any territory without depriving people of their property, guaranteed under the Fifth Amendment of the Constitution.

Southerners would still have welcomed the decision as verification that the federal government would uphold their right to protection of their property in slaves. Northern abolitionists would have expressed their outrage and attracted a few new converts to their cause, but most Northerners would have chosen compromise over conflict. They would have applied little political pressure to their leaders, many of whom would have viewed the court's ruling on most of the issues as opinions and would have agreed with the ruling that slaves were not citizens. The controversy would have received less attention and would have passed from national attention within a few months' time.

In the late 1850s, little-known militant abolitionist John Brown perhaps would have tried to raise funds to stage a small raid on the federal arsenal and armory at Harpers Ferry, Virginia (now West Virginia), but he would have attracted little attention, money, or followers. He would not have become a national figure because of the peaceful settlement of Kansas. He might have sought support from more prominent abolitionists, but would have failed to do so. Militant abolitionists, already challenged by their minority status in the North, would have feared being linked to a violent slave rebellion sure to bring censure from both sections of the country. Brown would have been forced to abandon any such plan and would have returned to his work on the Underground Railroad.

At the end of this now quiet decade, the upcoming 1860 presidential election would have attracted the country's attention. When the Democratic convention met in Charleston, South Carolina, incumbent President Stephen Douglas would have enjoyed widespread support in both sections of the country. Although a few radical Southern Democrats would have demanded a platform plank guaranteeing the right of slavery in any federal territory, most delegates would have dismissed the idea in favor of ensuring a strong chance at victory in the upcoming election. A few dissatisfied radical Southerners might have held their own convention to create a platform with a federal slave code, but this splinter group would have received little support or attention.

The small Republican Party would still have nominated Abraham Lincoln, a moderate, as their candidate. Although the renowned Lincoln-Douglas debates would never have occurred, Lincoln would have received national attention as a senator from Illinois when he delivered a speech claiming that the country could not endure permanently half slave and half free. The Republican platform once again would have called for the exclusion of slavery from the federal territories, but it would not have attacked slavery where it already existed. Instead it would have stated that each state would "order and control its own domestic institutions," according to Eric Foner in *Politics and Ideology in the Age of the Civil War*. The Know-Nothings would have

once again nominated Millard Fillmore. While the party would have
grown in strength, it still would have been no match for the powerful
Democrats and their nominee. Douglas, renowned statesman and architect of the Great Compromise, would have handily won the election in
a result that would have surprised almost no one.

Sectional tensions, however, could not have been ignored much
longer. As lands continued to be settled and new territories and states
were established in a Trans-Missouri West geographically unsuited to
slavery, Southerners would have become more and more disturbed by
the growing imbalance of power between slave and free states in the
Senate. Their attention would have turned to Mexico, Central America,
and the Caribbean as possible areas of U.S. expansion that would be
suited for slavery's growth. Schemes such as William Walker's plan to
take over Nicaragua would have received much more overt support
from Southern politicians. U.S. anger over French violation of the
1823 Monroe Doctrine by the installation of puppet dictator
Maximilian of Austria as head of Mexico would have provided an
incentive for Southerners to call for another war with Mexico.

Northerners would have been increasingly alarmed over the
Southern demands. Many of them had been willing to allow slavery
to exist and had supported popular sovereignty when it appeared that
most new states would be free, but they would not be willing to continue such views in the face of slavery's possible widespread expansion. Southern "Fire-Eaters," fearful of growing Northern dominance,
would have rallied the Deep South to their cause. Moderate
Southerners, however, would have viewed the continued rise of
industry and urbanization and the recognition that much Western
land was unsuitable to slavery as a sign of the eventual extinction of
the "peculiar institution."

The Deep South would have felt threatened enough to attempt
secession in the 1870s, but these states would not have been joined
by the remaining Southern states. The New South movement toward
industrialization would have become popular in the upper South and
border states, which would not support talk of secession over what
they saw as a doomed institution. The Democrats would not have
sought to eliminate slavery because of the need to appease the numerous Southern states that would have remained loyal, but its expansion
would have been prohibited. Instead, the Democrats would have
instituted a program of gradual emancipation with economic compensation to former slave owners. The constitutional amendment outlawing slavery would not have been added until the turn of the
century. There would have been no enforced Reconstruction period,
meaning that African-American suffrage and other rights would not
have been granted until the later civil rights movement of the twentieth century.

Meanwhile, Know-Nothings would have gained enough representatives in Congress by the 1860s to begin pushing through their
nativist agenda. Stricter immigration laws and the establishment of
quotas would have severely restricted immigration to the United States
by the late 1800s. As a result, the great migration of African Americans

to the Northern job markets would have occurred sooner, during the late 1800s, fueling racial tensions in the North. The sectional controversy and the absence of an immigration-fueled population explosion would have delayed settlement of the Trans-Missouri West and subsequent Native American wars until the early twentieth century. As a result, a slower-growing United States would probably have remained isolationist well into the twentieth century and probably would not have become involved in areas such as Alaska, Hawaii, and the Panama Canal.

Marcella Bush Trevino

Discussion Questions

1. In the alternate history presented in this chapter, the spirit of compromise prevents severe sectional splits during the 1850s and the Civil War is avoided. In actual history, the issues of Fugitive Slave Law enforcement and popular sovereignty in Kansas kept up tensions between North and South. Why do you think the voices of compromise did not win out in actual history?

2. If Stephen Douglas had been presented and accepted as a compromise candidate in 1860 and Lincoln had drawn only a small vote in the North, where do you think that vote would have been concentrated?

3. If the Know-Nothing Party had become a major influence in American politics in the 1870s and later, what effect would that have had on issues of civil rights?

4. If the United States had not welcomed European immigration from the 1870s through the 1920s, how would that have affected the cultural makeup of the nation? How would East Coast cities be different? What impact would such a policy have had on the social makeup of the rest of the nation?

5. If the Civil War had not occurred in the period 1861–1865, the 600,000 Americans who died in that war would have lived on for several decades. What impact would their presence have had on American life, culture, and the economy?

Bibliography and Further Reading

Fehrenbacher, Don E. *Slaveholding Republic: An Account of the United States Government's Relations to Slavery*. New York: Oxford University Press, 2002.

Foner, Eric. *Politics and Ideology in the Age of the Civil War*. New York: Oxford University Press, 1980.

Grant, Susan-Mary. *North over South: Northern Nationalism and American Identity in the Antebellum Era*. Lawrence: University Press of Kansas, 2000.

Holt, Michael F. *The Political Crisis of the 1850s.* New York: John Wiley, 1978.

Huston, James L. *Calculating the Value of the Union: Slavery, Property Rights, and the Economic Origins of the Civil War.* Chapel Hill: University of North Carolina Press, 2003.

Levine, Bruce C. *Half Slave and Half Free: The Roots of the Civil War.* New York: Hill and Wang, 1992.

Library of Congress. "Compromise of 1850." *Primary Documents in American History.* www.loc.gov/rr/program/bib/ourdocs/Compromise1850.html (accessed October 16, 2005).

Morrison, Michael A. *Slavery and the American West: The Eclipse of Manifest Destiny and the Coming of the Civil War.* Chapel Hill: University of North Carolina Press, 1997.

Norton, Anne. *Alternative Americas: A Reading of Antebellum Political Culture.* Chicago: University of Chicago Press, 1986.

Peterson, Merrill D. *The Great Triumvirate: Webster, Clay, and Calhoun.* New York: Oxford University Press, 1987.

Potter, David. *The Impending Crisis, 1848–1861.* New York: Harper and Row, 1976.

Remini, Robert V. *Henry Clay: Statesman for the Union.* New York: W.W. Norton, 1991.

Walther, Eric H. *The Fire-Eaters.* Baton Rouge: Louisiana State University Press, 1992.

Waugh, John C. *On the Brink of Civil War: The Compromise of 1850 and How It Changed the Course of American History.* Wilmington, DE: Scholarly Resources, 2003.

Wilson, Carol. "Active Vigilance Is the Price of Liberty: Black Self-Defense against Fugitive Slave Recapture and Kidnapping of Free Blacks." In *Antislavery Violence: Sectional, Racial, and Cultural Conflict in Antebellum America*, edited by John R. McKivigan and Stanley Harrold. Knoxville: University of Tennessee Press, 1999.

TURNING POINT

The first meetings of the Republican Party took place in 1854. What if the organization of the party dissolved in disagreement?

INTRODUCTION

To understand the need for and development of political parties and interest groups in the United States, one first must understand the disorder in the political system that was caused by the lack of cohesive groups. Although some people may not think of a political party as an interest group, they have to realize that the purpose of a party is to create a platform and lobby to assure that legislation supporting that platform is developed and passed, that taxing situations favor the party's interest, and that tariffs support its position whether this involves creating additional tariffs or removing those that already exist.

European settlers in the newly formed United States knew the power of the party system and attempted to avoid a strong centralized government reflective of the British Crown, the same government that had caused many of them to flee their homeland and had brought them "taxation without representation"—and the onset of the Revolutionary War.

After the Revolution, most new Americans embraced the idea of implementing a loose form of central government. The settlers had come to the New World to escape the political systems of Europe—and most of all to separate themselves from the politics of the Crown. European rule was dominated by a personal interest system in which birthright, social standing, wealth, and even in some cases religion determined what a person could or could not accomplish in life. Risking everything to come to the New World, settlers again put everything on the line to win their freedom from the Crown. Settlers were not anxious to create a strong centralized government that would tax them, since experience made it difficult to imagine the benefits; instead they imagined how a centralized government could control them.

Thus, the first document binding the republic together did not allow for a strong federal or centralized government. States, and in some cases even cities or individuals with large tracts of land, created and enforced laws that applied to individuals when within those boundaries. The

KEY CONCEPT   Divine Right

Many Europeans who emigrated to the American colonies came to escape the concept of divine right, which allowed monarchs to ascend thrones by virtue of belonging to particular family lines. It was divine right that placed Prussian-born King George III (1738–1820) on the British throne at the time the American colonists were rebelling against taxes levied against the colonies by the English Parliament. When the Declaration of Independence was written in 1776, author Thomas Jefferson (1743–1826) included a long list of grievances against the king who refused to acknowledge the rights of the colonists as English citizens.

The colonists' grievances against King George III, which explained why it was necessary to dissolve the political bonds that connected the American colonies to the mother country, included the king's waging war, refusing to acknowledge American laws, imposing laws passed without the consent of the colonists, dissolving duly elected legislative bodies, interfering with the execution of justice, quartering British soldiers in private homes, and interfering with foreign trade. The colonists did not list any grievances against the British Parliament because they refused to acknowledge that this legislative body in which they had no representation had any power over them.

When the American colonists rebelled against the British throne, they were following the teachings of British philosopher Thomas Hobbes (1588–1679), who rejected the inherent right of monarchs to govern in favor of government by social contract. Hobbes accepted the right of the people to choose an absolute monarch as sovereign but not the right of governments to force illegitimate sovereigns upon the people. In *Leviathan* in 1651, Hobbes argued that under the present British political system, the commonwealth (the Leviathan) had created a sovereign with an "artificial soul" that overrode the rights of rational beings

---

Articles of Confederation allowed only for a legislative branch of government. Although it was now representative, the body did not have the authority to tax. Without a method of raising money, the centralized government could not fund a militia or a navy. The legislature was able to create laws but not enforce them.

For example, there was no central bank. States had their own currency. Some backed their paper currency with gold or silver, but that value varied from state to state. Currency was devalued to meet mounting debt. A central federal bank or money system was needed. Some roads were maintained by individuals who charged travelers tolls for using them. The central government had no funds for roads or road improvements and the states had other and more important items to fund.

States imposed tariffs on imports from other states, just as one country would do to another. Instead of being a united republic, the post-Revolution union was more like thirteen separate countries than a confederation of United States.

As differences arose, it became apparent that the Articles of Confederation were not sufficient. Currency issues and the trade disputes fueled a pressing need to revise the Articles or abandon them for a document establishing and endorsing a more centralized federal government that would bring the nation together. At a meeting held in Philadelphia to discuss strengthening the federal government, representatives from twelve states named seventy-four delegates to a Constitutional Convention. George Washington, the famed Revolutionary War leader, was elected president of

to seek their own rulers. Hobbes hypothesized that, left to their own devices, individuals would create their own governments to provide the basic security essential to human survival. Once a contract was agreed upon, Hobbes accepted no natural right to break it.

In 1690, in *Two Treatises of Government*, British empiricist philosopher John Locke (1632–1704) expanded on Hobbes's theories to develop the concept of inherent rights that were translated into the Declaration of Independence as "certain unalienable Rights," which included the right to "Life, Liberty, and the pursuit of Happiness." Locke agreed with Hobbes that rational beings should be allowed to create their own governments by social contract, but he disagreed with Hobbes that contracts could not be broken. Locke accepted an innate right of rebellion whenever original participants refused to honor the terms of the contract. Locke was a direct influence on the writing of the United States Constitution in 1787.

In 1776, the same year that the Declaration of Independence was written, Scottish economist Adam Smith (1723–1790) further expanded on the works of Hobbes and Locke when he published *An Inquiry into the Nature and Causes of the Wealth of Nations*. Smith's work led to the eventual overturn of mercantilism in Europe by suggesting that governments best served the economy by allowing it to regulate itself instead of invoking laws designed to favor the fiscal interests of the selected few (mercantilists). The emerging nation of the United States of America adopted Smith's ideas, allowing capitalism to flourish. As a result of the Great Depression, which began in 1929 and continued until the outbreak of World War II in Europe, Smith's classical economic theories provided the greatest influence on American economic policies. In the 1980s, Republicans under the guidance of President Ronald Reagan (1911–2004) revitalized Adam Smith's economic theories through what became known as "Reaganomics."

the Constitutional Convention, and eventually became the first president of the United States.

Washington believed that men in the new United States had fought hard enough for the new union to ensure that legislation would be drawn for the benefit of the union rather than for an individual. A staunch opponent of the party system, Washington remains the only president to be elected and reelected without a party affiliation. Before leaving office, but after serving two terms, Washington warned in his farewell address that the party system would allow personal and special interests to divide a country now united. Even at that time, a strong two-party system already existed.

The Federalists, supported by Alexander Hamilton and John Adams, Washington's vice president and successor, supported a strong national government with centralized authority. Thomas Jefferson, Adams's vice president, was a member of the Democratic-Republican Party (also known as Jeffersonian Republicans) that supported a modest centralized government, favored the agrarian community, and was less partial to trade and commercial activities. Jefferson's ideas and ideals supported limited growth and expansion. In 1828, the Democratic-Republican Party split into two separate parties.

Andrew Jackson took the lead of the Democratic-Republicans who still believed in limiting centralized national government. John Quincy Adams led the other faction, the National Republican Party, which favored the Federalist point of view, supporting strong economic nationalism. The

Federalists had ceased to exist as a political party after the presidency of James Monroe.

This would not be the end of splits in the party system. Jackson's association with Free Masonry resulted in the first independent party—or third party to exist. His opponents formed the Anti-Masonic Party—a primary example of what Washington had warned against: a group of people specifically using politics to gain revenge on another group of people. The split in the National Republican Party resulted in another new party, the Whigs, led by Henry Clay and Daniel Webster. Their platform included expanding national government, increasing commercial development, and encouraging a cautious move westward.

Other parties with specific agendas formed and dissolved over time. America's push westward created new issues. The Free Soil Party wanted to ban slavery in the new territories. The Know-Nothing Party (American Party), a group composed mostly of former Democrats, opposed immigration. The Republican Party, as we know it today, drew in Whigs, Free Soilers, and Know-Nothings. Their strongest point in their early platform was the abolition of slavery and some freedom for blacks.

TURNING POINT

The founders of the Republican Party were men who split away from the nearly defunct Whig Party. Some of the founders were Free Soilers, a group of men who believed that slavery should be prohibited in any territory acquired from Mexico, and some members of the Know-Nothing Party, also called the American Party, which was composed of mostly Northern Democrats who objected to Catholic immigrants entering the United States. The issue that bound this new group together was the abolition of slavery.

In the first fifty years of the 1800s, slavery had become a larger social and economic issue than it had been in the century before. Ideas such as the American System, implemented after the War of 1812, appeared to unite states by creating a system of tariffs that internalized production and consumption of goods within the United States. But there were social issues, such as slavery, that demonstrated such unity among the states could not exist.

As settlement expanded westward, the question of slavery (the ownership of human beings as property) was challenged. There were those who believed that any new territories should abolish this practice as all citizens of the United States had the same rights; others believed that slavery should be allowed to continue. The first official step in supporting the abolitionists' cause came in 1808 when the importation of slaves from other countries was banned by Congress. Slaves already in the states, and their offspring, since they were also considered property, could still be purchased or sold.

In 1818, the territory of Missouri applied for admission into the United States. It took two years to work out the Missouri Compromise, which in 1820 was put into effect to retain the balance of slave and free states and to "forever prohibit" slavery in all territories gained by the Louisiana Purchase north of Missouri's southern border, except for Missouri itself. The Missouri Compromise also precluded slavery in states that were to be formed north of the 36°30′ line of latitude.

As the name infers, the "compromise" took something and gave something back. Until the admission of the Missouri territory, slave states and free states had been equal in number, maintaining a balance in the Senate where two senators, regardless of the state's size or population, represented each state. Missouri's admission as a slave state would have caused an imbalance in favor of slave states. As a compromise, Maine, a free state, was formed out of land given up by Massachusetts, and the balance of power in the Senate was preserved.

The Missouri Compromise and the slavery issue drew another line, one which was as apparent and nearly as defined as a line of latitude. That line eventually split the Democrats, the Whigs, and the nation. With issues that caused irreparable divisions, the once strong and united Democratic Party split into Northern and Southern Democrats and became a minority. The agrarian faction in the South supported slavery while the industrial faction in the North did not. That breach helped to catapult the Republican Party to success.

Southern Democrats, many of them large-scale planters, argued that without cheap labor they would not be able to produce their crops for profit. Northern Democrats, who did not gain the same advantage from owning slaves, often agreed with slavery as it existed in the South but did not support the expansion of slavery into the new territories.

A power struggle and the issue of slavery also created a dispute within the Whig Party. Some powerful Whigs moved their support to the Free Soil Party. Conscience Whigs, or Higher-Law Whigs (referring to a law from a power "higher" than the Constitution) were the names associated with members of the Whig Party who opposed slavery. Cotton Whigs, or Lower-Law Whigs (referring to the lower law of man—such as the men who created the Constitution) was the name associated with Whigs who were the pro-slavery members of the party.

Congress was not separated from the issues. Many Northerners and Southerners expressed strong opinions on the slavery issue. John C. Calhoun, a Southerner from South Carolina, who had already caused an uproar when serving as Andrew Jackson's vice president, spoke out clearly and strongly in favor of a man's right to own slaves. William Seward was on the opposing side of the argument. A staunch antislavery representative in the Senate, Seward served as a Whig and then as a Republican in the Senate. Then there were those like Senator Henry Clay of Kentucky, a slave owner himself, but a great compromiser. It was Clay who was instrumental in compiling what is known as the Compromise of 1850. This agreement allowed California to enter the Union as a free state and abolished the slave trade in the nation's capital, Washington, D.C. In exchange, the territories that would become New Mexico and Utah would be popular sovereignty states. Popular sovereignty, an unpopular idea brought to the table by Zachary Taylor, allowed the people who lived in a state or territory to decide whether slavery would be permitted in that state or territory.

A large area north of Missouri was being considered as a possible separate territory. Although the Missouri Compromise was clear in forever banning slavery in territories north of Missouri, the issue of slavery in the new territory again became a topic of heated congressional discussion. In May 1854, Congress passed the Kansas Nebraska Act that nullified the terms of the Missouri Compromise, creating two territories: Kansas and Nebraska. The population had the right to decide whether to allow slavery in their newly created territory. After the Kansas Nebraska Act was passed, slavery became the major issue uniting Americans and dividing them as well.

ACTUAL HISTORY

The Whig Party was the seed for the Republican Party. Although the Whig platform was clear from the onset, the infighting from which the party was born remained apparent up to at least the Civil War. In 1824, without benefit of organization and only a name, the National Republican Party was formed. The Whig Party would evolve from this group. Throughout their existence, the Whigs seemed to be fueled by separation rather than unification.

In the election of 1836, three Whigs ran for president: Daniel Webster represented the New England Whigs, William Henry Harrison the Midwest Whigs, and Hugh Lawson White those of the Southwest. The Democrat Martin Van Buren won easily. By the election of 1840, the Whigs realized that they could defeat a Democrat only by unifying the party. They united behind William Henry Harrison, who emerged victorious and become the first Whig president. For all that effort, his presidency was short. Harrison died after only a month in office and was replaced by his vice president, John Tyler of Virginia.

Tyler's policy of vetoing bills passed by the legislative branch of government was viewed as excessive power in the executive branch. Andrew Jackson had earned the same reputation years before, and two strong Whigs, Clay and Webster, had founded the Whig party as a protest against Jackson. Tyler's vetoes created a breach in the Whig party, and at Clay's urging, members of the party abandoned Tyler as a Whig. Clay ran as the Whig candidate in the election of 1844, losing to Democrat James K. Polk. By the presidential election of 1848, the New York Whigs had enough power to support Zachary Taylor, a commander in the Mexican War, as their candidate for the presidency. Taylor died in office. His vice president, Millard Fillmore, finished out the term.

Clay and Webster, the Whig's strongest leaders, died during the campaign of 1852. Winfield Scott, the Whig candidate, won only forty-two electoral votes. Once again the party was split. Conscience Whigs and Cotton Whigs were at odds with one another over the issue of slavery. The Higher-Law Whigs and the Lower-Law Whigs argued about the rights of slaves. The party, and the party platform, never recovered.

Some Whigs joined the separated Democratic Party; some followed Fillmore into the Know-Nothing Party. Some Whigs joined the abolitionists. Some joined forces in 1854 with the newly formed Republican Party. At about the same time, antislavery activity was beginning to become more public and popular. The terms of the Kansas Nebraska Bill—which allowed voters in

Kansas and Nebraska to decide whether they would allow slavery—became the focus of antislavery meetings and the topic of books and newspapers.

On February 28, 1854, a Whig, Alvan E. Bovay held an antislavery meeting in Ripon, Wisconsin. At that meeting a resolution was passed to create a new party that would support the antislavery platform if the Kansas Nebraska Bill passed. Another meeting, attended by fifty-three men, was held in Ripon on March 20, 1854, at which a committee was formed that would meet on July 6, 1854, in Jackson, Michigan. The Jackson meeting would be to consider a name and platform for the new party. It was at that meeting that the first Republican gathering took place.

Even without the benefit of national party, Republicans had a successful year in 1854. The new party showed its unity and power by having forty-four Republicans elected to the House. In addition, they added several new Republican senators and governors.

Although there had been various gatherings of Republicans prior to the organizational convention, the national party was officially established on February 22, 1856, according to Lewis Gould in *The Grand Old Party: A History of the Republicans*. On that date a group of Republicans met in Pittsburgh, Pennsylvania, for an "informal convention" with the purpose of "perfecting the National Organization." The National Organization met once more that year, again in Pittsburgh. This convention, held in Lafayette Hall, a building at the intersection of Fourth and Wood, was the Republican's first presidential nominating convention.

Some historians dispute the number of delegates attending that first convention. The *Pittsburgh Post* reported counting fewer than 1,000 delegates. The *Dispatch*, on the other hand, counted closer to 2,000 delegates. A known fact is that one of the most famous early Republicans, Abraham Lincoln, did not attend that first nominating convention. The Republicans' first candidate for the office of president was Senator John C. Frémont. Ironically, the Democrats had also asked Fremont to run as their candidate but he declined because he felt that the Democratic Party supported slavery. Fremont ran on the slogan "Free Speech, Free Press, Free Soil, Free Men, Fremont, and Victory."

The Democrats ran James Buchanan against Fremont. They argued that Fremont's position would separate the Southern states from the Union. They also hinted that his ideas could result in Civil War. Fremont carried eleven states, Buchanan carried nineteen, and the Democrats won the election. Buchanan's inauguration in 1857 was followed almost immediately by the Dred Scott decision. In that decision, the Supreme Court decided that black people were not citizens and therefore were not entitled to the rights of white individuals. It also added that, because they were not citizens, limiting the spread of slavery—and therefore a part of the Missouri Compromise—was unconstitutional.

The Republican Party did not split based on the Dred Scott decision. Instead, it focused on continuing to fight for a platform that would

The Republicans' first candidate for the office of president was Senator John C. Fremont. (Library of Congress)

IN CONTEXT   Dred Scott Decision

When the U.S. Supreme Court handed down the decision *Dred Scott v. Sandford* (60 U.S.393) in 1857, the country was in great turmoil over the issue of slavery. A compromise between the North and South when the U.S. Constitution was written in 1787 had banned the importation of slaves after 1808, but slavery continued to flourish throughout the Deep South and in a number of territories. Battle lines were drawn as various territories sought state-hood by attempting to maintain the balance of slave and free states. In 1820, when debating the entry of Missouri into the Union, Congress enacted the Missouri Compromise, which admitted Missouri as a free state while accepting northern Massachusetts as the free state of Maine. This compromise, thus, maintained balance, with twelve free and twelve slave states. In addition to achieving balance, Congress drew an imaginary line at 36 degrees 30 minutes north latitude, asserting that all

sections of the Louisiana Territory north of the line would be free of slavery. The Missouri Compromise also upheld the right of slave owners to reclaim their "property" whenever slaves escaped into free states and territories.

Within the context of the battle over slavery, a slave named Dred Scott attempted to challenge the right of slave states to treat as property blacks who had lived in free states and territories. To support his challenge, Scott showed that he and his family had lived in Illinois, a free state, for two years and in Wisconsin, a free territory, with his owner Dr. John Emerson, an Army surgeon, before returning to the slave state of Missouri. After the death of Dr. Emerson and the remarriage of his widow, John Sandford, Emerson's brother-in-law and a citizen of New York, gained control of Dred Scott. Under the Judiciary Act of 1789, the Supreme Court could choose to accept jurisdiction of cases involving

repeal the Kansas Nebraska Act, would encourage the building of a transcontinental railroad, would support a homestead act that would make it easier to settle the western territories, and would back the enactment of higher tariffs so that goods would be cheaper to export than import. The Republicans also were in favor of a liberal immigration law so that the manufacturers in the Northeast would be able to import labor. Many of the Republican interests were economic rather than humanitarian.

The party made an effort to win political control of the North so it could put a Republican in the office of president. They succeeded in the election of 1860 when Abraham Lincoln, a Whig turned Republican from Illinois, was elected to that office. His election was helped by divisions in other parties. The Southern Democrats ran a candidate; the Conservative Whigs and Know-Nothing Party banded together to create the Constitutional Union Party and they ran a candidate. The Republicans remained unified and Lincoln was elected on November 6, 1860.

Southerners, aware of Lincoln's position on slavery, rejected his election as president. South Carolina seceded from the Union on December 20, 1860, before Lincoln took the oath of office. Six more states: Alabama, Florida, Georgia, Louisiana, Mississippi, and Texas followed South Carolina and seceded in January and February 1861. Lincoln did not recognize the action of the Southern states and when inaugurated on March 4, 1861, he considered himself president of the Union. War broke out on April 12, 1861. After Lincoln's inauguration and the firing on Federal forces at Fort Sumter in Charleston Harbor, Arkansas, North Carolina, Tennessee, Texas, and Virginia joined the Confederacy.

IN CONTEXT   *Dred Scott Decision (Continued)*

citizens of different states. Scott argued that as a citizen of Missouri, he had the right to sue for his freedom. A clerk mistakenly entered Sanford's name as Sandford, and the case officially became *Dred Scott v. Sandford* (60 U.S. 393).

When the case reached the Supreme Court, the majority of the justices were pro-slavery. Chief Justice Roger B. Taney and four other justices were from the South, and two other justices were pro-slavery Northern Democrats. Writing for the Court, Taney rejected Scott's challenge, asserting that black Americans "were not and could never become citizens of the United States," according to Donald G. Nieman in *Promises to Keep: African-Americans and the Constitutional Order, 1776 to the Present.*

Taney went so far as to deny the humanity of blacks, upholding the right of slave owners to treat slaves as articles "of merchandise and traffic, whenever profit could be made by it" and contending that

blacks were not included in the phrase "all men are created equal" in the Declaration of Independence, according to *Promises to Keep*.

In order to justify their actions in Dred Scott, the Court also overturned the Missouri Compromise, which had declared Wisconsin a free territory.

Not until the Civil War ended in 1865 and the process of Reconstruction began was slavery abolished throughout the United States by the Thirteenth Amendment. In 1868, the Fourteenth Amendment stipulated that citizens would henceforth be defined as "All persons born or naturalized in the United States, and subject to the jurisdiction thereof." State citizenship was based on residency in individual states. In 1870, the Fifteenth Amendment was ratified, guaranteeing that "the right of citizens of the United States to vote shall not be denied or abridged by the United States or by any state on account of race, color, or previous condition of servitude."

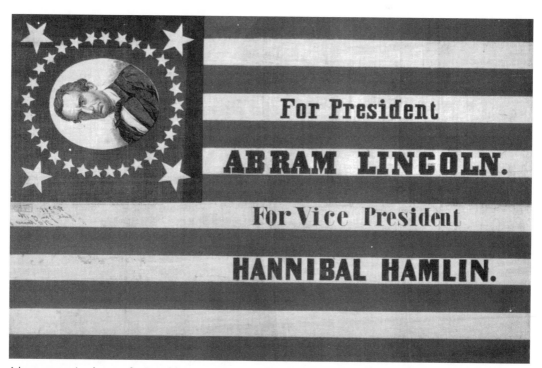

A large campaign banner for Republican presidential candidate Abraham Lincoln and running mate Hannibal Hamlin. (Library of Congress)

Lincoln, like many wartime presidents, was not popular during his term of office. Until the war truly seemed about to end, near the close of his first term of office, many thought he would not be reelected. However, Lincoln won reelection in 1864 by a margin of 212 electoral votes to 12 earned by his opponent. The war ended on April 9, 1865, when General Robert E. Lee surrendered to General Ulysses S. Grant at the Appomattox Court House in Virginia. Louisiana almost immediately applied for re-admission into the Union.

Feelings were mixed on whether the states that left the Union should be readmitted. In what would be his last public speech, Lincoln commented on this, remarking that although the government in Louisiana was not perfect, would it be "wiser to take it as it as and help improve it, or to reject and disperse it?"(according to "The Republican Party—The First Republican," on the Republican Party website, www.gop.com).

The battle over civil rights and the role of federal rule versus states' rights is one that is still unsettled today. Lincoln's role in politics ended with his assassination on April 14, 1865, at Ford's Theatre. John Wilkes Booth shot the president in the head and Lincoln died the next morning.

Andrew Johnson, Lincoln's vice president, assumed the presidency. He was faced with a split in the party that included Northern radicals and moderates who were on the opposite ends of the spectrum as to what should be done with the Southern states and how they should be punished for the war. Johnson adopted Lincoln's policies and made attempts to carry them out but was met with the anger of a large number of strong radicals. In 1868 Johnson was impeached by the House but was saved from impeachment by a single vote in the Senate. Southerners were not

Arrival of the delegates to the Republican convention in Chicago in 1868. (Library of Congress)

happy, either. The Southern states had to agree to follow federal laws before being readmitted into the Union.

What was left of the Democratic Party was centered mostly in the South. Grant, another Republican, followed Johnson into the White House for two terms during which America continued to expand. His administration, however, suffered from scandal and corruption associated with Reconstruction, although Grant was not personally involved.

Rutherford B. Hayes, who ran for president and promised to remove the federal troops from the South, served for four years. His election was similar to the one in 2000. The Democratic candidate, Samuel Tilden, received the most popular votes but Hayes was awarded the election by the electoral commission, made up primarily of Republicans.

The Hayes administration ended Reconstruction. It also reformed the civil service and stabilized the money system. Hayes was unpopular with the strongholds of the party and did not seek reelection. James Garfield was nominated in 1880 and served only a year before he was assassinated and his vice president, Chester A. Arthur, finished out Garfield's term. Under Arthur's administration, the Pendleton Act was passed, creating a merit system for civil service jobs.

The Republican Party did not renominate Arthur for the presidency and instead ran George G. Blaine of Maine. In a heated and tumultuous election, Blaine lost the White House by a small margin and for the first time in almost a quarter of a century, it was home to a Democrat, Grover Cleveland. The Republicans regained the keys to the White House in 1888. Benjamin Harrison won the presidential election based on electoral votes. Harrison had 233 to Cleveland's 168, but Harrison

"Principles of the Republican Party of the United States of America"—An 1888 campaign poster. (Library of Congress)

had 100,000 fewer popular votes than Cleveland. The party next suffered its greatest defeat since 1874: Harrison was renominated to run in 1892 but lost to Cleveland, who this time defeated Harrison by a landslide.

William McKinley ran against William Jennings Bryan in the election of 1896. McKinley, the Republican, won by a substantial margin. In this election, the geographical lines of interest were very apparent. McKinley received support of the industrial Northeast and business interests. Bryan depended on the agrarian South and the laborers of the West. These lines of loyalty seem to be the ones that are still associated with these specific political parties. In 1900, McKinley ran again, needing a new vice president. As Garret Hobart had died, Theodore Roosevelt was chosen. McKinley was assassinated in 1901 and Roosevelt became president. Roosevelt served out McKinley's term and was elected for one additional term. Roosevelt chose not to run again. The Roosevelt years saw much legislation dealing with economic and political reforms.

William Howard Taft was nominated to follow Roosevelt. He won election but his conservative policies alienated the liberals within the party. Led by Robert M. La Follette they organized the National Progressive Republican Party.

Roosevelt, not wanting Taft to serve another term, attempted to win the nomination; when he was not nominated by the Republicans, he went to La Follette's party and ran against Taft. Roosevelt became a spoiler—the

Robert M. La Follette organized the splinter National Progessive Republican Party. (Library of Congress)

split Republican vote allowed Woodrow Wilson, a Democrat, to serve for the next eight years. The 1920 election again saw Republicans in the White House. Warren Harding, with Calvin Coolidge as his vice president, was elected to serve a term. Harding died in office. Coolidge inherited Harding's scandals but wisely appointed two special prosecutors to investigate the scandals and he won a second term in 1924. Coolidge did not want to run in 1928. Herbert Hoover was nominated instead and he won with a large margin over Alfred E. Smith. The Republicans also had control of both houses of Congress.

A worldwide depression resulting from World War I was an issue many thought Hoover addressed too late and in 1932, the country was in its depths. Hoover ran for another term but was defeated by Democrat Franklin D. Roosevelt. This Roosevelt served as president for three terms plus part of a fourth before dying in office in 1945. He was followed by Harry S Truman, another Democrat who served for two terms. After twenty years, the White House was finally returned to a Republican in the 1953 election.

Dwight D. Eisenhower, a World War II hero, won thirty-nine states (out of 48 at that time). Eisenhower and his vice president Richard Nixon won the 1956 election as well. In 1960, Nixon lost his bid for the White House to John F. Kennedy, a popular young liberal Democrat. Kennedy was assassinated while in office and his vice president, Lyndon B. Johnson, completed Kennedy's term. Johnson won in a landslide when the Republican Party ran ultra-conservative Barry M. Goldwater against Johnson in 1964.

The Republicans returned to the White House in 1968 when Nixon was nominated and elected. He was reelected but in 1974 resigned under the shadow of severe political wrongdoing. Nixon's vice president at the time was Gerald Ford who had been appointed to office after Spiro T. Agnew, the elected vice president, was forced to resign. Ford completed Nixon's term, and ran against Democrat Jimmy Carter. Ford lost the election.

Ronald Reagan of California easily beat Carter in the election of 1980. Reagan's win was bolstered by the Republicans' winning

Dwight and Mamie Eisenhower watching television coverage of the Republican National Convention in Chicago in 1952. (Library of Congress)

President Gerald Ford, First Lady Betty Ford, Senator Bob Dole, and Elizabeth Dole celebrate winning the Republican nomination in 1976. (Library of Congress)

twelve new seats in the Senate, and after a quarter century, they again had a majority control of that body. Reagan won reelection against Walter F. Mondale in 1984. His vice president, George H. W. Bush, served one term in the White House, but domestic issues made Democrat Bill Clinton's optimistic rhetoric a welcome message to Americans. Clinton, not without preelection personal scandal and considerable personal scandal throughout his two terms, held the White House for the next eight years and remained a charismatic speaker and fund-raiser for his party.

In 2000, George W. Bush, governor of Texas and son of the former President Bush, was awarded the election in a very close race with Clinton's vice president, Al Gore. Gore won the popular vote but Bush was awarded Florida's electoral votes. The highly contested election resulted from voting irregularities on the local level. Bush was declared winner by a Republican attorney general serving under Florida's governor, Jeb Bush, George W.'s brother. George W. Bush won his second term against John Kerry, a senator from Massachusetts.

ALTERNATE HISTORY

The divide over slavery in the 1850s was not getting any better and it seemed as if compromise was out of the question. The radicals were crying out that compromise had not worked before and were almost unwilling to discuss any resolution. They insisted that when a rule had been set down, such as the Missouri Compromise, it should not be reversed when a new person was elected to the White House, Senate, or House of Representatives.

Several statesmen, however, might have gathered in Washington, D.C., seeking a resolution. Their suggestion might have shocked the nation, but at the same time it would have brought a great amount of peace to the population. Realizing that different sections of the country had different interests and philosophies, they might have decided to create Four Nations.

In the South, slave owners, mostly large tobacco and cotton farmers, would have been unable to turn a profit if they had had to pay for their labor. Many were indebted to European firms, and the South, having little interest in developing industry, would have found themselves with low tariffs.

The northeasterners, mostly industrialists and factory owners, had an opposite view from Southerners on tariffs. Some northeasterners thought slavery should be abolished but at the same time wanted to decrease the restrictions on immigration so that they could import cheap labor from Europe. Although they paid wages to their employees, many employees were paying off ocean passage to America, paid rents to live in company housing, were forced to buy supplies from company stores, and were never able to earn enough to work themselves out of what amounted to legal bondage. A large number of the workers were exploited children.

The West offered opportunity for homesteading, farming, mining, and eventually, manufacturing. Dividing that great expanse into a southwest nation and a northwest nation would have promised to some degree that slave and free territories would remain equal.

Sadly, the statesmen would have agreed that although the Union had been bound together by the Constitution, the great differences in this vast land were now causing separation rather than unification. The idea of popular sovereignty had come up in the Compromise of 1850 and again in the Kansas Nebraska Bill; perhaps it was time for a nation this large and with so many different resources to divide. The statesmen would have set up boundaries and agreed that the presidents of each nation should meet once a year for a week to resolve any issues they might have between their countries, thereby keeping them united and divided at the same time.

Not all statesmen immediately would have agreed with this idea. A group of Northerners—who called themselves Republicans—would have continued to believe that a balance could be maintained and that the United States as envisioned by their forefathers could exist. They would have felt strongly that slavery did not have to expand into the new territories. To many, however, the division of the country into four nations seemed to offer opportunities. Had the Republicans failed to get a sufficient number of supporters, they would have agreed to discuss the division.

Washington, D.C., would probably have been selected as a common center to resolve issues between the separate but United Nations. The nations would have had to agree that they must be united in spirit, realizing they were divided only in philosophical aspects of their existence. The new committee to create the Four Nations would have looked closely at what had happened to the United States prior to the ratification of the Constitution. They would have realized that a haphazard division of power would result in chaos as they set specific plans for the new nations.

Nation One would be made up of the states north of Washington, D.C., and would extend as far west as the Mississippi River. States or territories with names would retain their governments and borders but combined they would be called Nation One. Stephen Douglas would have been elected president of this nation. The orator who had lived in Illinois for a while had been at odds with Abraham Lincoln on the slave issue. Their debates (in both actual and alternate history) were followed by the politically interested on both sides of the issue.

Douglas believed that popular sovereignty—the right of the population to decide—was the method for settling the slavery issue. Lincoln, on the other hand, believed in limiting the extension of slavery into federal-held western territories, even though he never became an abolitionist. Soon after taking office, Douglas would have wanted to change the capital of Nation One to his home in Brandon, Vermont, but Boston, Massachusetts, would have been selected by popular vote.

Nation Two would be the states south of Washington, D.C. This nation would extend west to just east of the Mississippi River. The state governments, borders, and identities would have also been retained. To the south, tradition and family values had always been important. More than one man had lost his life defending the family name. Creating a new nation that erased history would have been unacceptable.

The Third Nation would be the lands west of the Mississippi River and north of the Missouri line with the exception of Illinois, which was east of the Mississippi and excluded from being part of Nation One by agreement. Prior to the Kansas Nebraska Bill, this land had already been mandated as mostly free (nonslave) area. Slavery still would not have been permitted except where two-thirds of the population determined that they wanted to own and maintain slaves.

Abraham Lincoln, a lawyer-politician who now resided in Springfield, Illinois, would have been nominated and accepted the position of president of this nation. In our alternate history, he was often thought of as being antislavery, but he would not be one to take radical action. He was a Whig and thought about supporting the Republican platform but would only have done so if they had organized into a national party. Lincoln proposed that children born to slaves be free, creating a slow death for the practice of slavery, as he also supported the prior law of outlawing the importation of new slaves into the nation from other countries. Lincoln would have been determined to see that the next generation of African Americans would be free. Lincoln's idea of easing out slavery brought a solution to the problem and did not remove all the existing slave labor from farms, plantations, and homesteads, leaving the slave owners without labor and equally leaving those who had been bonded into slavery as undereducated free people, without resources and easily exploited. Lincoln would have believed every man should have the means to maintain his dignity and pride.

Nation Four, the southwest nation, would be the space west of the Mississippi and south of the northernmost border of Kansas. That space would have been open to slavery. The exception would again have been an area where two-thirds of the population agreed to abolish slavery in their specific state or area. John Charles Frémont would have been nominated and would have served as the first president of this nation. Fremont, a surveyor, had worked his way through the territory befriending Kit Carson, a frontiersman who guided young Fremont across the Southwest and into parts of the Northwest Territories as well. A Southerner by birth, Frémont married into a powerful Missouri family. Fremont would not have hidden his opinions on slavery, and sometimes would have been looked at as a traitor to the cause and existence of the southwest nation, where many proslavery advocates (including his father-in-law, a former Missouri senator) felt that their philosophy would flourish.

The division of the lands, as prescribed, would have been intended to maintain a balance within specific areas of the land once known as the United States and now known as the United Nations. The United Nations would have agreed on a common system for minting monies. Although each nation would issue its own currency, a proper amount of gold or silver reserve would be on deposit in Washington, D.C., to cover the value of any paper money issued.

It might have been believed that the newer territories would be at a disadvantage, but they allowed wealthy investors from the northeast, southeast, and Europe to fund projects within their borders. Gold, silver, and other precious minerals were found on the land and eventually the existence of oil would have made Nations Three and Four rich. Toll roads would have been maintained by their owners who would have been authorized to collect tolls for the roads' creation and maintenance. Over time, the nations themselves would have decided to fund the roads, collecting tolls for the same purpose. The four nations would have created joint armed forces. Each nation would have trained a percentage of young men to be ready in case they were needed to defend against an enemy. Each nation would have created and maintained a number of arsenals within the bounds of their nation.

Having looked over the issues of the past, the one still to be resolved would have been tariffs. Would one nation tax another for goods? At one time, in actual history after the War of 1812, the United States had implemented a plan, the American Spirit, that benefited trade between states. It failed because other issues interrupted the flow of trade. In our alternate history, it would have been decided that eliminating tariffs between the nations would have been in the best interests of all, although any visitor, whether for business or pleasure, would have been subject to the taxes and tariffs that the citizens of that nation paid. This decision would have assured the distribution of goods within the entire former United States without having the competition from the much richer—and for some time in the earlier days, more advanced—European market.

And so the United States—divided—would have prospered.

The northeast nation (Nation One) would have been ruled by a probusiness party called the Republicans. The eastern mills would have processed the Southern cotton into cloth, crafted the western silver into fine trinkets for the home and for European ladies, and bagged the milled crops from the Midwest for export to Europe. The tariffs in the Northeast would have always been low. The exchange rate with Europe would have been maintained by the central bank. At one time, the Northeasterners would have bought patented inventions from Europe but they would now have been adept enough to design their own, or sly enough to recreate what they had seen developed across the "pond," or the Atlantic Ocean.

Fish were abundant and the fishing fleets of the northeast could have caught sufficient stock for themselves as well as for export. Whale blubber made excellent lamp oil used for lights before the invention and mass distribution of electricity. There was very little waste in products from the ocean.

The southern nation's largest cash crops would have been tobacco and cotton. Their climate and soil were fine enough to grow vegetables and fruit for their own consumption. As their growing season was longer than that of their northern neighbors, they would sometimes have supplemented fruits and vegetables for the winter market. The South also would have had a fishing industry. Oysters, crabs, and clams were harvested off the shores of the Mid-Atlantic coast. Nation Two (the South) would have concentrated on farming and export crops. Tobacco was a favorite for most men of the time and although some tobacco would have been distributed within the four nations, it became frowned upon over time. There always would have been a sufficient amount sent to export, satisfying markets worldwide.

Cotton, sometimes in raw form, would have been loaded onto boats for the long trip to England and France. Some of the cotton would have gone to the mills in the northeast nation, where processing on a larger scale produced a better quality cloth than home weaving. Most then would have been exported from that nation, but some textiles would have been retained for use by consumers in Nation One. Some bolts of cloth goods would have been returned to the South as a part of trade, where they were handmade into fine dresses for upscale southern women, and tablecloths and curtains for the proper southern home. In the early years, before mass production and importing, practical clothing was made of a combination of cotton and wool.

Very little cotton or cloth would have gone to the western nations. In parts of the West, cotton would probably have been grown in limited amounts or sheep would have been raised for their wool. Warmer clothing would have been made from animal fur or tanned hides. The areas west of the Mississippi were not yet as refined. The southern portion, charted by Frémont and Carson, would have been wild. There were miles of deserts where water was nonexistent. The higher elevations were cold, sometimes snowy and difficult to access. Natives, whether man or beast, would not yet have been ready to give up space to settlers.

Buffalo and cattle would have been free to roam in the vast expanse. Mining for gemstones, minerals, and ore would have become a major activity in this area. But it was still dangerous territory. It would have been said that the "snakes" in Nation Four not only slithered on the ground but sometimes came with six legs: four on his horse and two of his own.

In time, residents of this region would find oil, but drilling, processing, and refining the "black gold," as it was sometimes called, would not have been fully developed because the United Nations would have found it cheaper to buy resources from other countries. Gold, found in the extreme western territories, would have made some people rich and California would have been quickly populated by hopeful gold miners, as it was in actual history.

The northern Midwest would have been excellent for farming and for raising livestock. Large tracts of flat land allowed farmers to plant wheat and corn and other grains in rows that extended miles instead of acres. Cows and sheep had large enough grazing areas. Hogs and chickens were easy animals to maintain, as in actual history.

The far north territories would have had too short a growing season to support farming. Mining in the northern territories would have brought in gold and other ores that eventually would have been essential to the manufacturing that would become a large part of the Midwest.

For the next 100 years, the American population would have remained spread out and there would have been large open areas in both Nation Three and Nation Four. But the originally established open-immigration policy among the Four Nations would have allowed for growth, and for freedom to live or work in them all.

Time and progress would have made their impact on the nations. Boston would have remained the capital city of the northeast nation. Richmond would have been the capital of the southeast nation. Chicago, although it was in the easterly corner of the territory, would have become the capital of the northwest nation. New Orleans, at the mouth of the Mississippi and on the Gulf Coast, would have been the capital of the southwest nation.

Thus, in our alternate history, the climate of distrust and anger that had been brewing at the creation of the United Nations had now been set aside and each nation would have been free to do what it felt it did best. Although there would have been some disagreements, peaceful resolve was always the selected option in this scenario. The four nations would have been satisfied with their progress and could have concentrated on the cultural and environmental issues that fueled their lifestyle.

America divided was never more united.

Rita E. Valenti

Discussion Questions

1. How has the Republican Party's image changed over the last century?
2. Republicans led the way toward abolishing slavery, granting women's suffrage, and ensuring freedom of speech. Do you see "rights" issues being fought for by the Republican Party today?
3. If the Democrats had not split on the slavery issue, do you believe that the Republican Party would have organized and survived?
4. Usually only two strong parties are represented in an election (although we have had spoilers—a third-party candidate strong enough to siphon votes from the candidate who would have otherwise won the election). Do you believe that two strong parties are enough to represent the multiple issues and interests of all Americans?
5. What Republican politicians, elected or appointed, do you believe have most changed the world and the country?

Bibliography and Further Reading

Becker, Carl Lotus. *The Declaration of Independence, a Study in the History of Political Ideas*. New York: P. Smith, 1922.

Foner, Eric. *Free Soil, Free Labor, Free Men, the Ideology of the Republican Party before the Civil War*. New York: Oxford University Press, 1995.

Freehling, William W. *The Road to Disunion Secessionists at Bay, 1776–1854*. New York: Oxford University Press, 1991.

Gienapp, William E. *The Origins of the Republican Party 1852–1856*. New York: Oxford University Press, 1988.

Gould, Lewis. *The Grand Old Party: A History of the Republicans*. New York: Random House, 2003.

Hobbes, Thomas. *Leviathan*. New York: Cambridge University Press, 1996.

Holt, Michael. *Political Crisis of the 1850s*. New York: W.W. Norton, 1983.

Holt, Michael. *The Rise and Fall of the American Whig Part: Jacksonian Politics and the Onset of the Civil War*. New York: Oxford University Press, 2003.

Huchshorn, Richard H. "The American Presidency." ap.grolier.com (accessed September 8, 2005).

Locke, John. *Two Treatises of Government*. London: Cambridge University Press, 1967.

Mayer, George H. "Republican Party." www.worldbookonline.com (accessed September 13, 2005).

Nieman, Donald G. *Promises to Keep: African-Americans and the Constitutional Order, 1776 to the Present*. New York: Oxford University Press, 1991.

Potter, Chris. *"You Had to Ask."* http://www.pittsburghcitypaper.ws/prev/archives (accessed September 15, 2005).

Quinn, Frederick, ed. *The Federalist Papers Reader and Historical Documents of Heritage*. Cabin John, MD: Seven Locks Press, 1997.

"The Republican Party—The First Republican." www.gop.com (accessed August 12, 2005).

Smith, Adam. *An Inquiry into the Nature and Causes of the Wealth of Nations*. New York: Random House, 1985.

TURNING POINT

The Lincoln-Douglas Debates brought the issues of slavery to the forefront of American politics. What if Abraham Lincoln had not so eloquently questioned the nation's history and course?

INTRODUCTION

On a hot day in June 1858, a tall and lanky frontier lawyer, dressed in an ill-fitting suit, stood before the excited members of the Illinois Republican Party at their state convention in Springfield. Well known in Illinois, but little known outside his own state, Abraham Lincoln had just been nominated the Republican candidate for senator in the upcoming election. He would face a formidable opponent, Senator Stephen A. Douglas, a two-term Democrat known as the "Little Giant." But Lincoln had decided there was an even more formidable opponent that he must take on in the race for the Illinois Senate seat. That enemy was the institution of slavery. He told the crowd, according to *The Lincoln-Douglas Debates*, that "a house divided against itself" cannot stand. The nation could no longer go on half-slave and half-free, and therefore slavery must go.

Slavery had come to the United States during colonial times. A Dutch ship brought the first Africans to Jamestown, Virginia, in 1619. However, during the next two generations, most Africans, who were brought north from the West Indies where they were "seasoned," were sold as indentured servants rather than as slaves in the English colonies. They went to work alongside indentured servants from Europe in the tobacco fields of Virginia and Maryland. By the 1680s, the English colonies in North America continued to import indentured servants from Europe, but now most Africans brought into the country were sold as slaves. There were soon slaves in every colony, but their numbers were far greater in the South. In fact, slaves outnumbered the white settlers in South Carolina where they did backbreaking labor on the many profitable rice plantations. Northern colonies like Rhode Island, Massachusetts, and New York also profited greatly from the institution through their participation in the Atlantic slave trade.

The development of slavery in the thirteen original colonies stood in stark contrast to the growing freedom available to individuals in British North America. Unlike Europe, where a rigid class system still prevailed, colonial America was a place where individuals could own land, start businesses, and participate in politics. Members of the royal and noble classes did not migrate to the harsh circumstances of colonial America. Instead, the colonies were built by the poorest commoners who came with little else but the determination to survive and the ambition to build a better life for themselves and their families. Similar opportunities were not available to the majority of people in Europe, where the class system developed in the Middle Ages held on even as the feudal economy gave way to capitalism. Captain John Smith was the first adventurer in English America who seemed to understand that a new way of life, filled with freedom and opportunity for the average man and woman, had opened for many people on the American shore. After traveling along the New England coast in 1614, he wrote in *The Advantages of New England with Historical Reflections*, "Here every man may be master and owner of his own labor and land . . . if he has nothing but his hands, he may set up his trade and by industry quickly grow."

The new American experience of freedom and opportunity for the average man was best expressed politically in the colonial assemblies. In most of the colonies, men who were at least twenty-one years of age and property owners were allowed to vote for representatives to the legislatures. These representatives made most of the laws for the colonies including, and perhaps most important, those related to taxation. The colonies also came to appreciate the many rights that came to them from their English heritage, such as protections in criminal and civil law, and rights that came to them from their American experience, like freedom of religion, speech, assembly, and the press. When the British, under the leadership of King George III and Parliament, attempted to take greater control of the colonies after the French and Indian War, the Americans, who had known a freedom unheard of in the rest of the world, objected in a variety of ways.

They argued that they must maintain their rights as Englishmen, even though they were colonists, and that they must defend the rights that came to them through their own history, especially the right of their colonial assemblies to levy taxes on them. They found comfort in the writings of thinkers like John Locke and Baron de Montesquieu, and used the ideas of these thinkers when protesting the Stamp Act, the Tea Act, and other measures taken against them by the British King and Parliament.

By the spring of 1775, the Americans were determined to pursue the freedom and equality that they had envisioned for themselves. This determination led to actual armed conflict when British soldiers and Massachusetts Minute Men fought at the Battles of Lexington and Concord. At first, the majority of Americans seemed to believe that they were fighting only in their own defense against a royal aggressor. But after the publication of Thomas Paine's moving pamphlet *Common Sense* in the winter of 1776, many American Patriots called for independence from Great Britain, the creation of a new nation, and an explanation to the world of the idealistic principles upon which their country would be founded.

At last, in the summer of 1776, the Second Continental Congress expressed the growing awareness in the country that America must be free. The members of Congress declared independence for the United

States of America from Great Britain on July 2, and two days later, they approved Thomas Jefferson's Declaration of Independence, which described the reasons for independence and the principles upon which the United States would be founded. In the most stirring phrase of the document, Jefferson captured the essence of the new ideals so cherished by Americans. He wrote, "We hold these truths to be self-evident, that all men are created equal, that they are endowed by their Creator with certain unalienable rights, and that among these are life, liberty, and the pursuit of happiness."

TURNING POINT

But did Americans actually believe these words? Nearly one-quarter of the two million people living in the United States were slaves. Although the founding principle of the country was that "all men were created equal," it was abundantly clear that Americans did not practice what they preached. The revolutionary generation, which won the nation its independence from Great Britain in 1783, struggled with this profound contradiction. Many of the nation's leaders, including Jefferson, James Madison, and George Washington who were slaveholders, believed that all men and women were equals in the sense that they were all part of the same human race descended from an original human couple.

They were convinced that God had created mankind as equals and not in some pre-ordained ordering of classes. All later social distinctions between people had been purely the invention of men themselves. Slavery, therefore, was a human and not a divine invention. The founding generation felt this so deeply that they passed many measures to end slavery. Northern states like Pennsylvania and Massachusetts outlawed the institution immediately; others like New York eliminated it over time. Manumission of slaves was allowed in the Upper South, while Congress outlawed slavery north of the Ohio River in 1787 by means of the Northwest Ordinance.

While many hoped that slavery would simply die out in the nation, others remained adamant that the institution was necessary for the economic survival of the South. At the Constitutional Convention in Philadelphia in 1787, Charles Pinkney, a wealthy planter from South Carolina, argued that as long as there were swamps to clear in his home state or anywhere else in the South, there would be slavery. The fifty-five representatives who had come to write the Constitution struck a series of compromises to hold together the slave and nonslave sections of the country. In the "three-fifths clause" under Article I, states were allowed to count three-fifths of their slaves as part of the total population when determining how many representatives should be sent to Congress. However, the Constitution also implied that the Atlantic slave trade would end by 1808.

For the next sixty-five years, Americans continued to practice the method they had developed to deal with slavery during the Constitutional

IN CONTEXT   Douglas and Kansas

Stephen Douglas gained national prominence during the effort to enact the separate pieces of the Compromise of 1850 when he helped steer through Congress the separate bills that made up the Compromise. Douglas hoped that his same ability to fashion a compromise could work in passing legislation to organize the territory of Kansas. If a railroad were to be built linking Chicago with the West Coast, it would need to pass through the unorganized lands lying west of the state of Missouri and east of the already organized territory of Utah, which at that time stretched from what is now mid-Colorado all the way to the California border. Until the territory between Utah and Missouri was organized, no land titles could be made legal, and lands could not be assigned to a railroad right-of-way.

Because Southern senators would not support a bill to organize those territories unless they were opened to slave settlement, and Northern senators would not support a bill that set up the territories as open to slavery, compromise seemed impossible. Douglas's solution was to apply the principle of local self-determination, or popular sovereignty, that had been a minor feature of the bills in the Compromise of 1850 that organized the territories of Utah and New Mexico. The new territory would be open to slave settlement, but the territorial legislature could set rules regarding slavery, with the legislature being chosen by local voters.

The bill that incorporated this principle was the Kansas Nebraska Act, passed in 1854. Immediately, pro-slavery settlers began flooding into the territory from nearby Missouri, including some who brought their slaves with them. Meanwhile, antislavery emigrants, some funded by abolitionist groups from as far away as New York and Massachusetts, also began moving into the state. Over the period 1855–1857, a series of local battles between contending militia units, sheriffs' posses, and outlaw gangs turned into a miniature civil war, known as "Bleeding Kansas." Meanwhile, antislavery Northerners, formerly

---

Convention. They compromised. Such compromises became more and more necessary when slavery did not die out as many in the revolutionary generation had hoped it would. Instead, the institution grew even stronger as white Southerners used slaves to produce the profitable cotton crop. Cultivation of cotton increased dramatically after the invention of the cotton gin and the development of the textile industry in Great Britain and New England. Once Native American nations like the Creeks had been defeated in the War of 1812, cotton and slavery quickly spread west through Alabama to the Mississippi River and beyond.

In 1820, the nation faced its first political crisis over slavery when Missouri petitioned Congress to enter the Union as a slave state. Congress struck a deal known as the Missouri Compromise. Missouri would enter the Union as a slave state, while Maine would enter the Union as a free state. An imaginary line would also be drawn from Missouri's southern border westward to the Pacific. All new states formed north of the line would be free; all those formed south of the line would be slave. The Missouri Compromise survived for the next thirty years in part because it matched the westward migration of the American people. During the 1820s, Southerners seeking more land for cotton plantations headed south of the line into the Mexican territory of Texas. By the 1840s, a migration was under way from the north to the Oregon Territory. Hundreds of thousands of people headed out of the Middle West especially down the Oregon Trail to the rich farmlands of the Pacific Northwest. At the conclusion of the Mexican War in 1848, more territory

---

IN CONTEXT   *Douglas and Kansas (Continued)*

Democrats, Whigs, or independents, rallied around to form the Republican Party. The main impetus for the formation of this party was the reaction against Douglas's attempt to build a compromise based on popular sovereignty that would open the territories to slavery. Thus when Lincoln and Douglas conducted their famous debates in 1858, the hot issue of the era was Douglas's own identification with the problems in Kansas.

Douglas sought to deflect the issue by pointing out that the question would not be a federal one, but a local one. Furthermore, he hoped people would realize that very few slaveholders would move to Kansas, as the land there was not particularly suitable to plantation crops, such as cotton or tobacco. Nevertheless, by 1858, opinions had hardened. In Illinois, antislavery voters disliked popular sovereignty because it allowed slavery to gain a foothold in a federal territory. Pro-slavery voters disliked the policy because it appeared that Douglas was insincere. Lincoln as a Republican, had an easier path. By frankly opposing the extension of slavery into the territories he could afford to point out the problems with popular sovereignty.

Under the *Dred Scott* decision of early 1857, the Supreme Court had ruled that slavery could not be outlawed in federal territories, suggesting a flaw in the popular sovereignty compromise. At Freeport, Lincoln pointed this out, and Douglas attempted to evade the question by suggesting that a territorial legislature, by simply not enacting laws to protect slavery, would be able to preserve a territory as a non-slave region. That pathway through the problem only made Douglas appear devious and two-faced to any remaining pro-slavery voters in his own Democratic Party. It was partly for this reason that the Democratic Party split in 1860, with only Northern Democrats supporting Douglas and Southern Democrats endorsing a more frankly pro-slavery candidate, John Cabell Breckinridge, a senator from Kentucky. With Democrats divided, and Northern antislavery voters rallying around Lincoln, the stage was set for the election that would divide the nation along sectional lines and lead to the secession of slave states.

---

was added in the Southwest but much was dry desert, not suitable for either Northern or Southern farming. The discovery of gold in California in 1848 provided a temporary place for adventurers from both the North and South to seek a better life for themselves.

As long as there was room for both the North and the South to grow, the problem of slavery could be avoided, at least for awhile. However, by the decade of the 1850s, as Americans found they had nowhere else to grow, the issue of slavery had to be met head on. Northern abolitionists called for the immediate end of the evil institution. In contrast, white Southerners came to defend slavery as a moral and God-ordained institution. The Compromise of 1850 relieved some of the growing tension by giving certain benefits to the North, like the entrance of California into the Union as a free state and an end to the slave trade in Washington, D.C., and other benefits to the South, like the Fugitive Slave Act and money to Texas for damages in the Mexican War. But the compromise could not avoid the growing rift between the North and South over the question of slavery.

As Americans looked out at the Great Plains, the last empty stretch of farmland in America, both sides were determined to win this land only for free labor or slave labor. Senator Douglas of Illinois attempted to solve the problem by passing the Kansas Nebraska Act in 1853. The law called for "popular sovereignty," meaning that the people who settled in these territories could decide for themselves whether the new states were slave or free. During the next five years, the nation found that a compromise on the issue of slavery in the western territories was impossible. Kansas erupted in violence, the new Republican Party called for only free white labor in the Great Plains, and the Supreme Court decided in the *Dred Scott* decision that there could be no limits on slaveholding. As the nation spun out of control, one clear voice could be heard calling Americans back to the ideals of their revolutionary past. That voice belonged to Abraham Lincoln.

ACTUAL HISTORY

For a time, after making his now famous "House Divided" speech, Lincoln followed Douglas around the state of Illinois, speaking to crowds after the senator departed for other campaign stops. Many voters thought this made Lincoln appear desperate as he was always chasing Douglas and never seemed to catch up with him. Knowing that he was an excellent debater himself, Lincoln challenged Douglas to a series of one-on-one contests throughout the state where the voters could hear the deep differences that divided the two candidates. Even though as the incumbent he had everything to lose and not much to gain by accepting this challenge, Douglas took a chance and agreed to meet Lincoln in a series of debates. They would take place in seven of the nine congressional districts in the state. The first debate would be held in Ottawa on August 21 and the last would be in Alton on October 15. At four of the seven sites, Douglas would go first, speaking for an hour, then Lincoln would talk for an hour and a half, and finally Douglas would have the last half hour for a rebuttal. The process would be reversed at three other sites where Lincoln would go first.

At Ottawa, nearly 15,000 people crowded into the town square to listen to the debate and cheer on their favorite candidate. While Douglas's voice was a deep one that some said sounded like a barking dog, it could not reach to the farthest edges of the crowd. In contrast, Lincoln spoke in a high-pitched voice that could be heard and clearly understood by everyone present no matter how far away the listener stood. Douglas went on the attack first by mocking Lincoln's belief that the Founding Fathers truly believed in the equality of blacks and whites. He warned the crowd that Lincoln's lament of a house divided could only lead the nation into civil war. In contrast, his own call for "popular sovereignty" in the western territories would keep peace in the nation. It would allow his fellow Americans to choose whether future states in the Far West should be slave or free. He argued that this, and not a literal interpretation of the Declaration of Independence, was the true democracy laid out for us by the founding generation.

Lincoln responded by laying out a series of arguments that he would use to challenge the American people in the upcoming years. He said he did not advocate violence as he would make no attempt to end slavery immediately in the South where it currently existed. However, he boldly stated that slavery was wrong and it could not be allowed to extend into the western territories. Slavery must be set on the certain road to extinction where men like Washington, Jefferson, and Madison had placed it.

Talking to the many average people in the crowd who worked for a living, he made a point about the unfairness of slavery that struck home. He said a worker deserves to keep the fruits of his labor. He challenged the crowd to consider what their lives would be like if they had to turn over all their wages to someone else who had done none of the work himself. Surely everyone including Senator Douglas would agree that this was unfair.

The second debate came in Freeport. Another huge crowd of 15,000 people poured into the town. The excited crowd got to hear a three-hour "question and answer" session as Lincoln and Douglas responded to issues that each one had brought up against the other one in Alton. Lincoln said again he hoped slavery would die a certain death someday, but he would make no attempt to interfere with it where it now existed. He attacked Douglas for not understanding that the *Dred Scott* decision had effectively killed the doctrine of popular sovereignty. Since the Supreme Court said no limits could be placed on slavery, how could the people in a new territory vote to outlaw it? Douglas struck back with what the nation would soon call the Freeport Doctrine. He said it did not matter what the Supreme Court said! People made laws for themselves at the

Rival presidential nominees Lincoln and Douglas are matched in a footrace, in which Lincoln's long stride is a clear advantage. (Library of Congress)

KEY CONCEPT   Senators Selected, Not Elected

Even though Lincoln "won" the debates in 1858, with more voters turning out to support Republican legislators than Democratic ones, Stephen Douglas, the Democratic candidate, was selected to serve in the U.S. Senate. The reason for such an outcome has to do with the way U.S. senators were chosen under the Constitution.

Article I, Section 3, of the Constitution of the United States reads, "The Senate of the United States shall be composed of two Senators from each State, chosen by the legislature thereof, for six years; and each Senator shall have one vote." That method of selection of U.S. Senators remained in place until the

elections held in 1914, after the ratification of the Seventeenth Amendment to the Constitution. That amendment, proposed in 1912, was declared ratified May 31, 1913. The Seventeenth Amendment read in part, "The Senate of the United States shall be composed of two Senators from each State, elected by the people thereof, for six years; and each Senator shall have one vote." In 1858, however, the state legislatures still chose the U.S. Senators, under the original terms of the Constitution. Strictly speaking, Senators were chosen or selected, not elected.

So when Lincoln and Douglas debated in 1858, they were not exactly running for the Senate. Instead,

local level as soon as they moved into a new territory. They passed police regulations that would protect or not protect the institution of slavery. Even before a territorial legislature met, the people had already decided if they were for or against slavery. Cotton plantations and the slaves who must work them simply could not go where the majority of the people did not want them.

The debate in Jonesboro three weeks later drew little attention. There was much greater excitement at the fourth debate in Charleston where 12,000 people heard Douglas attack Lincoln as a hypocrite. He said Lincoln changed his argument depending on where he was speaking in the state. In the North, Lincoln's message was "pure black," in the middle, it was "mulatto," and in the South, it was "pure white!" This meant in the North he proclaimed the equality of everyone no matter what their color, but in the South, he toned down his message since many people there sympathized with the slaveholders across the Ohio River. Lincoln appeared to back down from his earlier stance against slavery when he said that emancipation of the slaves would probably take a century. However, he still argued that the end of slavery had to be seen as a necessary part of the process.

Three weeks later on October 7, the two candidates met at Galesburg in what many historians now consider the candidates' greatest debate. While both men were totally exhausted by their travels throughout the state, they were in top debating form. Douglas still taunted Lincoln as a hypocrite and a danger to the peace of the nation. But now he also gave a stirring vision of the country's future that lay just ahead if only Lincoln and his followers would drop their relentless attack on slavery. The Great Plains would fill up with towns and farms, and all the sections of the nation would live in peace together. While Douglas painted a bright picture of America's future, Lincoln looked backward to the summer of 1776 when the nation was founded on the principle that "all men are created equal." He said that Americans could not move into a better future if they

KEY CONCEPT   *Senators Selected, Not Elected (Continued)*

they were campaigning for the election of state legislators. The voters understood that if they were to elect Republican legislators, those legislators would vote to select Lincoln to serve in the U.S. Senate. Even though Lincoln garnered more votes for Republican candidates than Douglas did for Democratic candidates in 1858, the distribution of those votes in the state was such that Democrats still ended up holding a majority in the state legislature. In the legislative districts, forty-six Democratic legislators were elected, and forty-one Republicans, assuring the re-selection of Douglas by the legislature to serve another term in the U.S. Senate. In addition, thirteen state senators were held over from the previous election, of whom eight were Democrats. Even if the

selection of new members for the legislature had been exactly in proportion to the popular vote, the presence of the holdover members of the legislature would have ensured a vote for Douglas there.

Even though Lincoln did not get selected for the U.S. Senate, he had been able to make clear that he was more antislavery than Douglas, although he was not as strongly antislavery as some other Republicans, such as Senator William Seward from New York. Furthermore, with the nationwide publicity about his ability to stand up to Douglas and to represent a moderate antislavery position, Lincoln became a likely candidate for the Republican nomination for the presidency in the next presidential election, to be held in 1860.

---

forgot the heritage of freedom upon which their nation rested. That heritage was celebrated every fourth of July. By ignoring the fact that the Declaration of Independence applied to all people, Senator Douglas had "muzzled the cannon that thunders its annual joyous return," Lincoln said according to *The Lincoln-Douglas Debates*. By allowing the possibility of slavery in America's future, Douglas was "blowing out the moral lights around us."

In the final debates in Quincy and Alton, the two candidates repeated many of their earlier themes. Douglas demanded that all parts of the country, including the South, have a say in the direction the American nation would take on the Great Plains. Lincoln described the unfairness of slavery in a simple sentence, according to *The Lincoln-Douglas Debates*: "You toil and work and make bread, and I'll eat it!" He again reminded the crowds that the Founding Fathers had believed in the equality of all people and had set the nation on a future course where slavery would disappear forever. He challenged the Americans of his own generation to commit themselves to living up to the original principles of their nation and so end the evil institution once and for all.

When the votes were finally counted, 125,275 people had voted for Republican candidates to the state legislature who supported Lincoln, while 121,090 people had voted for Democratic candidates who supported Douglas. However, the final total did not matter because at this time the state legislature picked the U.S. senator. Even though fewer people had voted for the Democrats, the party had won more seats in the state house. This meant that Douglas was soon on his way to Washington, D.C., to serve another term as a senator from Illinois. Although Douglas claimed victory, he knew that Lincoln had made his mark on Illinois and the nation, and that the two men might well meet again as candidates for president.

Two years later in 1860, Lincoln and Douglas did oppose each other in the race for the White House. Lincoln's call for the American people to remember their revolutionary heritage frightened white Southerners who refused to give up slavery. In fact, they were so committed to the institution that they would rather see the Union dismembered than give up their slaves. The Southern states seceded from the Union and formed the Confederate States of America. Now Abraham Lincoln had to prosecute a civil war that would preserve the Union and lead it back to its revolutionary ideals. In four bloody years of fighting from 1861 until 1865, hundreds of thousands of soldiers were killed or wounded as the nation fought to settle the question of slavery once and for all. Lincoln moved cautiously as he set the war objectives. At first, he argued only that he fought to preserve the Union, but after the bloody battle at Antietam in September 1862, he made the end of slavery a goal of the war. On New Year's Day in 1863, he declared the Emancipation Proclamation, which set the slaves free in all rebel territory not then controlled by the Union Army. Later in the year when he dedicated the battlefield at Gettysburg, he expressed a third and final war aim. Democracy must survive in the United States for the good of the whole world. In the final speech of his life, given just days before the South was defeated and the Civil War ended, he told Americans that they must prepare for the full equality of the freed slaves.

Lincoln was killed by an assassin's bullet in April 1865, but the ideals he had so eloquently set forth for the nation could not be silenced. Even when the nation could not live up to them in the next century, they remained a quiet but steady background calling Americans to remember their revolutionary heritage. Lincoln's ideal of equality was added to the Constitution through the Thirteenth Amendment, which ended slavery (1865); the Fourteenth Amendment, which guaranteed full citizenship for all Americans (1868); and the Fifteenth Amendment, which gave black men the right to vote (1870). Sadly, between the ending of Reconstruction and the coming of World War II, the United States again turned its back on the revolutionary ideal of equality of all people. Segregation of blacks and whites became the rule, and African Americans became second-class citizens.

Attitudes finally changed as the nation moved out onto the world stage to fight the racism of the Nazi dictator Adolf Hitler. Now America held itself up as the leader of the Allies who fought for democracy and freedom for all. But if the United States truly meant to lead the world toward equality for all, then it must practice this principle at home. The civil rights movement began in the 1950s as blacks and whites, echoing Lincoln at his best, called for an end to segregation. The Supreme Court ordered an end to segregation in public schools with "all deliberate speed." Douglas's own party, the Democrats, took the lead under Presidents Harry Truman, John Kennedy, and Lyndon Johnson to win full civil rights for all Americans regardless of their race, ethnic origin, sex, or religion. Life is still not perfect in the United States, but the nation today is closer to living up to its revolutionary ideals than ever before in its history. We can now look back to see that the nation had gone off course in the direction set for us by the Founding Fathers, and that Abraham Lincoln helped us make a fundamental course correction when he bravely stood up in the great debates with Stephen Douglas and reminded us that this nation was truly founded on the principle that all men are created equal.

ALTERNATE HISTORY

It's hard to imagine what the United States would be like today if Abraham Lincoln had not made such a powerful impact on the nation during his debates with Stephen Douglas. His essential arguments that slavery was morally wrong, that the nation had been founded on the principle of equality, as clearly stated in the Declaration of Independence, and that slavery must come to an end one day were truly shining lights in the dark storm raging in the 1850s over the future of the nation. Lincoln reminded all who would listen that never in the history of the world had another nation been founded on such high principles as America had been in 1776. By the middle of the nineteenth century, it seemed impossible for Americans to live up to these high principles, as nine million men, women, and children were enslaved, and most of them were working to raise the nation's most valuable export: cotton. If it was impossible to live up to ideals set forth by the Founding Fathers, then why not simply forget them? What would be wrong with letting the "moral lights" go out all around us?

If Lincoln's own moral compass had not been so powerful in the debates against Douglas in 1858, and later in his speeches as president of the United States, our nation's own moral lights might well have flickered out around us. Lincoln himself could have turned his back on the ideals of the nation by avoiding the issue of slavery in the 1858 senatorial race and concentrating instead on local issues that concerned only the people of Illinois. One issue was the growing divide in wealth between the thriving city of Chicago in the north and the poorer farming counties in the south along the Ohio River. Lincoln could have raised concerns about the countless immigrants pouring into the nation from Europe. He could have won much support from many voters by arguing that these newcomers from places like Ireland and Germany had no right to the vast grasslands that swept westward from Illinois to the Rocky Mountains. He might even have joined into the debate that had gone on for the last decade about just where the transcontinental railroad should be built across the Great Plains. Why should Chicago be the destination of the many trains that would come from the east to head west on the new transcontinental line? Why shouldn't Springfield, his home town, be the hub? If Lincoln had kept to such local issues, he might have won the Senate race. But after he had gone to Washington, D.C., to serve out

Poster for reenactment of the Lincoln-Douglas debate to be held at the Du Page County, Illinois, Centennial. (Library of Congress)

In his debates with Douglas, Lincoln showed the nation a moral direction. (Library of Congress)

his term, he would surely today be as forgotten as most other senators who head to the capitol to serve only their state and not their nation.

A possible alternate outcome to the legendary contest between Abraham Lincoln and Stephen Douglas rests not just on Lincoln's shoulders, but on Douglas's, too. If Douglas had been better able to shape a positive view of his own vision for America's future, then today we might look back to the debates as a time when Douglas, rather than Lincoln, came to the forefront as a national leader. In the actual debates, Douglas attacked Lincoln on many counts, but most especially with the charge that Lincoln was an abolitionist who wanted the immediate end of slavery. He accused Lincoln of wanting whites and blacks to intermarry, and so he played on the fears of racists who dreaded the creation of a mulatto or mixed race nation. He mocked blacks as the inferiors of whites and ridiculed Lincoln for suggesting that Jefferson meant to include them with his illustrious words, "We hold these truths to be self evident, that all men are created equal." From Ottawa and Freeport to Quincy and Alton, Douglas ridiculed Lincoln's insistence that America live up to its founding principle of equality for all people, black and white.

Today we read the words of Stephen Douglas and wince at their cruelty. But imagine what might have happened to the country if Douglas had toned down his racism and had instead placed greater emphasis on his own positive vision of America's future in the many speeches he gave throughout Illinois in the late summer and early fall of 1858. Slavery was really an issue, Douglas could have argued, only if we wrongly believed that cotton could grow on the Great Plains. In the hot and arid world across the Mississippi River, called the Kansas and Nebraska Territories, slavery would not go because cotton could simply not grow there. Why must Lincoln, and all the other radical abolitionists, make such an issue over an outdated economic institution that would die a natural death in the West? Why try so hard to keep slavery out of the Great Plains when this hot and arid land would end the institution once and for all? Why not just sit back and let nature take its course instead of raising divisive issues that could only lead to misery? Even white Southerners would have to come to their senses eventually and give up the dream of taking cotton plantations out onto the Great Plains. Once they did that, in the not too distant future slavery would have ended and the United States could have moved on to a more peaceful and prosperous future.

Douglas could also have portrayed Lincoln as a man who clung to his own perfected sense of morality at the expense of the nation. If

Lincoln's logic was followed through to its inevitable conclusion, Douglas could have argued, then surely the nation was heading directly into civil war. Did Lincoln have some kind of death wish that made him want to send hundreds of thousands of young men into one bloody battle after another? Why was he setting a timetable that would only throw white Southerners into a panic and force them into secession and thus bring about the destruction of the United States? Slavery had existed in America for at least 200 years. Couldn't it be allowed to exist for just one more generation? Wouldn't its slow death on the hot and dry Great Plains be preferable to civil war? Douglas could have made these arguments.

A suggestion from Douglas that the nation should remain calm and patient over the issue of slavery in order to avoid war might well have struck a deep chord with the American people. If Douglas had coupled this caution with a glowing vision of America's future, he might have been able to counter Lincoln's "long look backward" to the ideals of the Founding Fathers. Lincoln had a masterful way of tugging on people's heartstrings. He spoke his greatest lines of sheer poetry calling Americans back to the past when their ideals were first set. But what if Douglas had spoken with equal power about what lay ahead for Americans, especially if they were able to avoid civil war? He might have said in even bolder terms that the Great Plains would quickly fill up as the American people raced west. Soon the entire country from the Mississippi to the Rockies, from Texas to the Canadian border would be filled with towns and farms, factories and railroad lines. New states would enter the Union with no memory of slavery but instead with a vision of a peaceful and prosperous future for Americans.

Douglas could have argued that if Americans would stop looking back, as Lincoln wanted them to do, and would instead look forward, as Douglas wanted them to do, then they would look into a glittering future where they would be the most prosperous nation on the face of the earth. Immigrants would pour in from all over the world to help build up their new nation and also fulfill the dreams they had for themselves and their families. Surely if we headed into this kind of a future where men and women could live in such freedom and opportunity, then we would have fulfilled the destiny carved out for us by the Founding Fathers. Slavery would simply and quietly disappear in the race toward a better future. These could have been Douglas's arguments.

With a stirring vision like this one as the main theme of his debates in 1858, Douglas might well have won a smashing victory over Abraham Lincoln in the race for the Illinois Senate seat. Hailed as a political genius, he could have gone on to win a smashing victory against any opponent in the 1860 presidential contest. His calm view about the slow but inevitable end of slavery might have temporarily stilled the angry voices of the abolitionists who called for an immediate end to the institution. Douglas could have painted the abolitionists as selfish moralists bent on the destruction of their nation in civil war, and so silenced them. His vision of a prosperous future might have led bankers, business leaders, and railroad owners alike to invest not just in the West but also in the South. President Douglas would have worked to help the South transition from an outdated economy, based on one or two cash crops and slave labor, to a more modern and diversified economy built on farming, industry, transportation, banking, and commerce. He would have gone down in history as one of our greatest presidents because he had helped his nation avoid civil war and instead pass into a tremendous future.

But what would have been lost under a Douglas presidency? The founding principles of our nation would have become a distant memory. The stirring words of the Declaration of Independence would be studied by historians, but the American people would feel no pressure to live up to these forgotten ideals. The Civil War would have been avoided, but as a consequence, the nation would not have taken a stand against slavery. The nation would also have failed to codify a stance against slavery in the Constitution. The Thirteenth, Fourteenth, and Fifteenth Amendments would never have been written. Slavery might well have died out in another generation, but without the protections written into the Constitution, African Americans would never be full citizens of the United States. Instead, they would be second-class citizens who would never be treated as the equals of white Americans. They would have become a permanent underclass, surviving as poorly paid agricultural workers or common laborers. The many contributions that our nation's African-American citizens have made since the Civil War would never have occurred. Without the renewed guarantees of equality for all written into the Constitution—in the Fourteenth Amendment especially—other groups like women and Native Americans would never have been able to fight for their equality in modern America.

With Douglas and his philosophy of pragmatic prosperity coming to the forefront of American life in the late nineteenth century, the United States would have come onto the world stage at the dawn of the twentieth century with no special vision to guide the world. We would have lost our ideals of equality for all and the need to build democratic government on this principle. We would simply have been a wealthy nation, separated from the troubles of the world by two oceans. When the European nations stumbled into the Great War in 1914, later called World War I, the United States would not have entered. No one would have felt the need to "make the world safe for democracy." No matter how many wars Europe and the rest of the world would have fallen into, the United States would have stayed aloof, preferring only to trade with everyone in order to maintain its own prosperity. We would have had no revolutionary ideals to share with the world, only our goods and services. We would be remembered in the history books today as a people who had for a time believed that all men were created equal, but who blew out their moral lights in the mid-nineteenth century. Americans would now play no leadership role in the world where government of the people, by the people, and for the people would have disappeared from the earth.

Mary Stockwell, Ph.D.

Discussion Questions

1. Douglas had the idea in the Freeport Doctrine that people could decide whether to allow slavery in a territory by deciding whether to enact local slave codes. Do you think that such an application of popular sovereignty could have avoided further conflict over slavery in Kansas?

2. In actual history, Stephen Douglas died in June 1861. If he had been elected president in 1860 and inaugurated in March 1861, who do you think might have been the vice president to take his place? Would the succeeding vice president have carried out the compromise policies suggested in the alternate history in this chapter, or would that person have instituted policies that could cause a civil war?

3. If compromise policies between North and South such as those proposed in this alternate history by Stephen Douglas had been implemented, how would the status of African Americans have altered between 1860 and 1940? What would be similar between the alternate history and actual history in this regard?

4. Even though Lincoln was not selected by the Illinois legislature to serve in the Senate, his performance in the debates in 1858 brought him national fame as a moderate antislavery Republican. What could he have said or done during the debates that would have resulted in his selection as U.S. senator in that year, if anything?

5. Politicians besides Lincoln attacked slavery much more vehemently than he did on the grounds of its incompatibility with the ideals of the founding fathers and its contradiction of many Christian values. William Seward, who was more antislavery than Lincoln, almost won the nomination of the Republican Party for the presidency in 1860. If Seward had run as a Republican against Douglas as a Democrat in that year, what would the outcome have been?

Bibliography and Further Reading

Douglas, Stephen, and Lincoln, Abraham. *The Lincoln-Douglas Debates.* Mineola, NY: Dover, 2004.

Fehrenbacher, Donald E. *Prelude to Greatness: Lincoln in the 1850's.* Stanford, CA: Stanford University Press, 1962.

Holzer, Harold, ed. *The Lincoln-Douglas Debates: The First Complete Unexpurgated Text.* New York: HarperCollins, 1993.

Jaffa, Harry V. *Crisis of the House Divided: An Interpretation of the Lincoln-Douglas Debates.* Garden City, NY: Doubleday, 1958.

Johannsen, Robert W. *Stephen A. Douglas.* New York: Oxford University Press, 1973.

Nevins, Allen. *The Emergence of Lincoln.* New York: Charles Scribner's Sons, 1950.

Oates, Stephen B. *With Malice toward None: The Life of Abraham Lincoln.* New York: Harper and Row, 1977.

Sigelschiffer, Saul. *The American Conscience: The Drama of the Lincoln-Douglas Debates*. New York: Horizon Press, 1973.

Smith, John. *On the Advantages of New England with Historical Reflections*. Charles Webster, 1887.

Thomas, John L., ed. *Abraham Lincoln and the American Political Tradition*. Amherst: University of Massachusetts Press, 1986.

Zarefsky, David. *Lincoln, Douglas and Slavery in the Crucible of Public Debate*. Chicago and London: University of Chicago Press, 1990.

Major Documents Related to Manifest Destiny

LOUISIANA PURCHASE TREATY: APRIL 30, 1803

Treaty between the United States of America and the French Republic

The President of the United States of America and the First Consul of the French Republic in the name of the French People desiring to remove all Source of misunderstanding relative to objects of discussion mentioned in the Second and Fifth articles of the Convention of the 8th Vendémiaire on 9/30 September 1800 relative to the rights claimed by the United States in virtue of the Treaty concluded at Madrid the 27 of October 1795, between His Catholic Majesty & the Said United States, & willing to Strengthen the union and friendship which at the time of the Said Convention was happily reestablished between the two nations have respectively named their Plenipotentiaries to wit The President of the United States, by and with the advice and consent of the Senate of the Said States; Robert R. Livingston Minister Plenipotentiary of the United States and James Monroe Minister Plenipotentiary and Envoy extraordinary of the Said States near the Government of the French Republic; And the First Consul in the name of the French people, Citizen Francis Barbé Marbois Minister of the public treasury who after having respectively exchanged their full powers have agreed to the following Articles.

Article I

Whereas by the Article the third of the Treaty concluded at St Ildefonso the 9th Vendémiaire on 1st October 1800 between the First Consul of the French Republic and his Catholic Majesty it was agreed as follows.

"His Catholic Majesty promises and engages on his part to cede to the French Republic six months after the full and entire execution of the conditions and Stipulations herein relative to his Royal Highness the Duke of Parma, the Colony or Province of Louisiana with the Same extent that it now has in the hand of Spain, & that it had when France possessed it; and Such as it Should be after the Treaties subsequently entered into between Spain and other States."

And whereas in pursuance of the Treaty and particularly of the third article the French Republic has an incontestible title to the domain and to the possession of the said Territory—The First Consul of the French Republic desiring to give to the United States a strong proof of his friendship doth hereby cede to the United States in the name of the French Republic for ever and in full Sovereignty the said territory with all its rights and appurtenances as fully and in the Same manner as they have been acquired by the French Republic in virtue of the above mentioned Treaty concluded with his Catholic Majesty.

Article II

In the cession made by the preceeding article are included the adjacent Islands belonging to Louisiana all public lots and Squares, vacant lands and all public buildings, fortifications, barracks and other edifices which are not private property.—The Archives, papers & documents relative to the domain and Sovereignty of Louisiana and its dependances will be left in the possession of the Commissaries of the United States, and copies will be afterwards given in due form to the Magistrates and Municipal officers of such of the said papers and documents as may be necessary to them.

Article III

The inhabitants of the ceded territory shall be incorporated in the Union of the United States and admitted as soon as possible according to the principles of the federal Constitution to the enjoyment of all these rights, advantages and immunities of citizens of the United States, and in the mean time they shall be maintained and protected in the free enjoyment of their liberty, property and the Religion which they profess.

Article IV

There Shall be Sent by the Government of France a Commissary to Louisiana to the end that he do every act necessary as well to receive from the Officers of his Catholic Majesty the Said country and its dependances in the name of the French Republic if it has not been already done as to transmit it in the name of the French Republic to the Commissary or agent of the United States.

Article V

Immediately after the ratification of the present Treaty by the President of the United States and in case that of the first Consul's shall have been previously obtained, the commissary of the French Republic shall remit all military posts of New Orleans and other parts of the ceded territory to the Commissary or Commissaries named by the President to take possession—the troops whether of France or Spain who may be there shall cease to occupy any military post from the time of taking possession and shall be embarked as soon as possible in the course of three months after the ratification of this treaty.

Article VI

The United States promise to execute Such treaties and articles as may have been agreed between Spain and the tribes and nations of Indians until by mutual consent of the United States and the said tribes or nations other Suitable articles Shall have been agreed upon.

Article VII

As it is reciprocally advantageous to the commerce of France and the United States to encourage the communication of both nations for a limited time in the country ceded by the present treaty until general arrangements relative to commerce of both nations may be agreed on; it has been agreed between the contracting parties that the French Ships coming directly from France or any of her colonies loaded only with the produce and manufactures of France or her Said Colonies; and the Ships of Spain coming directly from Spain or any of her colonies loaded only with the produce or manufactures of Spain or her Colonies shall be admitted during the Space of twelve years in the Port of New-Orleans and in all other legal ports-of-entry within the ceded territory in the Same manner as the Ships of the United States coming directly from France or Spain or any of their Colonies without being Subject to any other or greater duty on merchandize or other or greater tonnage than that paid by the citizens of the United States.

During that Space of time above mentioned no other nation Shall have a right to the Same privileges in the Ports of the ceded territory—the twelve years Shall commence three months after the exchange of ratifications if it Shall take place in France or three months after it Shall have been notified at Paris to the French Government if it Shall take place in the United States; It is however well understood that the object of the above article is to favour the manufactures, Commerce, freight and navigation of France and of Spain So far as relates to the importations that the French and Spanish Shall make into the Said Ports of the United States without in any Sort affecting the regulations that the United States may make concerning the exportation of the produce and merchandize of the United States, or any right they may have to make Such regulations.

Article VIII

In future and for ever after the expiration of the twelve years, the Ships of France shall be treated upon the footing of the most favoured nations in the ports above mentioned.

Article IX

The particular Convention Signed this day by the respective Ministers, having for its object to provide for the payment of debts due to the Citizens of the United States by the French Republic prior to the 30th Sept. 1800 (8th Vendémiaire an 9) is approved and to have its execution in the Same manner as if it had been inserted in this present treaty, and it Shall be ratified in the same form and in the Same time So that the one Shall not be ratified distinct from the other.

Another particular Convention Signed at the Same date as the present treaty relative to a definitive rule between the contracting parties is in the like manner approved and will be ratified in the Same form, and in the Same time and jointly.

Article X

The present treaty Shall be ratified in good and due form and the ratifications Shall be exchanged in the Space of Six months after the date of the Signature by the Ministers Plenipotentiary or Sooner if possible.

In faith whereof the respective Plenipotentiaries have Signed these articles in the French and English languages; declaring nevertheless that the present Treaty was originally agreed to in the French language; and have thereunto affixed their Seals.

Done at Paris the tenth day of Floreal in the eleventh year of the French Republic; and the 30th of April 1803.

Robt R Livingston
Jas. Monroe
Barbé Marbois

THE TEXAS DECLARATION OF INDEPENDENCE: MARCH 2, 1836

The Unanimous Declaration of Independence made by the Delegates of the People of Texas in General Convention at the town of Washington on the 2nd day of March 1836.

When a government has ceased to protect the lives, liberty and property of the people, from whom its legitimate powers are derived, and for the advancement of whose happiness it was instituted, and so far from being a guarantee for the enjoyment of those inestimable and inalienable rights, becomes an instrument in the hands of evil rulers for their oppression.

When the Federal Republican Constitution of their country, which they have sworn to support, no longer has a substantial existence, and the whole nature of their government has been forcibly changed, without their consent, from a restricted federative republic, composed of sovereign states, to a consolidated central military despotism, in which every interest is disregarded but that of the army and the priesthood, both the eternal enemies of civil liberty, the everready minions of power, and the usual instruments of tyrants.

When, long after the spirit of the constitution has departed, moderation is at length so far lost by those in power, that even the semblance of freedom is removed, and the forms themselves of the constitution discontinued, and so far from their

petitions and remonstrances being regarded, the agents who bear them are thrown into dungeons, and mercenary armies sent forth to force a new government upon them at the point of the bayonet.

When, in consequence of such acts of malfeasance and abdication on the part of the government, anarchy prevails, and civil society is dissolved into its original elements. In such a crisis, the first law of nature, the right of self-preservation, the inherent and inalienable rights of the people to appeal to first principles, and take their political affairs into their own hands in extreme cases, enjoins it as a right towards themselves, and a sacred obligation to their posterity, to abolish such government, and create another in its stead, calculated to rescue them from impending dangers, and to secure their future welfare and happiness.

Nations, as well as individuals, are amenable for their acts to the public opinion of mankind. A statement of a part of our grievances is therefore submitted to an impartial world, in justification of the hazardous but unavoidable step now taken, of severing our political connection with the Mexican people, and assuming an independent attitude among the nations of the earth.

The Mexican government, by its colonization laws, invited and induced the Anglo-American population of Texas to colonize its wilderness under the pledged faith of a written constitution, that they should continue to enjoy that constitutional liberty and republican government to which they had been habituated in the land of their birth, the United States of America.

In this expectation they have been cruelly disappointed, inasmuch as the Mexican nation has acquiesced in the late changes made in the government by General Antonio Lopez de Santa Anna, who having overturned the constitution of his country, now offers us the cruel alternative, either to abandon our homes, acquired by so many privations, or submit to the most intolerable of all tyranny, the combined despotism of the sword and the priesthood.

It has sacrificed our welfare to the state of Coahuila, by which our interests have been continually depressed through a jealous and partial course of legislation, carried on at a far distant seat of government, by a hostile majority, in an unknown tongue, and this too, notwithstanding we have petitioned in the humblest terms for the establishment of a separate state government, and have, in accordance with the provisions of the national constitution, presented to the general Congress a republican constitution, which was, without just cause, contemptuously rejected.

It incarcerated in a dungeon, for a long time, one of our citizens, for no other cause but a zealous endeavor to procure the acceptance of our constitution, and the establishment of a state government.

It has failed and refused to secure, on a firm basis, the right of trial by jury, that palladium of civil liberty, and only safe guarantee for the life, liberty, and property of the citizen.

It has failed to establish any public system of education, although possessed of almost boundless resources, (the public domain,) and although it is an axiom in political science, that unless a people are educated and enlightened, it is idle to expect the continuance of civil liberty, or the capacity for self government.

It has suffered the military commandants, stationed among us, to exercise arbitrary acts of oppression and tyrany, thus trampling upon the most sacred rights of the citizens, and rendering the military superior to the civil power.

It has dissolved, by force of arms, the state Congress of Coahuila and Texas, and obliged our representatives to fly for their lives from the seat of government, thus depriving us of the fundamental political right of representation.

It has demanded the surrender of a number of our citizens, and ordered military detachments to seize and carry them into the Interior for trial, in contempt of the civil authorities, and in defiance of the laws and the constitution.

It has made piratical attacks upon our commerce, by commissioning foreign desperadoes, and authorizing them to seize our vessels, and convey the property of our citizens to far distant ports for confiscation.

It denies us the right of worshipping the Almighty according to the dictates of our own conscience, by the support of a national religion, calculated to promote the temporal interest of its human functionaries, rather than the glory of the true and living God.

It has demanded us to deliver up our arms, which are essential to our defence, the rightful property of freemen, and formidable only to tyrannical governments.

It has invaded our country both by sea and by land, with intent to lay waste our territory, and drive us from our homes; and has now a large mercenary army advancing, to carry on against us a war of extermination.

It has, through its emissaries, incited the merciless savage, with the tomahawk and scalping knife, to massacre the inhabitants of our defenseless frontiers.

It hath been, during the whole time of our connection with it, the contemptible sport and victim of successive military revolutions, and hath continually exhibited every characteristic of a weak, corrupt, and tyrranical government.

These, and other grievances, were patiently borne by the people of Texas, until they reached that point at which forbearance ceases to be a virtue. We then took up arms in defence of the national constitution. We appealed to our Mexican brethren for assistance. Our appeal has been made in vain. Though months have elapsed, no sympathetic response has yet been heard from the Interior. We are, therefore, forced to the melancholy conclusion, that the Mexican people have acquiesced in the destruction of their liberty, and the substitution therfor of a military government; that they are unfit to be free, and incapable of self government.

The necessity of self-preservation, therefore, now decrees our eternal political separation.

We, therefore, the delegates with plenary powers of the people of Texas, in solemn convention assembled, appealing to a candid world for the necessities of our condition, do hereby resolve and declare, that our political connection with the Mexican nation has forever ended, and that the people of Texas do now constitute a free, Sovereign, and independent republic, and are fully invested with all the rights and attributes which properly belong to independent nations; and, conscious of the rectitude of our intentions, we fearlessly and confidently commit the issue to the decision of the Supreme arbiter of the destinies of nations.

LINCOLN-DOUGLAS DEBATE: AUGUST 27, 1858 (Second Debate with Stephen A. Douglas at Freeport, Illinois)

The Lincoln-Douglas debates consisted of seven debates between the two candidates for the U.S. Senate seat from Illinois in 1858: incumbent Democrat Stephen Douglas and Republican Abraham Lincoln. The head-to-head format and direct appeals to the people of the state were unusual, as state legislatures still chose U.S. senators at that time. The debates focused on the contentious sectional issues of slavery and states' rights that were dividing the country and the Democratic Party on the eve of the Civil War, bringing the debates a national audience and assuring their prominent place in American political history. Lincoln's famous "House Divided" speech, which implied the idea of an irrevocable conflict to make the country all slave or all free, became a key subject of the debates and helped make slavery a moral issue.

Lincoln felt that Douglas's doctrine of popular sovereignty, allowing the people of a territory to decide the slavery question, represented a conspiracy that would allow slavery to spread throughout the nation. Douglas claimed that economic and geographic factors would restrict slavery's expansion and that the people of a territory or state could exclude slavery, despite the Supreme Court ruling to the contrary in Dred Scott v. Sandford, by not protecting the institution under local laws. This latter belief became known as the Freeport Doctrine. Douglas also supported the rights of the separate sovereign states and claimed that Lincoln instead sought a federal government that would have more power than that of the individual states. Both men pledged not to interfere with slavery where it already existed and agreed that there was not equality between the races.

Douglas won his bid for reelection and remained the front-runner for the Democratic presidential nomination in 1860, but he alienated himself from his party's southern wing, including President James Buchanan. Lincoln gained national attention and became a leading candidate for the Republican presidential nomination in 1860, an election he would go on to win.

Marcella Trevino

Mr. Lincoln's Speech

Mr. Lincoln was introduced by Hon. Thomas J. Turner, and was greeted with loud cheers. When the applause had subsided, he said:

Ladies and Gentlemen: On Saturday last, Judge Douglas and myself first met in public discussion.... I propose to devote myself during the first hour to the scope of what was brought within the range of his half-hour speech at Ottawa.... In the course of that opening argument Judge Douglas proposed to me seven distinct interrogatories. In my speech of an hour and a half, I attended to some other parts of his speech, and incidentally, as I thought, answered one of the interrogatories then.... I do him no injustice in saying that he occupied at least half of his reply in dealing with me as though I had *refused* to answer his interrogatories. I now propose that I will answer any of the interrogatories, upon condition that he will answer questions from me not exceeding the same number....

[Owing to the press of people against the platform, our reporter did not reach the stand until Mr. Lincoln had spoken to this point. The previous remarks were taken by a gentleman in Freeport, who has politely furnished them to us.]

I have supposed myself, since the organization of the Republican party at Bloomington, in May, 1856, bound as a party man by the platforms of the party, then and since. If in any interrogatories which

I shall answer I go beyond the scope of what is within these platforms, it will be perceived that no one is responsible but myself.

Having said thus much, I will take up the Judge's interrogatories as I find them printed in the Chicago *Times*, and answer them *seriatim*....

Question 1. "I desire to know whether Lincoln to-day stands, as he did in 1854, in favor of the unconditional repeal of the Fugitive Slave law?"

Answer. I do not now, nor ever did, stand in favor of the unconditional repeal of the Fugitive Slave law. [Cries of "Good," "Good."]

Q. 2. "I desire him to answer whether he stands pledged to-day, as he did in 1854, against the admission of any more slave States into the Union, even if the people want them?"

A. I do not now, or ever did, stand pledged against the admission of any more slave States into the Union.

Q. 3. "I want to know whether he stands pledged against the admission of a new State into the Union with such a Constitution as the people of that State may see fit to make?"

A. I do not stand pledged against the admission of a new State into the Union, with such a Constitution as the people of that State may see fit to make. [Cries of "good," "good."]

Q. 4. "I want to know whether he stands to-day pledged to the abolition of slavery in the District of Columbia?"

A. I do not stand to-day pledged to the abolition of slavery in the District of Columbia.

Q. 5. "I desire him to answer whether he stands pledged to the prohibition of the slave-trade between the different States?"

A. I do not stand pledged to the prohibition of the slave-trade between the different States.

Q. 6. "I desire to know whether he stands pledged to prohibit slavery in all the Territories of the United States, North as well as South of the Missouri Compromise line?"

A. I am impliedly, if not expressly, pledged to a belief in the *right* and *duty* of Congress to prohibit slavery in all the United States Territories.

Q. 7. "I desire him to answer whether he is opposed to the acquisition of any new territory unless slavery is first prohibited therein?"

A. I am not generally opposed to honest acquisition of territory; and, in any given case, I would or would not oppose such acquisition, accordingly as I might think such acquisition would or would not

agravate [sic] the slavery question among ourselves. [Cries of "good", "good".]

Now, my friends, it will be perceived upon an examination of these questions and answers, that so far I have only answered that I was not *pledged* to this, that or the other.... But ... I am rather disposed to take up at least some of these questions, and state what I really think upon them.

As to the first one, in regard to the Fugitive Slave law, I have never hesitated to say, and I do not now hesitate to say, that I think, under the Constitution of the United States, the people of the Southern States are entitled to a Congressional Fugitive Slave law. Having said that, I have had nothing to say in regard to the existing Fugitive Slave law, further than that I think it should have been framed so as to be free from some of the objections that pertain to it, without lessening its efficiency....

In regard to the other question, of whether I am pledged to the admission of any more slave States into the Union, I state to you very frankly that I would be exceedingly sorry ever to be put in a position of having to pass upon that question. I should be exceedingly glad to know that there would never be another slave State admitted into the Union; but I must add, that if slavery shall be kept out of the Territories during the territorial existence of any one given Territory, and then the people shall, having a fair chance and a clear field, when they come to adopt the Constitution, do such an extraordinary thing as to adopt a slave Constitution, uninfluenced by the actual presence of the institution among them, I see no alternative, if we own the country, but to admit them into the Union. [Applause.]

The third interrogatory is answered by the answer to the second....

The fourth one is in regard to the abolition of slavery in the District of Columbia. In relation to that, I have my mind very distinctly made up. I should be exceedingly glad to see slavery abolished in the District of Columbia. [Cries of "good, good."] I believe that Congress possesses the constitutional power to abolish it. Yet as a member of Congress, I should not with my present views, be in favor of *endeavoring* to abolish slavery in the District of Columbia, unless it would be upon these conditions: *First*, that the abolition should be gradual. *Second*, that it should be on a vote of the majority of qualified voters in the District; and *third*, that compensation should be made to unwilling owners....

In regard to the fifth interrogatory, I must say here, that as to the question of the abolition of the slave-trade between the different States, I can truly answer, as I have, that I am *pledged* to nothing about it.... I must say, however, that if I should be of opinion that Congress does possess the constitutional power to abolish the slave-trade among the different States, I should still not be in favor of the exercise of that power unless upon some conservative principle as I conceive it, akin to what I have said in relation to the abolition of slavery in the District of Columbia.

My answer as to whether I desire that slavery should be prohibited in all the Territories of the United States, is full and explicit within itself, and cannot be made clearer by any comments of mine....

I now proceed to propound to the Judge the interrogatories, so far as I have framed them.

...

The first one is:

Question 1. If the people of Kansas shall, by means entirely unobjectionable in all other respects, adopt a State Constitution, and ask admission into the Union under it, *before* they have the requisite number of inhabitants according to the English bill—some ninety-three thousand—will you vote to admit them? [Applause.]

Q. 2. Can the people of a United States Territory, in any lawful way, against the wish of any citizen of the United States, exclude slavery from its limits prior to the formation of a State Constitution? [Renewed applause.]

Q. 3. If the Supreme Court of the United States shall decide that States cannot exclude slavery from their limits, are you in favor of acquiescing in, adopting and following such decision as a rule of political action? [Loud applause.]

Q. 4. Are you in favor of acquiring additional territory, in disregard of how such acquisition may affect the nation on the slavery question? [Cries of "good," "good."]

As introductory to these interrogatories which Judge Douglas propounded to me at Ottawa, he read a set of resolutions which he said Judge Trumbull and myself had participated in adopting, in the first Republican State Convention, held at Springfield, in October, 1854. He insisted that I and Judge Trumbull, and perhaps the entire Republican party, were responsible for the doctrines contained in the set of resolutions which he read, and I understand that it was from that set of resolutions that he

deduced the interrogatories which he propounded to me.... I do not now, nor never did, recognize any responsibility upon myself in that set of resolutions. ... Now it turns out that he had got hold of some resolutions passed at some Convention or public meeting in Kane county. [Renewed laughter.] I wish to say here, that I don't conceive that in any fair and just mind this discovery relieves me at all.... I am just as much responsible for the resolutions at Kane county as those at Springfield, the amount of the responsibility being exactly nothing in either case; no more than there would be in regard to a set of resolutions passed in the moon. [Laughter and loud cheers.]

I allude to this extraordinary matter in this canvass for some further purpose than anything yet advanced. Judge Douglas did not make his statement upon that occasion as matters that he believed to be true, but he stated them roundly as *being true*... when we consider who Judge Douglas is—that he is a distinguished Senator of the United States—that he has served nearly twelve years as such—that his character is not at all limited as an ordinary Senator of the United States, but that his name has become of world-wide renown—it is *most extraordinary* that he should so far forget all the suggestions of justice to an adversary, or of prudence to himself, as to venture upon the assertion of that which the slightest investigation would have shown him to be wholly false.... [Cheers.]

And I may add that another extraordinary feature of the Judge's conduct in this canvass—made more extraordinary by this incident—is, that he is in the habit, in almost all the speeches he makes, of charging falsehood upon his adversaries, myself and others....

I have been in the habit of charging as a matter of belief on my part, that, in the introduction of the Nebraska bill into Congress, there was a conspiracy to make slavery perpetual and national. I have arranged from time to time the evidence which establishes and proves the truth of this charge. I recurred to this charge at Ottawa....

But to draw your attention to one of the points I made in this case, beginning at the beginning. When the Nebraska bill was introduced, or a short time afterward, by an amendment, I believe, it was provided that it must be considered "the true intent and meaning of this act not to legislate slavery into any State or Territory, or to exclude it therefrom, but to leave the people thereof perfectly free to form and regulate their own domestic institutions in their own way, subject only to the Constitution of the United

States." I have called his attention to the fact that when he and some others began arguing that they were giving an increased degree of liberty to the people in the Territories over and above what they formerly had on the question of slavery, a question was raised whether the law was enacted to give such unconditional liberty to the people, and to test the sincerity of this mode of argument, Mr. Chase, of Ohio, introduced an amendment, in which he made the law—if the amendment were adopted—expressly declare that the people of the Territory should have the power to exclude slavery if they saw fit. I have asked attention also to the fact that Judge Douglas and those who acted with him, voted that amendment down, notwithstanding it expressed exactly the thing they said was the true intent and meaning of the law. I have called attention to the fact that in subsequent times, a decision of the Supreme Court has been made, in which it has been declared that a Territorial Legislature has no constitutional right to exclude slavery. And I have argued and said that for men who did intend that the people of the Territory should have the right to exclude slavery absolutely and unconditionally, the voting down of Chase's amendment is wholly inexplicable. It is a puzzle—a riddle. But I have said that with men who did look forward to such a decision, or who had it in contemplation, that such a decision of the Supreme Court would or might be made, the voting down of that amendment would be perfectly rational and intelligible. It would keep Congress from coming in collision with the decision when it was made. Any body can conceive that if there was an intention or expectation that such a decision was to follow, it would not be a very desirable party attitude to get into for the Supreme Court—all or nearly all its members belonging to the same party—to decide one way, when the party in Congress had decided the other way. Hence it would be very rational for men expecting such a decision, to keep the niche in that law clear for it. After pointing this out, I tell Judge Douglas that it looks to me as though here was the reason why Chase's amendment was voted down. I tell him that as he did it, and knows why he did it, if it was done for a reason different from this, *he knows what that reason was, and can tell us what it was.* I tell him, also, it will be vastly more satisfactory to the country for him to give some other plausible, intelligible reason *why* it was voted down than to stand upon his dignity and call people liars. [Loud cheers.] Well, on Saturday he did make his answer, and what do you think it was?

He says if I had only taken upon myself to tell the whole truth about that amendment of Chase's, no explanation would have been necessary on his part—or words to that effect. Now, I say here, that I am quite unconscious of having suppressed any thing material to the case, and I am very frank to admit if there is any sound reason other than that which appeared to me material, it is quite fair for him to present it. . . .

I pass one or two points I have because my time will very soon expire, but I must be allowed to say that Judge Douglas recurs again, as he did upon one or two other occasions, [to] the enormity of Lincoln—an insignificant individual like Lincoln—upon his *ipse dixit* charging a conspiracy upon a large number of members of Congress, the Supreme Court and two Presidents, to nationalize slavery. I want to say that, in the first place, I have made no charge of this sort upon my *ipse dixit.* I have only arrayed the evidence tending to prove it, and presented it to the understanding of others, saying what I think it proves, but giving you the means of judging whether it proves it or not. . . . On this occasion, I wish to recall his attention to a piece of evidence which I brought forward at Ottawa on Saturday, showing that he had made substantially the *same charge* against substantially the *same persons,* excluding his dear self from the category. I ask him to give some attention to the evidence which I brought forward, that he himself had discovered a "fatal blow being struck" against the right of the people to exclude slavery from their limits, which fatal blow he assumed as in evidence in an article in the Washington *Union,* published "by authority." I ask by whose authority? He discovers a similar or identical provision in the Lecompton Constitution. Made by whom? The framers of that Constitution. Advocated by whom? By all the members of the party in the nation, who advocated the introduction of Kansas into the Union under the Lecompton Constitution. . . .

I must again be permitted to remind him, that although my *ipse dixit* may not be as great as his, yet it somewhat reduces the force of his calling my attention to the *enormity* of my making a like charge against him. [Loud applause.]

Go on, Judge Douglas.

Mr. Douglas's Speech

Ladies and Gentlemen . . .

I am glad that at last I have brought Mr. Lincoln to the conclusion that he had better define his position on certain political questions to which I called his attention at Ottawa. He there showed no disposition, no inclination, to answer them.... I laid the foundation for those interrogatories by showing that they constituted the platform of the party whose nominee he is for the Senate.... I will first respond to these which he has presented to me....

First, he desires to know if the people of Kansas shall form a Constitution by means entirely proper and unobjectionable and ask admission into the Union as a State, before they have the requisite population for a member of Congress, whether I will vote for that admission. Well, now, I regret exceedingly that he did not answer that interrogatory himself.... But I will answer his question.... I will not make Kansas an exceptional case to the other States of the Union. (Sound, and hear, hear).... Either Kansas must come in as a free State, with whatever population she may have, or the rule must be applied to all the other Territories alike. (Cheers.) I therefore answer at once, that it having been decided that Kansas has people enough for a slave State, I hold that she has enough for a free State. ("Good," and applause.) I hope Mr. Lincoln is satisfied with my answer; ("he ought to be," and cheers,) and now I would like to get his answer to his own interrogatory—whether or not he will vote to admit Kansas before she has the requisite population. ("Hit him again.") I want to know whether he will vote to admit Oregon before that Territory has the requisite population....

The next question propounded to me by Mr. Lincoln is, can the people of a Territory in any lawful way, against the wishes of any citizen of the United States, exclude slavery from their limits prior to the formation of a State Constitution? I answer emphatically ... that in my opinion the people of a Territory can, by lawful means, exclude slavery from their limits prior to the formation of a State Constitution.... He heard me argue the Nebraska bill on that principle all over the State in 1854, in 1855, and in 1856, and he has no excuse for pretending to be in doubt as to my position on that question. It matters not what way the Supreme Court may hereafter decide as to the abstract question whether slavery may or may not go into a Territory under the Constitution, the people have the lawful means to introduce it or exclude it as they please, for the reason that slavery cannot exist a day or an hour anywhere, unless it is supported by local police regulations. ("Right, right.") Those police regulations can only be established by the local legislature, and

if the people are opposed to slavery they will elect representatives to that body who will by unfriendly legislation effectually prevent the introduction of it into their midst. If, on the contrary, they are for it, their legislation will favor its extension. Hence, no matter what the decision of the Supreme Court may be on that abstract question, still the right of the people to make a slave Territory or a free Territory is perfect and complete under the Nebraska bill....

[Deacon Bross spoke.]

In this connection, I will notice the charge which he has introduced in relation to Mr. Chase's amendment. I thought that I had chased that amendment out of Mr. Lincoln's brain at Ottawa; (laughter) but it seems that still haunts his imagination, and he is not yet satisfied. I had supposed that he would be ashamed to press that question further. He is a lawyer, and has been a member of Congress, and has occupied his time and amused you by telling you about parliamentary proceedings. He ought to have known better than to try to palm off his miserable impositions upon this intelligent audience. ("Good," and cheers.) The Nebraska bill provided that the legislative power, and authority of the said Territory, should extend to all rightful subjects of legislation consistent with the organic act and the Constitution of the United States. It did not make any exception as to slavery, but gave all the power that it was possible for Congress to give, without violating the Constitution to the Territorial Legislature.... What more could Mr. Chase give by his amendment? Nothing. He offered his amendment for the identical purpose for which Mr. Lincoln is using it, to enable demagogues in the country to try and deceive the people. ("Good, hit him again," and cheers.)

[Deacon Bross spoke.]

His amendment was to this effect. It provided that the Legislature should have the power to exclude slavery: and General Cass suggested, "why not give the power to introduce as well as exclude?" The answer was, they have the power already in the bill to do both. Chase was afraid his amendment would be adopted if he put the alternative proposition.... He offered it for the purpose of having it rejected. He offered it, as he has himself avowed over and over again, simply to make capital out of it for the stump.... ("Good, good.") Lincoln knows that the Nebraska bill, without Chase's amendment, gave all the power which the Constitution would permit.... We gave all a full grant, with no exception in regard to slavery one way or the other. We left that question as we left all others, to be decided by the people for themselves....

The third question which Mr. Lincoln presented is, if the Supreme Court of the United States shall decide that a State of this Union cannot exclude slavery from its own limits, will I submit to it.... It is true that the Washington *Union*, in an article published on the 17th of last December, did put forth that doctrine, and I denounced the article on the floor of the Senate, in a speech which Mr. Lincoln now pretends was against the President. The *Union* had claimed that slavery had a right to go into the free States, and that any provision in the Constitution or laws of the free States to the contrary were null and void. I denounced it in the Senate, as I said before, and I was the first man who did. Lincoln's friends, Trumbull, and Seward, and Hale, and Wilson, and the whole Black Republican side of the Senate, were silent. They left it to me to denounce it. (Cheers).... He casts an imputation upon the Supreme Court of the United States, by supposing that they would violate the Constitution of the United States....

The fourth question of Mr. Lincoln is, are you in favor of acquiring additional territory, in disregard as to how such acquisition may affect the Union on the slavery questions? This question is very ingeniously and cunningly put.

[Deacon Bross here spoke, *sotto voce*,—the reporter understanding him to say, "Now we've got him."]

The Black Republican creed lays it down expressly, that under no circumstances shall we acquire any more territory unless slavery is first prohibited in the country. I ask Mr. Lincoln whether he is in favor of that proposition. . . . When I ask him whether he stands up to that article in the platform of his party, he turns, Yankee-fashion, and without answering it, asks me whether I am in favor of acquiring territory without regard to how it may affect the Union on the slavery question. ("Good.") I answer that whenever it becomes necessary, in our growth and progress, to acquire more territory, that I am in favor of it, without reference to the question of slavery, and when we have acquired it, I will leave the people free to do as they please, either to make it slave or free territory, as they prefer. [Here Deacon Bross spoke, the reporter believes that he said, "That's bold." It was said solemnly.] It is idle to tell me or you that we have territory enough....We have

enough now for the present, but this is a young and a growing nation....I tell you, increase, and multiply, and expand, is the law of this nation's existence. ("Good") . . . our destiny require additional territory in the North, in the South, or on the Islands of the ocean, I am for it, and when we acquire it, will leave the people, according to the Nebraska bill, free to do as they please on the subject of slavery and every other question. ("Good, good, hurra for Douglas.")

I trust now that Mr. Lincoln will deem himself answered on his four points. He racked his brain so much in devising these four questions that he exhausted himself, and had not strength enough to invent the others. (Laughter.) As soon as he is able to hold a council with his advisers, Lovejoy, Farnsworth, and Fred Douglass, he will frame and propound others. [Good, good, &c. Renewed laughter, in which Mr. Lincoln feebly joined, saying that he hoped with their aid to get seven questions, the number asked him by Judge Douglas, and so make *conclusions* even.] You Black Republicans who say good, I have no doubt think that they are all good men. ("White, white.") I have reason to recollect that some people in this country think that Fred Douglass is a very good man. The last time I came here to make a speech, while talking from the stand to you, people of Freeport, as I am doing to-day, I saw a carriage, and a magnificent one it was, drive up and take a position on the outside of the crowd; a beautiful young lady was sitting on the box-seat, whilst Fred Douglass and her mother reclined inside, and the owner of the carriage acted as driver. (Laughter, cheers, cries of right, what have you to say against it, &c.) I saw this in your own town. ("What of it.") All I have to say of it is this, that if you, Black Republicans, think that the negro ought to be on a social equality with your wives and daughters, and ride in a carriage with your wife, whilst you drive the team, you have perfect right to do so. I am told that one of Fred Douglass' kinsmen, another rich black negro, is now traveling in this part of the State making speeches for his friend Lincoln as the champion of black men. ("White men, white men," and "what have you to say against it?" That's right, &c.) All I have to say on that subject is, that those of you who believe that the negro is your equal and ought to be on an equality with you socially, politically, and legally, have a right to entertain those opinions, and of course will vote for Mr. Lincoln. ("Down with the negro," no, no, &c.)

I have a word to say on Mr. Lincoln's answer to the interrogatories contained in my speech at

Ottawa, and which he has pretended to reply to here to-day. Mr. Lincoln makes a great parade of the fact that I quoted a platform as having been adopted by the Black Republican party at Springfield in 1854, which, it turns out, was adopted at another place. Mr. Lincoln loses sight of the thing itself in his ecstacies over the mistake I made in stating the place where it was done. He thinks that that platform was not adopted on the right "spot."

When I put the direct questions to Mr. Lincoln to ascertain whether he now stands pledged to that creed—to the unconditional repeal of the Fugitive Slave law, a refusal to admit any more slave States into the Union even if the people want them, a determination to apply the Wilmot Proviso, not only to all the territory we now have, but all that we may hereafter acquire, he refused to answer, and his followers say, in excuse, that the resolutions upon which I based my interrogatories were not adopted at the "*right spot*." (Laughter and applause.) Lincoln and his political friends are great on "*spots*." (Renewed laughter.) In Congress, as a representative of this State, he declared the Mexican war to be unjust and infamous, and would not support it, or acknowledge his own country to be right in the contest, because he said that American blood was not shed on American soil in the "*right spot*." ("Lay on to him.") And now he cannot answer the questions I put to him at Ottawa because the resolutions I read were not adopted at the "*right spot*." It may be possible that I was led into an error as to the *spot* on which the resolutions I then read were proclaimed, but I was not, and am not in error as to the fact of their forming the basis of the creed of the Republican party when that party was first organized. [Cheers.] I will state to you the evidence I had, and upon which I relied for my statement that the resolutions in question were adopted at Springfield on the 5th of October, 1854. Although I was aware that such resolutions had been passed in this district, and nearly all the northern Congressional Districts and County Conventions, I had not noticed whether or not they had been adopted by any State Convention. In 1856, a debate arose in Congress between Major Thomas L. Harris, of the Springfield District, and Mr. Norton, of the Joliet District, on political matters connected with our State, in the course of which, Major Harris quoted those resolutions as having been passed by the first Republican State Convention that ever assembled in Illinois. I knew that Major Harris was remarkable for his accuracy, that he was a very conscientious and sincere man, and I also noticed that Norton did not question the accuracy of this statement. I therefore took it for granted that it was so, and the other day when I concluded to use the resolutions at Ottawa, I wrote to Charles H. Lanphier, editor of the *State Register*, at Springfield, calling his attention to them, telling him that I had been informed that Major Harris was lying sick at Springfield, and desiring him to call upon him and ascertain all the facts concerning the resolutions, the time and the place where they were adopted. In reply, Mr. Lanphier sent me two copies of his paper, which I have here. The first is a copy of the *State Register*, published at Springfield, Mr. Lincoln's own town, on the 16th of October 1854, only eleven days after the adjournment of the Convention, from which I desire to read the following:

"During the late discussions in this city, Lincoln made a speech, to which Judge Douglas replied. In Lincoln's speech he took the broad ground that, according to the Declaration of Independence, the whites and blacks are equal. From this he drew the conclusion, which he several times repeated, that the white man had no right to pass laws for the government of the black man without the nigger's consent. This speech of Lincoln's was heard and applauded by all the Abolitionists assembled in Springfield. So soon as Mr. Lincoln was done speaking, Mr. Codding arose and requested all the delegates to the Black Republican Convention to withdraw into the Senate chamber. They did so, and after long deliberation, they laid down the following Abolition platform as the platform on which they stood. We call the particular attention of all our readers to it."

Then follows the identical platform, word for word, which I read at Ottawa. (Cheers.) Now, that was published in Mr. Lincoln's own town, eleven days after the Convention was held, and it has remained on record up to this day never contradicted....

Now, I will show you that if I have made a mistake as to the place where these resolutions were adopted—and when I get down to Springfield I will investigate the matter and see whether or not I have—that the principles they enunciate were adopted as the Black Republican platform ("white, white,") in the various counties and Congressional Districts throughout the north end of the State in 1854. This platform was adopted in nearly every county that gave a Black Republican majority for the Legislature in that year. . . . I will now read the resolutions adopted at the Rockford Convention on the 30th of August, 1854, which nominated Washburne for Congress. You elected him on the following platform:

Resolved, That the continued and increasing aggressions of slavery in our country are destructive of the best rights of a free people, and that such aggressions cannot be successfully resisted without the united political action of all good men.

Resolved, That the citizens of the United States hold in their hands peaceful, constitutional and efficient remedy against the encroachments of the slave power, the ballot-box, and, if that remedy is boldly and wisely applied, the principles of liberty and eternal justice will be established.

Resolved, That we accept this issue forced upon us by the slave power, and, in defense of freedom, will co-operate and be known as Republicans, pledged to the accomplishment of the following purposes:

To bring the Administration of the Government back to the control of first principles; to restore Kansas and Nebraska to the position of free Territories; to repeal and entirely abrogate the Fugitive Slave law; to restrict slavery to those States in which it exists; to prohibit the admission of any more slave States into the Union; to exclude slavery from all the Territories over which the General Government has exclusive jurisdiction, and to resist the acquisition of any more Territories unless the introduction of slavery therein forever shall have been prohibited.

Resolved, That in furtherance of these principles we will use such constitutional and lawful means as shall seem best adapted to their accomplishment, and that we will support no man for office under the General or State Government who is not positively committed to the support of these principles, and whose personal character and conduct is not a guaranty that he is reliable and shall abjure all party allegiance and ties.

Resolved, That we cordially invite persons of all former political parties whatever in favor of the object expressed in the above resolutions to unite with us in carrying them into effect.

[Senator Douglas was frequently interrupted in reading these resolutions by loud cries of "Good, good," "that's the doctrine," and vociferous applause]....

In the adoption of that platform, you not only declared that you would resist the admission of any more slave States, and work for the repeal of the Fugitive Slave law, but you pledged yourselves not to vote for any man for State or Federal offices who was not committed to these principles. You were thus committed. Similar resolutions to those were adopted in your county Convention here, and now with your admissions that they are your platform and embody your sentiments now as they did then, what do you think of Mr. Lincoln, your candidate for the U.S. Senate, who is attempting to dodge the responsibility of this platform, because it was not adopted in the right spot....

Gentlemen, I have shown you what your platform was in 1854. You still adhere to it....I wish now to call your attention to the action of your representatives in the Legislature when they assembled together at Springfield. In the first place, you must remember that this was the organization of a new party. It is so declared in the resolutions themselves, which say that you are going to dissolve all old party ties and call the new party Republican. The old Whig party was to have its throat cut from ear to ear, and the Democratic party was to be annihilated and blotted out of existence, whilst in lieu of these parties the Black Republican party was to be organized on this Abolition platform. You know who the chief leaders were in breaking up and destroying these two great parties. Lincoln on the one hand and Trumbull on the other, being disappointed politicians, and having retired or been driven to obscurity by an outraged constituency because of their political sins, formed a scheme to abolitionize the two parties and lead the old line Whigs and old line Democrats captive, bound hand and foot, into the Abolition camp. Giddings, Chase, Fred Douglass and Lovejoy were here to christen them whenever they were brought in. Lincoln went to work to dissolve the old line Whig party. Clay was dead, and although the sod was not yet green on his grave, this man undertook to bring into disrepute those great Compromise measures of 1850, with which Clay and Webster were identified. Up to 1854 the old Whig party and the Democratic party had stood on a common platform so far as this slavery question was concerned. You Whigs and we Democrats differed about the bank, the tariff, distribution, the specie circular and the sub-treasury, but we agreed on this slavery question and the true mode of preserving the peace and harmony of the Union. The Compromise measures of 1850 were introduced by Clay, were defended by Webster, and supported by

Cass, and were approved by Fillmore, and sanctioned by the National men of both parties. They constituted a common plank upon which both Whigs and Democrats stood. In 1852 the Whig party, in its last National Convention at Baltimore, indorsed and approved these measures of Clay, and so did the National Convention of the Democratic party, held that same year. Thus the old line Whigs and the old line Democrats stood pledged to the great principle of self-government, which guaranties to the people of each Territory the right to decide the slavery question for themselves. In 1854, after the death of Clay and Webster, Mr. Lincoln, on the part of the Whigs, undertook to Abolitionize the Whig party, by dissolving it, transferring the members into the Abolition camp and making them train under Giddings, Fred Douglass, Lovejoy, Chase, Farnsworth, and other Abolition leaders. Trumbull undertook to dissolve the Democratic party by taking old Democrats into the Abolition camp. Mr. Lincoln was aided in his efforts by many leading Whigs throughout the State. Your member of Congress, Mr. Washburne, being one of the most active. Trumbull was aided by many renegades from the Democratic party, among whom were John Wentworth, Tom Turner, and others, with whom you are familiar....

When the bargain between Lincoln and Trumbull was completed for Abolitionizing the Whig and Democratic parties, they "spread" over the State, Lincoln still pretending to be an old line Whig, in order to "rope in" the Whigs, and Trumbull pretending to be as good a Democrat as he ever was, in order to coax the Democrats over into the Abolition ranks. They played the part that "decoy ducks" play down on the Potomac river. In that part of the country they make artificial ducks and put them on the water in places where the wild ducks are to be found, for the purpose of decoying them. Well, Lincoln and Trumbull played the part of these "decoy ducks" and deceived enough old line Whigs and old line Democrats to elect a Black Republican Legislature. When that Legislature met, the first thing it did was to elect as Speaker of the House, the very man who is now boasting that he wrote the Abolition platform on which Lincoln will not stand. I want to know of Mr. Turner whether or not, when he was elected, he was a good embodiment of Republican principles?

Mr. Turner: "I hope I was then and am now."

Mr. Douglas: He swears that he hopes he was then and is now. He wrote that Black Republican

platform, and is satisfied with it now. I admire and acknowledge Turner's honesty. Every man of you know that what he says about these resolutions being the platform of the Black Republican party is true, and you also know that each one of these men who are shuffling and trying to deny it are only trying to cheat the people out of their votes for the purpose of deceiving them still more after the election. I propose to trace this thing a little further, in order that you can see what additional evidence there is to fasten this revolutionary platform upon the Black Republican party. When the Legislature assembled, there was a United States Senator to elect in the place of Gen. Shields, and before they proceeded to ballot, Lovejoy insisted on laying down certain principles by which to govern the party. It has been published to the world and satisfactorily proven that there was, at the time the alliance was made between Trumbull and Lincoln to Abolitionize the two parties, an agreement that Lincoln should take Shields's place in the United States Senate, and Trumbull should have mine so soon as they could conveniently get rid of me. When Lincoln was beaten for Shields's place, in a manner I will refer to in a few minutes, he felt very sore and restive; his friends grumbled, and some of them came out and charged that the most infamous treachery had been practiced against him; that the bargain was that Lincoln was to have had Shields's place, and Trumbull was to have waited for mine, but that Trumbull having the control of a few Abolitionized Democrats, he prevented them from voting for Lincoln, thus keeping him within a few votes of an election until he succeeded in forcing the party to drop him and elect Trumbull. Well, Trumbull having cheated Lincoln, his friends made a fuss, and in order to keep them and Lincoln quiet, the party were obliged to come forward, in advance, at the last State election, and make a pledge that they would go for Lincoln and nobody else. Lincoln could not be silenced in any other way.

... As I have before said, Lovejoy demanded a declaration of principles on the part of the Black Republicans of the Legislature before going into an election for United States Senator. He offered the following preamble and resolutions which I hold in my hand:

WHEREAS, Human slavery is a violation of the principles of natural and revealed rights; and whereas, the fathers of the Revolution, fully imbued with the spirit of these principles, declared freedom to be the inalienable birthright of all men; and whereas, the preamble to the Constitution of the United States avers that that instrument was ordained to establish justice, and secure the blessings of liberty to ourselves and our posterity; and whereas, in furtherance of the above principles, slavery was forever prohibited in the old North-west Territory, and more recently in all that Territory lying west and north of the State of Missouri, by the act of the Federal Government; and whereas, the repeal of the prohibition last referred to, was contrary to the wishes of the people of Illinois, a violation of an implied compact, long deemed sacred by the citizens of the United States, and a wide departure from the uniform action of the General Government in relation to the extension of slavery; therefore,

Resolved, by the House of Representatives, the Senate concurring therein, That our Senators in Congress be instructed, and our Representatives requested to introduce, if not otherwise introduced, and to vote for a bill to restore such prohibition to the aforesaid Territories, and also to extend a similar prohibition to all territory which now belongs to the United States, or which may hereafter come under their jurisdiction.

Resolved, That our Senators in Congress be instructed, and our Representatives requested, to vote against the admission of any State into the Union, the Constitution of which does not prohibit slavery, whether the territory out of which such State may have been formed shall have been acquired by conquest, treaty, purchase, or from original territory of the United States.

Resolved, That our Senators in Congress be instructed, and our Representatives requested, to introduce and vote for a bill to repeal an act entitled "an act respecting fugitives from justice and persons escaping from the service of their masters;" and, failing in that, for such a modification of it as shall secure the right of *habeas corpus* and trial by jury before the regularly-constituted authorities of the State, to all persons claimed as owing service or labor.

Those resolutions were introduced by Mr. Lovejoy immediately preceding the election of Senator. They declared first, that the Wilmot Proviso must be applied to all territory north of 36 deg. 30 min. Secondly, that it must be applied to all territory south of 36 deg. 30 min. Thirdly, that it must be applied to all the territory now owned by the United States, and finally, that it must be applied to

all territory hereafter to be acquired by the United States. The next resolution declares that no more slave States shall be admitted into this Union under any circumstances whatever.... The next resolution demands the unconditional repeal of the Fugitive Slave law, although its unconditional repeal would leave no provision for carrying out that clause of the Constitution of the United States which guaranties the surrender of fugitives. If they could not get an unconditional repeal, they demanded that that law should be so modified as to make it as nearly useless as possible. Now, I want to show you who voted for these resolutions. When the vote was taken on the first resolution it was decided in the affirmative—yeas 41, nays 32. You will find that this is a strict party vote, between the Democrats on the one hand, and the Black Republicans on the other. [Cries of "White, white," and clamor.] I know your name, and always call things by their right name. The point I wish to call your attention to, is this: that these resolutions were adopted on the 7th day of February, and that on the 8th they went into an election for a United States Senator, and that day every man who voted for these resolutions, with but two exceptions, voted for Lincoln for the United States Senate. ["Give us their names."] I will read the names over to you if you want them, but I believe your object is to occupy my time.

On the next resolution the vote stood-yeas 33, nays 40, and on the third resolution-yeas 35, nays 47. I wish to impress it upon you, that every man who voted for those resolutions, with but two exceptions, voted on the next day for Lincoln for U. S. Senator. Bear in mind that the members who thus voted for Lincoln were elected to the Legislature pledged to vote for no man for office under the State or Federal Government who was not committed to this Black Republican platform....

...Thus you see every member from your Congressional District voted for Mr. Lincoln, and they were pledged not to vote for him unless he was committed to the doctrine of no more slave States, the prohibition of slavery in the Territories, and the repeal of the Fugitive Slave law. Mr. Lincoln tells you today that he is not pledged to any such doctrine. Either Mr. Lincoln was then committed to those propositions, or Mr. Turner violated his pledges to you when he voted for him. Either Lincoln was pledged to each one of those propositions, or else every Black Republican Representative from this Congressional District violated his pledge of honor to his constituents by voting for him. . . . Either Mr. Lincoln was committed to those propositions, or your members violated their faith. Take either horn of the dilemma you choose. There is no dodging the question; I want Lincoln's answer. . . . I put the question to him distinctly, whether he indorsed that part of the Black Republican platform which calls for the entire abrogation and repeal of the Fugitive Slave law. He answers no! that he does not indorse that, but he does not tell what he is for, or what he will vote for. His answer is, in fact, no answer at all. Why cannot he speak out and say what he is for and what he will do?

In regard to there being no more slave States, he is not pledged to that. He would not like, he says, to be put in a position where he would have to vote one way or another upon that question. I pray you, do not put him in a position that would embarrass him so much. Gentlemen, if he goes to the Senate, he may be put in that position, and then which way will he vote?

[A Voice: "How will you vote?"]

Mr. Douglas: I will vote for the admission of just such a State as by the form of their Constitution the people show they want; if they want slavery, they shall have it; if they prohibit slavery it shall be prohibited. They can form their institutions to please themselves, subject only to the Constitution; and I for one stand ready to receive them into the Union. Why cannot your Black Republican candidates talk out as plain as that when they are questioned? . . .

Mr. Lincoln made a speech when he was nominated for the United States Senate which covers all these Abolition platforms. He there lays down a proposition so broad in its abolitionism as to cover the whole ground.

"In my opinion it [the slavery agitation] will not cease until a crisis shall have been reached and passed. 'A house divided against itself cannot stand.' I believe this Government cannot endure permanently half slave and half free. I do not expect the house to fall—but I do expect it will cease to be divided. It will become all one thing or all the other. Either the opponents of Slavery will arrest the further spread of it, and place it where the public mind shall rest in the belief that it is in the course of ultimate extinction, or its advocates will push it forward till it shall become alike lawful in all the States—old as well as new, North as well as South." . . .

He tells you the Union cannot exist unless the States are all free or all slave; he tells you that he is opposed to making them all slave, and hence he is for making them all free, in order that the Union may exist; and yet he will not say that he will not vote against another slave State, knowing that the Union must be dissolved if he votes for it. I ask you if that is fair dealing? The true intent and inevitable conclusion to be drawn from his first Springfield speech is, that he is opposed to the admission of any more slave States under any circumstance. If he is so opposed, why not say so? . . .

Mr. Lincoln says that he believes that this Union cannot continue to endure with slave States in it, and yet he will not tell you distinctly whether he will vote for or against the admission of any more slave States, but says he would not like to be put to the test. (Laughter.) I do not think he will be put to the test. (Renewed laughter.) I do not think that the people of Illinois desire a man to represent them who would not like to be put to the test on the performance of a high constitutional duty. (Cries of "good.") I will retire in shame from the Senate of the United States when I am not willing to be put to the test in the performance of my duty. I have been put to severe tests. ("That is so.") I have stood by my principles in fair weather and in foul, in the sunshine and in the rain. I have defended the great principles of self-government here among you when Northern sentiment ran in a torrent against me, (A VOICE—"that is so") and I have defended that same great principle when Southern sentiment came down like an avalanche upon me. I was not afraid of any test they put to me. I knew I was right—I knew my principles were sound—I knew that the people would see in the end that I had done right, and I knew that the God of Heaven would smile upon me if I was faithful in the performance of my duty. (Cries of "good," cheers, and laughter.)

Mr. Lincoln makes a charge of corruption against the Supreme Court of the United States, and two Presidents of the United States, and attempts to bolster it up by saying that I did the same against the Washington *Union*. Suppose I did make that charge of corruption against the Washington *Union*, when it was true, does that justify him in making a false charge against me and others? That is the question I would put. He says that at the time the Nebraska bill was introduced, and before it was passed, there was a conspiracy between the Judges of the Supreme Court, President Pierce, President Buchanan and myself by that bill, and the decision of the court to break down the barrier and establish slavery all over the Union. Does he not know that that charge is historically false as against President Buchanan? He knows that Mr. Buchanan was at that time in England, representing this country with distinguished ability at the Court of St. James, that he was there for a long time before, and did not return for a year or more after. He knows that to be true, and that fact proves his charge to be false as against Mr. Buchanan. (Cheers.) Then again, I wish to call his attention to the fact that at the time the Nebraska bill was passed, the Dred Scott case was not before the Supreme Court at all; it was not upon the docket of the Supreme Court; it had not been brought there, and the Judges in all probability knew nothing of it. Thus the history of the country proves the charge to be false as against them. As to President Pierce, his high character as a man of integrity and honor is enough to vindicate him from such a charge, (laughter and applause,) and as to myself, I pronounce the charge an infamous lie, whenever and wherever made, and by whomsoever made. I am willing that Mr. Lincoln should go and rake up every public act of mine, every measure I have introduced, report I have made, speech delivered, and criticise them, but when he charges upon me a corrupt conspiracy for the purpose of perverting the institutions of the country, I brand it as it deserves. I say the history of the country proves it to be false, and that it could not have been possible at the time. But now he tries to protect himself in this charge, because I made a charge against the Washington *Union*. My speech in the Senate against the Washington *Union* was made because it advocated a revolutionary doctrine, by declaring that the free States had not the right to prohibit slavery within their own limits. Because I made that charge against the Washington *Union*, Mr. Lincoln says it was a charge against Mr. Buchanan. Suppose it was; is Mr. Lincoln the peculiar defender of Mr. Buchanan? Is he so interested in the Federal Administration, and so bound to it, that he must jump to the rescue and defend it from every attack that I may make against it? (Great laughter and cheers.) I understand the whole thing. The Washington *Union*, under that most corrupt of all men, Cornelius Wendell, is advocating Mr. Lincoln's claim to the Senate. Wendell was the printer of the last Black Republican House of Representatives; he was a candidate before the present Democratic House, but was ignominiously kicked out, and then he took the money which he had made out of the public printing by means of the Black Republicans,

bought the Washington *Union*, and is now publishing it in the name of the Democratic party, and advocating Mr. Lincoln's election to the Senate. Mr. Lincoln therefore considers an attack upon Wendell and his corrupt gang as a personal attack upon him. (Immense cheering and laughter.) This only proves what I have charged, that there is an alliance between Lincoln and his supporters, and the Federal office-holders of this State, and Presidential aspirants out of it, to break me down at home.

[A VOICE. "That is impossible," and cheering.]

Mr. Lincoln feels bound to come in to the rescue of the Washington *Union*. In that speech which I delivered in answer to the Washington *Union*, I made it distinctly against the *Union*, and against the *Union* alone. I did not choose to go beyond that. If I have occasion to attack the President's conduct, I will do it in language that will not be misunderstood. When I differed with the President, I spoke out so that you all heard me. ("That you did," and cheers). ...Whenever the great principle of self-government— the right of the people to make their own Constitution, and come into the Union with slavery or without it, as they see proper, shall again arise, you will find me standing firm in defense of that principle, and fighting whoever fights it. ("Right, right." "Good, good," and cheers.) If Mr. Buchanan stands, as I doubt not he will, by the recommendation contained in his Message, that hereafter all State Constitutions ought to be submitted to the people before the admission of the State into the Union, he will find me standing by him firmly, shoulder to shoulder, in carrying it out. I know Mr. Lincoln's object; he wants to divide the Democratic party, in order that he may defeat me and get to the Senate.

Mr. Douglas' time here expired, and he stopped on the moment.

MR. LINCOLN'S REJOINDER.

As Mr. Lincoln arose he was greeted with vociferous cheers. He said:

My friends: It will readily occur to you that I cannot, in half an hour, notice all the things that so able a man as Judge Douglas can say in an hour and a half....I can but take up some of the points that he has dwelt upon....

Now, my friends, I come to all this long portion of the Judge's speech—perhaps half of it—which he has devoted to the various resolutions and platforms that have been adopted in the different counties in the different Congressional Districts, and in the Illinois Legislature—which he supposes are at variance with the positions I have assumed before you to-day. It is true that many of these resolutions are at variance with the positions I have here assumed.... I happen to know, the Judge's opinion to the contrary notwithstanding, that I have never tried to conceal my opinions, nor tried to deceive any one in reference to them. He may go and examine all the members who voted for me for United States Senator in 1855, after the election of 1854. They were pledged to certain things here at home, and were determined to have pledges from me, and if he will find any of these persons who will tell him any thing inconsistent with what I say now, I will resign, or rather retire from the race, and give him no more trouble. [Applause.] The plain truth is this: At the introduction of the Nebraska policy, we believed there was a new era being introduced in the history of the Republic, which tended to the spread and perpetuation of slavery. But in our opposition to that measure we did not agree with one another in every thing. The people in the north end of the State were for stronger measures of opposition than we of the central and Southern portions of the State, but we were all opposed to the Nebraska doctrine. We had that one feeling and that one sentiment in common. You at the north end met in your Conventions and passed your resolutions. We in the middle of the State and further south did not hold such Conventions and pass the same resolutions, although we had in general a common view and a common sentiment. So that these meetings which the Judge has alluded to, and the resolutions he has read from, were local, and did not spread over the whole State. We at last met together in 1856, from all parts of the State, and we agreed upon a common platform. You, who held more extreme notions, either yielded those notions, or if not wholly yielding them, agreed to yield them practically, for the sake of embodying the opposition to the measures which the opposite party were pushing forward at that time. We met you then, and if there was any thing yielded, it was for practical purposes. We agreed then upon a platform for the party throughout the entire State of Illinois, and now we are all bound as a party, *to that platform*. And I say here to you, if any one expects of me—in the case of my election— that I will do any thing not signified by our Republican platform and my answers here to-day, I tell you very frankly that person will be deceived.... For my part, I do hope that all of us, entertaining a common sentiment in opposition to what appears to us a design to nationalize and perpetuate slavery, will waive minor differences on questions which either belong to the dead pastor the distant future, and all pull together in this struggle. What are your sentiments? ["We will, we will," and loud cheers]....

The Judge complains that I did not fully answer his questions. If I have the sense to comprehend and answer those questions, I have done so fairly. If it can be pointed out to me how I can more fully and fairly answer him, I aver I have not the sense to see how it is to be done. He says I do not declare I would in any event vote for the admission of a slave State into the Union. If I have been fairly reported he will see that I did give an explicit answer to his interrogatories, I did not merely say that I would dislike to be put to the test; but I said clearly, if I were put to the test, and a Territory from which slavery had been excluded should present herself with a State Constitution sanctioning slavery—a most extraordinary thing and wholly unlikely to happen—I did not see how I could avoid voting for her admission....

He says if I should vote for the admission of a slave State I would be voting for a dissolution of the Union, because I hold that the Union cannot permanently exist half slave and half free. I repeat that I do not believe this Government *can* endure permanently half slave and half free, yet I do not admit, nor does it at all follow, that the admission of a single slave State will permanently fix the character and establish this as a universal slave nation. The Judge is very happy indeed at working up these quibbles. [Laughter and cheers]....

Judge Douglas says he made a charge upon the editor of the Washington *Union, alone*, of entertaining a purpose to rob the States of their power to exclude slavery from their limits. I undertake to say, and I make the direct issue, that he did *not* make his charge against the editor of the *Union* alone. [Applause.] I will undertake to prove by the record here, that he made that charge against more and higher dignitaries than the editor of the Washington *Union*.... Will he dodge it now by alleging that I am trying to defend Mr. Buchanan against the charge? Not at all. Am I not making the same charge myself? [Laughter and applause.] I am trying to show that you, Judge Douglas, are a witness on my side. [Renewed Laughter.] I am not defending Buchanan, and I will tell Judge Douglas that in my opinion, when he made that charge, he had an eye farther north than he was to-day. He was then fighting against people who called *him* a Black

Republican and an Abolitionist. . . . The Judge says that though he made this charge, Toombs got up and declared there was not a man in the United States, except the editor of the *Union*, who was in favor of the doctrines put forth in that article. And thereupon, I understand that the Judge withdrew the charge. Although he had taken extracts from the newspaper, and then from the Lecompton Constitution, to show the existence of a conspiracy to bring about a "fatal blow," by which the States were to be deprived of the right of excluding slavery, it all went to pot as soon as Toombs got up and told him it was not true. [Laughter.] . . .

Now, gentlemen, you may take Judge Douglas's speech of March 22d, 1858, beginning about the middle of page 21, and reading to the bottom of page 24, and you will find the evidence on which I say that he did not make his charge against the editor of the *Union* alone. . . . Judge Douglas said:

"Mr. President, you here find several distinct propositions advanced boldly by the Washington *Union* editorially and apparently *authoritatively*, and every man who questions any of them is denounced as an Abolitionist, a Freesoiler, a fanatic. The propositions are, first, that the primary object of all government at its original institution is the protection of persons and property; second, that the Constitution of the United States declares that the citizens of each State shall be entitled to all the privileges and immunities of citizens in the several States; and that, therefore, thirdly, all State laws, whether organic or otherwise, which prohibit the citizens of one State from settling in another with their slave property, and especially declaring it forfeited, are direct violations of the original intention of the Government and Constitution of the United States; and fourth, that the emancipation of the slaves of the Northern States was a gross outrage on the rights of property, inasmuch as it was involuntarily done on the part of the owner."

"Remember that this article was published in the *Union* on the 17th of November, and on the 18th appeared the first article giving the adhesion of the *Union* to the Lecompton Constitution. It was in these words:

"KANSAS AND HER CONSTITUTION. The vexed question is settled. The problem is solved. The dead point of danger is passed. All serious trouble to Kansas affairs is over and gone.

"And a column, nearly, of the same sort. Then, when you come to look into the Lecompton Constitution, you find the same doctrine incorporated in it which was put forth editorially in the *Union*. What is it?

"ARTICLE 7, *Section* 1. The right of property is before and higher than any constitutional sanction; and the right of the owner of a slave to such slave and its increase is the same and as invariable as the right of the owner of any property whatever.

"Then in the schedule is a provision that the Constitution may be amended after 1864 by a two-thirds vote.

"But no alteration shall be made to affect the right of property in the ownership of slaves.

"It will be seen by these clauses in the Lecompton Constitution that they are identical in spirit with this *authoritative* article in the Washington *Union* of the day previous to its indorsement of this Constitution.

"When I saw that article in the *Union* of the 17th of November, followed by the glorification of the Lecompton Constitution on the 18th of November, and this clause in the Constitution asserting the doctrine that a State has no right to prohibit slavery within its limits, I saw that there was a *fatal blow* being struck at the sovereignty of the States of this Union."

Here he says, "Mr. President, you here find several distinct propositions advanced boldly, and apparently *authoritatively*." By whose authority, Judge Douglas? [Great cheers and laughter.] Again, he says in another place, "It will be seen by these clauses in the Lecompton Constitution, that they are identical in spirit with this *authoritative* article." *By whose authority*? [Renewed cheers.] Who do you mean to say authorized the publication of these articles? He knows that the Washington *Union* is considered the organ of the Administration. *I* demand of Judge Douglas *by whose authority* he meant to say those articles were published, if not by the authority of the President of the United States and his Cabinet? I defy him to show whom he referred to, if not to these high functionaries in the Federal Government. More than this, he says the articles in that paper and the provisions of the Lecompton Constitution are "identical," and being identical, he argues that the authors are co-operating and conspiring together. He does not use the word "conspiring," but what other construction can you put upon it? He winds up with this:

"When I saw that article in the *Union* of the 17th of November, followed by the glorification of the

Lecompton Constitution on the 18th of November, and this clause in the Constitution asserting the doctrine that a State has no right to prohibit slavery within its limits, I saw that there was a *fatal blow* being struck at the sovereignty of the States of this Union."

I ask him if all this fuss was made over the editor of this newspaper. [Laughter.] It would be a terribly *"fatal* blow" indeed which a single man could strike, when no President, no Cabinet officer, no member of Congress, was giving strength and efficiency to the moment. Out of respect to Judge Douglas's good sense I must believe he didn't manufacture his idea of the "fatal" character of that blow out of such a miserable scapegrace as he represents that editor to be. But the Judge's eye is

farther south now. [Laughter and cheers.] Then, it was very peculiarly and decidedly north. His hope rested on the idea of visiting the great "Black Republican" party, and making it the tail of his new kite. [Great laughter.] He knows he was then expecting from day to day to turn Republican and place himself at the head [of] our organization. He has found that these despised "Black Republicans" estimate him by a standard which he has taught them none too well. Hence he is crawling back into his old camp, and you will find him eventually installed in full fellowship among those whom he was then battling, and with whom he now pretends to be at such fearful variance. [Loud applause and cries of "go on, go on."] I cannot, gentlemen, my time has expired.

GADSDEN PURCHASE: DECEMBER 30, 1853

By the President of the United States of America

A Proclamation

WHEREAS a treaty between the United States of America and the Mexican Republic was concluded and signed at the City of Mexico on the thirtieth day of December, one thousand eight hundred and fifty-three; which treaty, as amended by the Senate of the United States, and being in the English and Spanish languages, is word for word as follows:

IN THE NAME OF ALMIGHTY GOD:

The Republic of Mexico and the United States of America desiring to remove every cause of disagreement which might interfere in any manner with the better friendship and intercourse between the two countries, and especially in respect to the true limits which should be established, when, notwithstanding what was covenanted in the treaty of Guadalupe Hidalgo in the year 1848, opposite interpretations have been urged, which might give occasion to questions of serious moment: to avoid these, and to strengthen and more firmly maintain the peace which happily prevails between the two republics, the President of the United States has, for this purpose, appointed James Gadsden, Envoy Extraordinary and Minister Plenipotentiary of the same, near the Mexican government, and the President of Mexico has appointed as

Plenipotentiary "ad hoc" his excellency Don Manuel Diez de Bonilla, cavalier grand cross of the national and distinguished order of Guadalupe, and Secretary of State, and of the office of Foreign Relations, and Don Jose Salazar Ylarregui and General Mariano Monterde as scientific commissioners, invested with full powers for this negotiation, who, having communicated their respective full powers, and finding them in due and proper form, have agreed upon the articles following

Article I

The Mexican Republic agrees to designate the following as her true limits with the United States for the future: retaining the same dividing line between the two Californias as already defined and established, according to the 5th article of the treaty of Guadalupe Hidalgo, the limits between the two republics shall be as follows: Beginning in the Gulf of Mexico, three leagues from land, opposite the mouth of the Rio Grande, as provided in the 5th article of the treaty of Guadalupe Hidalgo; thence, as defined in the said article, up the middle of that river to the point where the parallel of 31 47' north latitude crosses the same; thence due west one hundred miles; thence south to the parallel of 31 20' north latitude; thence along the said parallel of 31 20' to the 111th meridian of longitude west of Greenwich; thence in a straight line to a point on the

Colorado River twenty English miles below the junction of the Gila and Colorado rivers; thence up the middle of the said river Colorado until it intersects the present line between the United States and Mexico. For the performance of this portion of the treaty, each of the two governments shall nominate one commissioner, to the end that, by common consent the two thus nominated, having met in the city of Paso del Norte, three months after the exchange of the ratifications of this treaty, may proceed to survey and mark out upon the land the dividing line stipulated by this article, where it shall not have already been surveyed and established by the mixed commission, according to the treaty of Guadalupe, keeping a journal and making proper plans of their operations. For this purpose, if they should judge it necessary, the contracting parties shall be at liberty each to unite to its respective commissioner, scientific or other assistants, such as astronomers and surveyors, whose concurrence shall not be considered necessary for the settlement and of a true line of division between the two Republics; that line shall be alone established upon which the commissioners may fix, their consent in this particular being considered decisive and an integral part of this treaty, without necessity of ulterior ratification or approval, and without room for interpretation of any kind by either of the parties contracting. The dividing line thus established shall, in all time, be faithfully respected by the two governments, without any variation therein, unless of the express and free consent of the two, given in conformity to the principles of the law of nations, and in accordance with the constitution of each country respectively.

In consequence, the stipulation in the 5th article of the treaty of Guadalupe upon the boundary line therein described is no longer of any force, wherein it may conflict with that here established, the said line being considered annulled and abolished wherever it may not coincide with the present, and in the same manner remaining in full force where in accordance with the same.

Article II

The government of Mexico hereby releases the United States from all liability on account of the obligations contained in the eleventh article of the treaty of Guadalupe Hidalgo; and the said article and the thirty-third article of the treaty of amity, commerce, and navigation between the United States of America and the United Mexican States concluded at Mexico, on the fifth day of April, 1831, are hereby abrogated.

Article III

In consideration of the foregoing stipulations, the Government of the United States agrees to pay to the government of Mexico, in the city of New York, the sum of ten millions of dollars, of which seven millions shall be paid immediately upon the exchange of the ratifications of this treaty, and the remaining three millions as soon as the boundary line shall be surveyed, marked, and established.

Article IV

The provisions of the 6th and 7th articles of the treaty of Guadalupe Hidalgo having been rendered nugatory, for the most part, by the cession of territory granted in the first article of this treaty, the said articles are hereby abrogated and annulled, and the provisions as herein expressed substituted therefor. The vessels, and citizens of the United States shall, in all time, have free and uninterrupted passage through the Gulf of California, to and from their possessions situated north of the boundary line of the two countries. It being understood that this passage is to be by navigating the Gulf of California and the river Colorado, and not by land, without the express consent of the Mexican government; and precisely the same provisions, stipulations, and restrictions, in all respects, are hereby agreed upon and adopted, and shall be scrupulously observed and enforced by the two contracting governments in reference to the Rio Colorado, so far and for such distance as the middle of that river is made their common boundary line by the first article of this treaty.

The several provisions, stipulations, and restrictions contained in the 7th article of the treaty of Guadalupe Hidalgo shall remain in force only so far as regards the Rio Bravo del Forte, below the initial of the said boundary provided in the first article of this treaty; that is to say, below the intersection of the 31 47'30'/ parallel of latitude, with the boundary line established by the late treaty dividing said river from its mouth upwards, according to the fifth article of the treaty of Guadalupe.

Article V

All the provisions of the eighth and ninth, sixteenth and seventeenth articles of the treaty of Guadalupe Hidalgo, shall apply to the territory ceded by the

Mexican Republic in the first article of the present treaty, and to all the rights of persons and property, both civil and ecclesiastical, within the same, as fully and as effectually as if the said articles were herein again recited and set forth.

Article VI

No grants of land within the territory ceded by the first article of this treaty bearing date subsequent to the day-twenty-fifth of September-when the minister and subscriber to this treaty on the part of the United States, proposed to the Government of Mexico to terminate the question of boundary, will be considered valid or be recognized by the United States, or will any grants made previously be respected or be considered as obligatory which have not been located and duly recorded in the archives of Mexico.

Article VII

Should there at any future period (which God forbid) occur any disagreement between the two nations which might lead to a rupture of their relations and reciprocal peace, they bind themselves in like manner to procure by every possible method the adjustment of every difference; and should they still in this manner not succeed, never will they proceed to a declaration of war, without having previously paid attention to what has been set forth in article twenty-one of the treaty of Guadalupe for similar cases; which article, as well as the twenty-second is here reaffirmed.

Article VIII

The Mexican Government having on the 5th of February, 1853, authorized the early construction of a plank and railroad across the Isthmus of Tehuantepec, and, to secure the stable benefits of said transit way to the persons and merchandise of the citizens of Mexico and the United States, it is stipulated that neither government will interpose any obstacle to the transit of persons and merchandise of both nations; and at no time shall higher charges be made on the transit of persons and property of citizens of the United States, than may be made on the persons and property of other foreign nations, nor shall any interest in said transit way, nor in the proceeds thereof, be transferred to any foreign government.

The United States, by its agents, shall have the right to transport across the isthmus, in closed bags, the mails of the United States not intended for distribution along the line of communication; also the effects of the United States government and its citizens, which may be intended for transit, and not for distribution on the isthmus, free of customhouse or other charges by the Mexican government. Neither passports nor letters of security will be required of persons crossing the isthmus and not remaining in the country.

When the construction of the railroad shall be completed, the Mexican government agrees to open a port of entry in addition to the port of Vera Cruz, at or near the terminus of said road on the Gulf of Mexico.

The two governments will enter into arrangements for the prompt transit of troops and munitions of the United States, which that government may have occasion to send from one part of its territory to another, lying on opposite sides of the continent. The Mexican government having e agreed to protect with its whole power the prosecution, preservation, and security of the work, the United States may extend its protection as it shall judge wise to it when it may feel sanctioned and warranted by the public or international law.

Article IX

This treaty shall be ratified, and the respective ratifications shall be exchanged at the city of Washington within the exact period of six months from the date of its signature, or sooner, if possible.

In testimony whereof, we, the plenipotentiaries of the contracting parties, have hereunto affixed our hands and seals at Mexico, the thirtieth (30th) day of December, in the year of our Lord one thousand eight hundred and fifty-three, in the thirty-third year of the independence of the Mexican republic, and the seventy-eighth of that of the United States.

JAMES GADSDEN, MANUEL DIEZ DE BONILLA, JOSE SALAZAR YLARBEGUI, AND J. MARIANO MONTERDE,

And whereas the said treaty, as amended, has been duly ratified on both parts, and the respective ratifications of the same have this day been exchanged at Washington, by WILLIAM L. MARCY, Secretary of State of the United States, and SENOR GENERAL DON JUAN N. ALMONTE, Envoy Extraordinary and Minister Plenipotentiary of the Mexican Republic, on the part of their respective Governments:

Now, therefore, be it known that I, FRANKLIN PIERCE, President of the United States of America, have caused the said treaty to be made public, to the end that the same, and every clause and article thereof, may be observed and fulfilled with good faith by the United States and the citizens thereof

In witness whereof I have hereunto set my hand and caused the seal of the United States to be affixed.

Done at the city of Washington, this thirtieth day of June, in the year of our Lord one thousand eight hundred and fifty-four, and of the Independence of the United States the seventy-eighth.

By the President:
Franklin Pierce,
W. L. Marcy, Secretary of State.

Chronology of Manifest Destiny, 1800–1860

1800   Thomas Jefferson (Democratic-Republican) is elected president in the "Revolution of 1800." Jefferson and running mate Aaron Burr receive equal numbers of electoral votes, so the election is decided in the House of Representatives. Jefferson's election represents the first and precedent-setting peaceful transfer of power between political parties in U.S. history.

1800   A planned slave insurrection led by Gabriel Prosser is uncovered and aborted in Virginia. Thirty-five, including Prosser, are hanged.

1800   The U.S. government is relocated to the new capital of Washington, D.C.

1801   In the Judiciary Act of 1801, outgoing President John Adams makes his "Midnight Appointees" to the Supreme Court in an effort to maintain Federalist control of the Court. Secretary of State James Madison refuses to deliver the new judges' commissions, effectively preventing them from assuming office, and Congress repeals the Act.

1801   John Marshall is appointed Chief Justice of the Supreme Court. He would serve until his death in 1835, presiding over a number of key, precedent-setting rulings.

1801   President Jefferson battles the Barbary States over piracy.

1802   The U.S. military academy at West Point is established.

1802   Governor William Henry Harrison of the Indiana Territory compels a number of Native American tribes in the area to cede several million acres to the United States in the Treaty of Vincennes. The Treaty establishes a precedent for future similar treaties in other areas.

1803   President Thomas Jefferson purchases the Louisiana Territory from the French Emperor Napoleon for $15 million. Although Jefferson believes that the Constitution does not grant the president authority to purchase territory, he goes against his belief in order to obtain the valuable farm-land. The 800,000 square mile territory doubles the size of the United States.

1803   The Supreme Court hands down its decision in *Marbury v. Madison*, declaring for the first time that a federal law is unconstitutional. This decision establishes the principle of judicial review, maintaining that the judiciary has the authority to declare federal and state laws unconstitutional.

1803	Ohio is admitted to the Union as a free state.
1803–1806	The Lewis and Clark Expedition explores the Louisiana Purchase and beyond, traveling 8,000 miles along the Missouri and Columbia Rivers to the Pacific Ocean and back.
1804	President Thomas Jefferson (Democratic-Republican) is reelected.
1804	The Twelfth Amendment to the U.S. Constitution is ratified. It allows members of the Electoral College to designate separate ballot choices for president and vice president.
July 11, 1804	Vice President Aaron Burr kills former Treasury Secretary Alexander Hamilton in a duel. Burr had been defeated in his run for the governorship of New York, and resented Hamilton's role in his loss.
1805	The *Essex* decision of a British prize court leads to increased British seizures of neutral American ships by stating that French West Indian goods transferred by American ships to American ports and on to France were not neutral cargo.
1805	U.S. Marines capture the port of Derna in Tripoli, ending the enslavement of American seamen and demands for tribute.
1806	In retaliation for the *Essex* decision Congress passes the Nonimportation Act forbidding the purchase of British products that could be made instead in the United States.
1806	Aaron Burr, along with Louisiana Territory Governor and secret Spanish agent General James Wilkinson, form an unclear plot to combine parts of the American West and Spanish Mexico into their own independent country. Wilkinson turns on Burr and informs President Jefferson of the scheme. Burr is charged with treason and acquitted.
1807	The *Chesapeake-Leopard* Affair: The British frigate *Leopard* attacks the U.S. warship *Chesapeake*, killing three Americans in an unprecedented attack on American sovereignty. The British also seize four deserters from the British Navy. The incident raises loud protests and calls for war throughout the United States.
1807	Robert Fulton's steamship the *Clermont* sails on the Hudson River in a round trip between Albany and New York City, marking the arrival of steam-powered transportation.
1807	Congress passes the Embargo Act in protest of European interference with American shipping. The Act prohibits American vessels from sailing to foreign ports and prohibits American goods aboard foreign ships. The embargo is met with widespread American protests, illegal smuggling, and economic hardship.
1808	James Madison (Democratic-Republican) is elected to the presidency.
January 1, 1808	The congressional prohibition of the African slave trade, outlined in Article I, Section 9, of the U.S. Constitution, goes into effect.
1809	Congress passes the Non-Intercourse Act, which repeals the 1807 Embargo Act and reopens all foreign trade with the exception of trade with Britain and France. The president was to restore the trading rights of these two countries if and when they stopped interfering with American shipping.

1810	Macon's Bill No. 2 repeals the Non-Intercourse Act restoring U.S. trade with Britain and France. It also contains the provision that if either country interfered with American shipping, the United States would reimpose trade restrictions with the other country.
1810	American settlers revolt in Spanish West Florida and President James Madison annexes the region to the United States.
1810	For the first time the Supreme Court strikes down a state law as unconstitutional in *Fletcher v. Peck*.
1811	In a close decision Congress votes not to renew the charter of the Bank of the United States.
1811	Construction begins on the National Road at Cumberland, Maryland.
1811	President Madison reimposes a ban on trade with Great Britain.
November, 1811	In Indiana, William Henry Harrison defeats Tecumseh and his brother Tenskwatawa (The Prophet) in the Battle of Tippecanoe. Tecumseh sought to form a Pan-Indian confederacy in order to stop white expansion. Many Americans believe the British had a hand in inciting the rebellion.
1812	President James Madison (Democratic-Republican) is reelected to the presidency.
1812	Louisiana is admitted to the Union as a slave state.
1812	Congress provides for a 35,000-man regular army and gives President James Madison the power to call up state militias for six-month service.
1812–1814	The War of 1812: The U.S. Congress declares war on Great Britain by a vote of 79–49 in the House and 19–13 in the Senate on June 18, 1812. Anger over interference with American shipping and the ongoing impressment of American sailors is responsible for the war declaration. News of a British repeal of trade restrictions does not reach America in time to forestall the declaration.
September 1, 1813	Captain Oliver Perry defeats British naval forces at the Battle of Lake Erie.
October 1813	General William Henry Harrison defeats the British and their Indian allies at the Battle of the Thames in Canada. Indian leader Tecumseh is killed, ending his dream of a Pan-Indian confederation. The British lose many of their Indian allies.
1814	New Englanders opposed to the War of 1812, most of them Federalists, call the Hartford Convention in Connecticut. Extremists call for secession from the Union. Official proposals include endorsing state nullifications of federal acts and seeking to limit the federal government's power over foreign affairs.
May 1814	General Andrew Jackson emerges victorious in the Creek War after defeating Chief Red Eagle in the Battle of Horse Shoe Bend. The Americans kill 800 Creeks, and the survivors sign a peace treaty surrendering a large amount of territory in Georgia and Alabama.
August 1814	The British enter Washington, D.C., unopposed, burning the White House, the Capitol, and numerous other public buildings.
September 1814	Francis Scott Key writes "The Star Spangled Banner" while held aboard a British warship during the attack on Fort McHenry in the harbor at Baltimore, Maryland. It is later adopted as the official national anthem.

September 1814	Commander Thomas McDonough defeats the British fleet at Plattsburgh on Lake Champlain in New York, ending a British invasion from Canada.
December 24, 1814	The United States and Great Britain sign the Treaty of Ghent in present-day Belgium, ending the War of 1812. The ambiguous treaty does not mention most of the key issues that had caused the war, such as impressment of sailors.
1815	Francis Cabot Lowell's Boston Manufacturing Company produces the first cotton cloth made by power machinery, the power loom. The business soon expands to Lowell, Massachusetts, and employs many women. The town provides workforce housing and a moral environment, and Lowell becomes one of the most famous businessmen of the time.
January 1815	General Andrew Jackson wins a victory over British forces at the Battle of New Orleans after the official end of the War of 1812. News of the Treaty of Ghent had not yet crossed the Atlantic Ocean to America. Jackson's victory ends British influence in the region and makes him a national hero.
1816	President James Monroe (Democratic-Republican) is elected to the presidency.
1816	The Tariff Act of 1816 protects U.S. industry from foreign competition for the first time.
1816	Congress charters the Second Bank of the United States.
1816–1818	The First Seminole War is fought in Spanish Florida. Generals Andrew Jackson and Edmund Gaines lead U.S. troops. A main dispute involves raids into Georgia by Seminoles and fugitive slaves who had earlier escaped to Spanish Florida. Jackson captures Pensacola and claims Florida for the United States.
1817	Mississippi is admitted to the Union as a slave state.
1817	The American Colonization Society is founded. Its mission is to return free African Americans to Africa. The Society would found the colony of Liberia on the west African coast.
1817	Britain and the United States sign the Rush-Bagot Agreement almost completely disarming the U.S.-Canadian border.
1819	The United States experiences its first major economic depression in the "Panic of 1819."
1819	In *McCulloch v. Maryland*, the Supreme Court declares unconstitutional a Maryland law taxing paper money issued by the Second Bank of the United States. The decision also rules that Congress has the authority to charter a national bank and that the states could not tax federal agencies.
1819	The Adams-Onis Treaty with Spain gives the United States the territory of Florida and establishes the western boundaries of the Louisiana Purchase. The United States also renounces its claim to Texas and Spain renounces claims to Oregon.
1819	Alabama is admitted to the Union as a slave state.
1819	To a bill granting Missouri statehood, Representative James Tallmadge of New York introduces an amendment that prohibits any further slaves from being introduced into the future state. All slave children in Missouri

would receive their freedom upon turning twenty-five. The amendment is never added, but causes violent debate over the issue.

1820   The Missouri Compromise admits Missouri as a slave state in 1821, balancing it with the admission of Maine as a free state in 1820. The remainder of the Louisiana Purchase is divided at 36 degrees, 30 minutes north latitude. All territory above the line is closed to slavery and all territory below the line is open to slavery.

1820   James Monroe (Democratic-Republican) is reelected to the presidency.

1822   Former slave Denmark Vesey attempts a slave insurrection in Charleston, South Carolina. A slave betrays the plot and thirty-five men, including Vesey, are hanged. The fear caused by such rebellions results in the passage of more stringent slave codes in many southern states.

1823   President James Monroe announces that the United States will not intervene in European affairs and that the Western hemisphere is closed to further colonization by European powers. This policy becomes known as the Monroe Doctrine.

1823   Stephen F. Austin establishes the first American colony in the Mexican territory of Texas with permission from the Mexican government.

1824   Senator Henry Clay first announces his "American System" favoring protective tariffs, federal expenditures on internal improvements, and a strong national bank. The system would later become the Whig Party platform.

1824   John Quincy Adams (Democratic-Republican) is elected to the presidency in the House of Representatives (no candidate won a majority of the electoral votes) in what Andrew Jackson supporters term the "corrupt bargain." Jackson had led in both the electoral and popular votes.

1825   Robert Owen founds the short-lived utopian community of New Harmony, Indiana.

1825   The Erie Canal connecting the Great Lakes to Albany, New York, is officially opened.

1828   The Baltimore and Ohio (B&O) Railroad is chartered. Such railroads linked port cities like Baltimore, which lacked good interior waterways, to the interior of the country.

1828   Congress passes the "Tariff of Abominations." John C. Calhoun's South Carolina Exposition and Protest, published anonymously, summarizes southern opposition to the tariff. It states that Congress did not possess the constitutional authority to pass a tariff whose high level would serve to exclude imports. The agricultural South relied on imports of cheap European manufactured goods and opposed the higher tariff rates on such goods that most Northerners favored for its protection of its own often higher-priced manufactured goods.

1828   Andrew Jackson (Democrat) is elected to the presidency. Jackson's dominant presidency would lead his opponents to dub him "King Andrew I" and create the Whig Party in opposition to his arbitrary power. Emergence of the Whig Party marks the Second Party System. Jackson's political philosophy came to be known as Jacksonian Democracy.

1829   Free black David Walker issues his militant *Appeal* in Boston, demanding immediate abolition and the end of discrimination.

1830   Joseph Smith founds the Mormon Church.

1830   Congress passes the Indian Removal Act in order to resettle those Native American tribes remaining in the eastern United States to lands west of the Mississippi River. The tribes would receive federal compensation and western land. The president is authorized to use force if necessary. The "Five Civilized Tribes" in the southeast (the Cherokee, Choctaw, Chickasaw, Creeks, and Seminoles) would be affected most by this act.

1831   Renowned abolitionist William Lloyd Garrison publishes the first issue of the antislavery newspaper the *Liberator*, advocating immediate abolition without compensation to owners.

1831   Slave and preacher Nat Turner plans the most famous and frightening slave insurrection in Virginia. Turner and his group of slaves kill over fifty whites before they are captured or killed by federal and state troops. Nat Turner is captured and executed several months later.

1832   Andrew Jackson (Democrat) is reelected to the presidency.

1832   The first school for the blind in the country opens. Dr. Samuel Gridley Howe serves as its director.

1832   The Supreme Court, led by Chief Justice John Marshall, upholds Cherokee land claims in *Worcester v. Georgia*. Marshall declares that they are a "domestic dependent nation" entitled to federal protection against the state's actions. President Andrew Johnson would defy the Court and force the Cherokee to march overland to Indian Territory in what became known as the "Trail of Tears."

1832   President Nicholas Biddle of the Second Bank of the United States seeks an early renewal of the bank's charter. Jackson vetoes the bill and removes federal government deposits, instigating what became known as the Bank War. It would become a major issue in that year's presidential election.

1832   The McCormick Reaper is invented.

1833   Samuel Colt invents the first handgun with a revolving barrel, known as a "six-shooter."

1833   Congress passes a Compromise Tariff, lowering import duties, and South Carolina revokes its Ordinance of Nullification. Congress also passes the Force Act, authorizing the president to enforce federal law in that state. South Carolina nullifies the Force Act, but the crisis passes.

1833   Oberlin College opens its doors. It is the first coeducational college in the United States. Two years later it would become the first college to admit African Americans.

1833   The American Anti-Slavery Society is founded in Philadelphia. It publishes abolitionist literature and lobbies for abolition in the nation's capital.

1834   The Senate censures President Andrew Jackson for removing federal government deposits from the Second Bank of the United States. The censure would be expunged in 1837.

January 30, 1835   In the U.S. Capitol, Richard Lawrence becomes the first person to attempt to assassinate a U.S. president. His attempt on the life of Andrew Jackson fails.

1835–1842	The Second Seminole War is fought in the Florida Territory. U.S. troops under General Zachary Taylor and other commanders attempt to capture those Seminoles who refuse to leave Florida for Indian Territory under the Indian Removal Act of 1830. It is the longest and most expensive of the Indian Wars fought by the U.S. government. In the end, several hundred Seminoles remain hidden in the Florida Everglades, calling themselves "the unconquered." They would later negotiate with the United States for reservations in Florida.
1836	Martin Van Buren (Democrat) is elected to the presidency.
1836	Arkansas is admitted to the Union as a slave state.
1836	The House of Representatives adopts the Gag Rule, which tabled any antislavery petitions without discussion. It would be lifted in 1844.
March 6, 1836	The Battle of the Alamo: after Santa Anna assumes power in Mexico and garrisons troops in Texas, a group of 182 Texans under William B. Travis attempt to defend the Alamo, a former mission. Davy Crockett and James Bowie also participate. After a siege, the Mexicans are able to storm the Alamo on March 6. All of the Texan defenders are killed, leading the Texans to adopt the battle cry "Remember the Alamo."
April 21, 1836	General Sam Houston's forces defeat Santa Anna at the Battle of San Jacinto, gaining the Republic of Texas its independence from Mexico.
1836	President Jackson issues the Species Circular, which states that the federal government now requires payment for public lands in gold or silver only. Critics blame the Species Circular for the Panic of 1837, which followed shortly thereafter.
1837	Michigan is admitted to the Union as a free state.
1837	John Deere introduces his steel-bladed plow.
1837	The country enters an economic depression started by the Panic of 1837.
1837	A pro-slavery mob murders the abolitionist Reverend Elijah Lovejoy in Alton, Illinois.
1838	*Letters on the Equality of the Sexes* by Quaker abolitionist and women's rights crusader Sarah Grimké is published.
1839	The Spanish ship *La Amistad* experiences a slave revolt and is captured off the coast of New York. The Supreme Court would later declare that the passengers on the ship had been illegally enslaved and grant their freedom.
1839	Antislavery forces form the Liberty Party. The party spoke out against a Slave Power Conspiracy of southern slave owners and sympathetic northern allies. It fielded a presidential candidate in the 1840 and 1844 elections but captured only a small percentage of votes.
1839	*American Slavery as It Is* by Theodore Weld is published. The book exposing the horrors of slavery sells thousands of copies in its first year.
1840	William Henry Harrison (Whig) is elected to the presidency. He would die on April 4, 1841, after one month in office and Vice President John Tyler would assume the presidency.

1840s   The Irish potato famine, begun by a blight that destroyed potato crops, sends over one million Irish immigrants to the United States.

1841   Congress passes the Pre-emption Act, allowing squatters to settle on public land and then to purchase up to 160 acres of it at low prices before a public sale.

1841   Beginning of the wagon trains that traveled from Independence, Missouri, to Oregon and California. Reports of cheap, fertile farmland leads to "Oregon Fever." At the time, the United States and Britain jointly occupied the Oregon Territory under a treaty of 1818.

1841   The utopian community Brook Farm is established near Boston, arising from the Transcendentalist movement and seeking to combine physical and intellectual work.

1842   The Webster-Ashburton Treaty between the United States and Great Britain settles border disputes with Canada, among other measures.

1844   James K. Polk (Democrat) is elected to the presidency.

1844   Samuel F. B. Morse sends the first message on his invention, the telegraph. He would also invent Morse code, the alphabet of dots and dashes used in such communications.

June 1844   Mormon founder Joseph Smith and his brother are murdered by an angry mob in Carthage, Illinois. The Mormons then leave for the Great Salt Lake area in present-day Utah. The first would arrive there a few years later.

1845   Texas and Florida are admitted to the Union as slave states.

1845   Editor John O'Sullivan first uses the phrase "manifest destiny" to describe the expansion of the United States from coast to coast, considered by many to be divinely ordained.

1845   The John Slidell Mission to Mexico City is unsuccessful in its attempt to negotiate the U.S. purchase of New Mexico and California from the Mexican government. Meanwhile, President Polk sends General Zachary Taylor to the north bank of the Rio Grande River, disputed territory along the Texas-Mexico border.

1846   Iowa is admitted to the Union as a free state.

1846   The United States and Britain agree to divide the Oregon Territory at the 49th parallel after talk of war over the area subsides.

July 1846   Author Henry David Thoreau refuses to pay a $1 poll tax in Massachusetts in protest of the federal government's involvement in slavery and the Mexican-American war. He spends time in jail and is later inspired to write the essay "Civil Disobedience," which advocates nonviolent protest against unjust government policies.

October 1846   The Mormon Donner Party is trapped for the winter in the Sierra Mountains by snows on their way to California. Only forty-seven of the eighty-two-member party would reach California the following spring. Stories of cannibalism and suffering would make them notorious.

1846–1848   The Mexican-American War is fought between the United States and Mexico.

1847   General Winfield Scott captures Veracruz and Mexico City.

1847	John Humphrey Noyes establishes Oneida, a communitarian experimental community, in western New York. The community succeeds economically, providing the basis for a renowned name-brand silverware company.
1848	Zachary Taylor (Whig) is elected to the presidency. He would die in office in 1850 and Vice President Milliard Fillmore would assume the presidency.
1848	Wisconsin is admitted to the Union as a free state.
1848	The Free Soil party is formed with a platform of preventing the expansion of slavery into the western territories. It is more moderate than the earlier Liberty Party.
January 24, 1848	Gold is discovered at John Sutter's sawmill near Sacramento, California. The California gold rush would soon follow. In 1849, mostly male gold prospectors known as forty-niners head to California by the thousands, swelling the territory's population.
1848	The Treaty of Guadalupe Hidalgo ends the Mexican-American War. The United States acquires the 339-million-acre Mexican Cession (California, Nevada, Utah, New Mexico, and parts of Arizona, Colorado, Kansas, and Wyoming) for $15 million and an assumption of debts owed by the Mexican government to U.S. citizens. The failed Wilmot Proviso of 1846 had sought to prohibit slavery in any territory gained as a result of the war, and the question of slavery's fate in the newly acquired territory continues to linger.
July 19–20, 1848	The first Woman's Rights Convention, organized by Elizabeth Cady Stanton and Lucretia Mott, is held in Seneca Falls, New York. The delegates issue a "Declaration of Sentiments" modeled on the Declaration of Independence, demanding women's suffrage among other measures.
1850	Congress passes a series of bills known as the Compromise of 1850. They admit California as a free state, establish the doctrine of popular sovereignty in the other areas of the Mexican Cession, abolish the slave trade in Washington, D.C., and create a more stringent Fugitive Slave Act.
1850	*The Scarlet Letter* by Nathaniel Hawthorne is published.
1850s	Several National Women's Rights conventions are held.
1851	*Moby-Dick* by Herman Melville is published.
1851	Maine adopts the first state law prohibiting the manufacture and sale of alcoholic beverages. Future prohibition laws would be thereafter called "Maine laws."
1852	Franklin Pierce (Democrat) is elected to the presidency.
1852	*Uncle Tom's Cabin* by Harriet Beecher Stowe is published, becoming an instant best seller. Its popularity gave rise to the anecdote that President Lincoln declared upon meeting Stowe, "Is this the little woman whose book made such a great war?"
1853	The Gadsden Purchase: the United States purchases 29,640 square miles of Mexican territory in present-day Arizona and New Mexico for $10 million.
1854	*Walden* by Henry David Thoreau is published.

1854   The Know-Nothing (American) Party, predicated on nativist fear of immigrants and the belief that "Americans must rule America," achieves notable electoral successes. Its success also reveals dissatisfaction with the Whigs and the Democrats.

1854   Senator Stephen Douglas introduces the Kansas Nebraska Act, dividing the Nebraska Territory into Kansas and Nebraska and introducing the doctrine of popular sovereignty there. The act repeals the Missouri Compromise, reigniting sectional controversy over slavery's expansion and leading to often-violent encounters between pro- and antislavery forces in the area that became known as "Bleeding Kansas." Pro-slavery forces establish a government in Lecompton and antislavery forces establish a government in Topeka. Both claim to be the legitimate territorial government.

1854   Antislavery Whigs and Democrats unite to form the Republican Party, leading to the rise of the Second Party System.

1854   Commodore Matthew Perry opens Japan to western trade under the Treaty of Kanagawa.

1854   Covert meetings among America's ministers to Spain, France, and Great Britain result in the secret Ostend Manifesto that becomes public. It justifies U.S. seizure of Cuba if Spain will not sell the island, confirming northern suspicions of a southern plot to extend slavery.

1855   *Leaves of Grass* by Walt Whitman is published.

1856   James Buchanan (Democrat) is elected to the presidency.

May 19, 1856   Senator Charles Sumner of Massachusetts delivers his "Crime against Kansas" speech in the U.S. Senate. Preston Brooks, nephew of a South Carolina senator insulted in Sumner's speech, later beats Sumner severely with a cane. Sumner requires several years to recover from the results of the beating.

1856   Pro-slavery forces destroy printing presses and burn several buildings in the antislavery town of Lawrence, Kansas. The incident would become known as the "Sack of Lawrence." In revenge, militant abolitionist John Brown would lead several men in an attack on a pro-slavery settlement on the banks of Pottawatomie Creek in the "Pottawatomie Massacre." His actions would touch off a wave of reprisals, in which one of his sons would be murdered.

1857   President James Buchanan accepts the pro-slavery Lecompton Constitution in Kansas in a controversial decision.

1857   The Supreme Court rules in the controversial *Dred Scott v. Sandford* case (the Dred Scott decision) that African Americans do not have federally protected constitutional rights and that Congress and territorial legislatures did not have the authority to exclude slavery from the territories.

1857   Inventor Elisha Otis installs the first passenger elevator in a New York department store.

1857   The country suffers an economic depression touched off by the "Panic of 1857."

1858   Minnesota is admitted to the Union as a free state.

August 21 to October 15, 1858	U.S. Senate candidates Stephen Douglas (Democrat) and Abraham Lincoln (Republican) hold a series of unusual face-to-face debates in Illinois. Douglas's Freeport Doctrine that territorial residents could exclude slavery by not protecting the institution through legislation further divides the Democratic Party along sectional lines. Lincoln achieves national recognition.
1859	Oregon is admitted to the Union as a free state.
1859	Edwin Drake strikes oil for the first time in Titusville, Pennsylvania.
October 16, 1859	Militant abolitionist John Brown and a small group of followers seize the federal arsenal at Harpers Ferry, Virginia (now West Virginia). U.S. forces under the command of Colonel Robert E. Lee later wound and capture Brown and several of his men. Brown is convicted of treason, among other charges, and sentenced to death in a Virginia state court. He would be hanged on December 2, leading him to be considered a martyr in much of the North.
1860	Publisher Erastus Beadle issues the first of the small paperback novels that would prove popular among lower- and middle-class readers. They would be widely referred to as "dime novels" although the first cost only a nickel.
1860	The Pony Express begins its overland mail service between Missouri and California.
1860	The Democratic Party breaks up along sectional lines, with northern and southern Democrats nominating different presidential candidates.
November 1860	Abraham Lincoln (Republican) is elected to the presidency despite receiving no electoral votes and few popular votes in the South. His election sets off a secession crisis in the southern states.
December 20, 1860	After a unanimous vote, South Carolina secedes from the Union.

Marcella Bush Trevino

This resource guide focuses on scholarly publications in the fields of American history, culture, and politics in the Manifest Destiny period. Included are a number of useful encyclopedias, biographical dictionaries, and other reference works as well as those works listed in the suggested readings following each chapter.

Books

Adams, Ephraim D. *The Power of Ideals in American History.* Port Washington, NY: Kennikat Press, 1969.

Adams, John. *The Adams-Jefferson Letters: The Complete Correspondence between Thomas Jefferson and Abigail and John Adams.*Chapel Hill: University of North Carolina Press, 1959.

Adams, William Howard, ed. *The Eye of Thomas Jefferson.*Charlottesville, VA: Thomas Jefferson Memorial Foundation, 1976.

Ambrose, Stephen E. *Undaunted Courage: Merriwether Lewis, Thomas Jefferson, and the Opening of the American West.* New York: Simon & Schuster, 1996.

Ammon, Harry. *James Monroe: The Quest for National Identity.* New York: McGraw-Hill, 1971.

Anderson, John Jacob. *Did the Louisiana Purchase Extend to the Pacific Ocean? And Our Title to Oregon.* San Francisco: Bacon, 1880.

Angle, Paul M., ed. *Created Equal? The Complete Lincoln-Douglas Debates of 1858.* Chicago: University of Chicago Press, 1985.

Baker, Vaughan Burdin, ed. *Visions and Revisions: Perspectives on Louisiana Society and Culture.* Lafayette: Center for Louisiana Studies, University of Louisiana, 2000.

Barbé-Marbois, Francois, marquis de. *The History of Louisiana, Particularly of the Cession of That Colony to the United States of America.* Philadelphia: Carey & Lea, 1830.

Barry, Louise. *The Beginning of the West: Annals of the Kansas Gateway to the American West, 1540–1854.*Topeka: Kansas State Historical Society, 1972.

Bean, Walton. *California: An Interpretive History.* New York: McGraw-Hill, 1968.

Blondheim, Menahem. *News over the Wires: The Telegraph and the Flow of Public Information in America, 1844–1897.* Boston: Harvard University Press, 1994.

Brooks, John. *Telephone: The First Hundred Years.* New York: Harper and Row, 1976.

Boime, Albert. *The Magisterial Gaze: Manifest Destiny and American Landscape Painting, c. 1830–1865.* Washington, DC: Smithsonian Institution Press, 1991.

Brack, Gene M. *Mexico Views Manifest Destiny: 1821–1846: An Essay on the Origins of the Mexican War.* Albuquerque: University of New Mexico Press, 1975.

Brackenridge, Henry Marie. *Views of Louisiana: Together with a Journal of a Voyage up the Missouri River, in 1811.* Chicago: Quadrangle Books, 1962.

Brasseaux, Carl A., ed. *A Refuge for All Ages: Immigration in Louisiana History.* Lafayette: University of Southwestern Louisiana Press, 1996.

Brown, Charles H. *Agents of Manifest Destiny: The Lives and Times of the Filibusters.* Chapel Hill: University of North Carolina Press, 1980.

Brown, Everett S. *The Constitutional History of the Louisiana Purchase, 1803–1812.* Berkeley: University of California Press, 1920.

Calloway, Colin G. *One Vast Winter Count: The Native American West before Lewis and Clark.* Lincoln: University of Nebraska Press, 2003.

Carlson, Laurie Winn. *Seduced by the West: Jefferson's America and the Lure of the Land beyond the Mississippi.* Chicago: Ivan R. Dee, 2003.

Carter, Alden R. The *Mexican War: Manifest Destiny.* New York: F. Watts, 1992.

Caughey, John Walton. *The California Gold Rush.* Berkeley: University of California Press, 1948.

Chambers, Henry Edward. *A History of Louisiana, Wilderness, Colony, Province, Territory, State, People.* Chicago: American Historical Society, 1925.

Chase, John Churchill. *Louisiana Purchase: An American Story Told in That Most American of All Forms of Expression, the Comic Strip.* New Orleans: Louisiana Purchase Sesquicentennial Commission, 1954.

Claiborne, William Charles Cole. *Official Letter Books of W. C. C. Claiborne, 1801–1816.* Jackson, MS: State Department of Archives and History, 1917.

Clarke, Thomas Curtis, et al. *The American Railway: Its Construction, Management, and Appliances.* New York: Arno Press, 1976.

Collier, Christopher. *Hispanic America, Texas, and the Mexican War, 1835–1850.* Tarrytown, NY: Benchmark Books, 1999.

Dargo, George. *Jefferson's Louisiana: Politics and the Clash of Legal Traditions.* Cambridge, MA: Harvard University Press, 1975.

De Conde, Alexander. *This Affair of Louisiana.* New York: Charles Scribner's Sons, 1976.

De Voto, Bernard Augustine. *Celebrating 150 years of the Louisiana Purchase.* New York: Collier, 1953.

Douglas, Stephen A. *A Brief Treatise Upon Constitutional and Party Questions, and the History of Political Parties.* New York: D. Appleton, 1866.

Douglas, William O. *Washington and Manifest Destiny; Address at the Opening of the Library of Congress Exhibition Commemorating the Centennial of the Territory of Washington, May 14, 1953.* Washington, DC: Library of Congress, 1953.

Drinnon, Richard. *Facing West: The Metaphysics of Indian-Hating and Empire Building.* Minneapolis: University of Minnesota Press, 1980.

Falconer, Thomas. *On the Discovery of the Mississippi, and on the Southwestern, Oregon, and Northwestern Boundary of the United States.* London: S. Clarke, 1844.

Fehrenbacher, Don E. *Manifest Destiny and the Coming of the Civil War, 1840–1861.* New York: Appleton-Century-Crofts, 1970.

Filler, Louis, and Allen Guttmann, eds. *The Removal of the Cherokee Nation: Manifest Destiny or National Dishonor?* Boston: Heath, 1962.

Fitzpatrick, John. *The Merchant of Manchac, the Letterbooks of John Fitzpatrick, 1768–1790.* Baton Rouge: Louisiana State University Press, 1978.

Foley, William E. *The Genesis of Missouri: From Wilderness Outpost to Statehood.* Columbia: University of Missouri Press, 1989.

Gluek, Alvin C. *Minnesota and the Manifest Destiny of the Canadian Northwest: A Study in Canadian-American Relations.* Toronto: University of Toronto Press, 1965.

Gold, Susan Dudley. *Land Pacts.* New York: Twenty-first Century Books, 1997.

Greenhow, Robert. *Memoir, Historical and Political, on the Northwest Coast of North America, and the Adjacent Territories.* Washington, DC: Blair and Rives, 1840.

Heckman, Richard Allen. *Lincoln vs. Douglas: The Great Debates Campaign.* Washington, DC: Public Affairs Press, 1967.

Hietala, Thomas R. *Manifest Design: Anxious Aggrandizement in Late Jacksonian America.* Ithaca, NY: Cornell University Press, 1990.

Hitchcock, Ripley. *The Louisiana Purchase and the Exploration, Early History and Building of the West.* Boston: Ginn, 1903.

Horsman, Reginald. *Race and Manifest Destiny: The Origins of American Racial Anglo-Saxonism.* Cambridge: Harvard University Press, 1981.

Hosmer, James Kendall. *The History of the Louisiana Purchase.* New York: D. Appleton, 1902.

Houck, Louis. *The Boundaries of the Louisiana Purchase: A Historical Study.* St. Louis: P. Roeder, 1901.

Howard, James Quay. *History of the Louisiana Purchase.* Chicago: Callaghan, 1902.

Jefferson, Thomas. *The Writings of Thomas Jefferson.* 20 vols. Washington, DC: Thomas Jefferson Memorial Association of the United States, 1905.

Jefferson, Thomas. *An Account of Louisiana, Being an Abstract of Documents, in the Offices of the*

Departments of State, and of the Treasury. Philadelphia: John Conrad & Co., 1803.

Jones, Breckinridge. *The Commercial Development of the Louisiana Purchase.* St. Louis: Nixon-Jones, 1899.

Jones, Howard, and Donald A. Rakestraw. *Prologue to Manifest Destiny: Anglo-American Relations in the 1840s.* Wilmington, DE: SR Books, 1997.

Kaplan, Lawrence S. *Thomas Jefferson: Westward the Course of Empire.* Wilmington, DE: SR Books, 1999.

Keats, John. *Eminent Domain: The Louisiana Purchase and the Making of America.* New York: Charterhouse, 1973.

Labbé, Dolores Egger, ed. *The Louisiana Purchase and Its Aftermath, 1800–1830.* Lafayette: University of Southwestern Louisiana, 1998.

LeMenager Stephanie. *Manifest and Other Destinies: Territorial Fictions of the Nineteenth-Century United States.* Lincoln: University of Nebraska Press, 2004.

Letcher, David M. *The Diplomacy of Annexation: Texas, Oregon and the Mexican War.* Columbia: University of Missouri Press, 1975

Lyon, Elijah Wilson. *The Man Who Sold Louisiana: The Career of François Barbé-Marbois.* Norman: University of Oklahoma Press, 1942.

Marshall, Thomas Maitland. *A History of the Western Boundary of the Louisiana Purchase, 1819–1841.* Berkeley: University of California Press, 1914.

Merk, Frederick. *Manifest Destiny and Mission in American History: A Reinterpretation.* New York: Alfred A. Knopf, 1970.

Merk, Frederick. *The Monroe Doctrine and American Expansion, 1843–1849.* New York: Alfred A. Knopf, 1966.

Merk, Frederick, and Lois Bannister Merk.*The Monroe Doctrine and American Expansionism, 1843–1849.* New York: Knopf, 1966.

Mills, Bronwyn. *The Mexican War.* New York: Facts On File, 1992.

Morrison, Michael A. *Slavery and the American West: The Eclipse of Manifest Destiny and the Coming of the Civil War.* Chapel Hill: University of North Carolina Press, 1997.

Nardo, Don. *The Mexican American War.* San Diego, CA: Lucent Books, 1999.

Owsley, Frank Lawrence. *Filibusters and Expansionists: Jeffersonian Manifest Destiny,* 1800–1821. Tuscaloosa: University of Alabama Press, 1997.

Paul, Rodman W. *California Gold: The Beginning of Mining in the Far West.* Lincoln: University of Nebraska Press, 1967.

Peterson, Merrill D. *Thomas Jefferson and the New Nation.* New York: Oxford University Press, 1970.

Peterson, Richard H. *Manifest Destiny in the Mines: A Cultural Interpretation of Anti-Mexican Nativism in California, 1848–1853.* San Francisco: R and E Research Associates, 1975.

Pichardo, José Antonia. *Pichardo's Treatise on the Limits of Louisiana and Texas, an Argumentative Historical Treatise with Reference to the Verification of the True Limits of the Provinces of Louisiana and Texas; written by Father José Antonia Pichardo, of the Congregation of the Oratory of San Felipe Neri, to Disprove the Claim of the United States That Texas Was Included in the Louisiana Purchase of 1803.* 4 vols. Austin: University of Texas Press, 1931–1946.

Pletcher, David M. *The Diplomacy of Annexation: Texas, Oregon and the Mexican War.* Columbia: University of Missouri Press, 1975.

Polk, James K. *The Diary of a President.* Chicago: Longman, 1952.

Rodriguez, Junius P., ed. *The Louisiana Purchase: A Historical and Geographical Encyclopedia.* Santa Barbara, CA: ABC-CLIO, 2002.

Rohrbough, Malcolm J. *Days of Gold: The California Gold Rush and the American Nation.* Berkeley: University of California Press, 1997.

Ruiz, Ramon E., ed. *The Mexican War: Was It Manifest Destiny?* Hinsdale, IL: Dryden Press, 1963.

Sigelschiffer, Saul. *The American Conscience: The Drama of the Lincoln-Douglas Debates.* New York: Horizon Press, 1973.

Smith, Walter Robinson. *Brief History of the Louisiana Territory.* St. Louis: St. Louis News Company, 1904.

Sprague, Marshall. *So Vast, so Beautiful a Land: Louisiana and the Purchase.* Boston: Little, Brown, 1974.

St. Louis City Art Museum. *Westward the Way: The Character and Development of the Louisiana Territory, as Seen by the Artists and Writers of the Nineteenth Century.* St. Louis: City Art Museum, 1954.

Stephanson, Anders. *Manifest Destiny: American Expansionism and the Empire of Right.* New York: Hill and Wang, 1995.

Stineback, David C., and Charles M. Segal. *Puritans, Indians, and Manifest Destiny.* New York: Putnam, 1977.

Stoddard, Amos. *Sketches, Historical and Descriptive, of Louisiana.* Philadelphia: M. Carey, 1812.

Stout, Joseph A. *The Liberators: Filibustering Expeditions into Mexico, 1848–1862 and the Last Thrust of Manifest Destiny.* Los Angeles: Westernlore Press, 1973.

Talbott, Wallace T. *The Osages: Dominant Power of Louisiana Territory.* New York: Carlton Press, 1989.

Tallant, Robert. *The Louisiana Purchase.* New York: Random House, 1952.

U.S. Department of State. *State Papers and Correspondence Bearing upon the Purchase of the Territory of Louisiana.* Washington, DC: U.S. Government Printing Office, 1903.

U.S. General Land Office. *Historical Sketch of "Louisiana" and the Louisiana Purchase, with Illustrative Maps Reproduced from the Exhibit of the General Land Office, Department of the Interior, Louisiana Purchase Exposition.* St. Louis, MO: 1904.

U.S. General Land Office. *Historical Sketch of "Louisiana" and the Louisiana Purchase, by Frank Bond, Chief Clerk General Land Office, with a Statement of other Acquisitions.* Washington, DC: U.S. Government Printing Office, 1912.

U.S. General Land Office. *The Louisiana Purchase, and Our Title West of the Rocky Mountains, with a Review of Annexation by the United States. By Binger Hermann, Commissioner of the General Land Office.* Washington, DC: U.S. Government Printing Office, 1898.

U.S. General Land Office. *The Louisiana Purchase: An Historical Sketch from the Files of the General Land Office Reprinted in Commemoration of the One Hundred Fiftieth Anniversary of the Louisiana Purchase, by Frank Bond.* Washington, DC: U.S. Government Printing Office, 1952.

U.S. National Archives and Records Service. *Territorial Papers of the United States: Territory of Louisiana-Missouri, 1803–1821.* Compiled and edited by Clarence Edwin Carter. Washington, DC: National Archives and Records Service, 1968.

Weinberg, Albert K. *Manifest Destiny: A Study of Nationalist Expansionism in American History.* Gloucester, MA: P. Smith, 1958.

Wood, W. Raymond. *Prologue to Lewis and Clark: The Mackay and Evans Expedition.* Norman: University of Oklahoma Press, 2003.

Journals

American Anthropologist
American Anthropological Association

American Antiquity
Society for American Archeology

American Historical Review
American Historical Association

American Quarterly
The Johns Hopkins University Press

Annals of Iowa

Annals of Kansas City, Missouri

Commercial Telegraphers' Union of America Journal

Essays in Economic and Business History

Journal of American History
Organization of American Historians

The Journal of the West

Macropolitics of Nineteenth-Century Literature: Nationalism, Exoticism, Imperialism

Mississippi Valley Historical Review
Organization of American Historians

Missouri Historical Society Collections
Missouri Historical Society

Ohio Archaeological and Historical Quarterly
Ohio State Archaeological and Historical Society

Railroad History

Retrieving the American Past
Ohio State University

Reviews in American History
The Johns Hopkins University Press

University Studies

William and Mary Quarterly
Omohundro Institute of Early American History

Internet

American West
www.americanwest.com/

Discovering Lewis and Clark
www.loc.gov/wiseguide/index-flash.html

From Revolution to Reconstruction
http://odur.let.rug.nl/~usa/index.htm

Library of Congress
www.loc.gov

Louisiana Purchase U.S. Census Statistics
www.loc.gov/wiseguide/index-flash.html

Manifest Destiny
www.accd.edu/pac/history/hist1302/ManifestDestiny.html

PBS: Gold Rush
www.pbs.org/goldrush

PBS: Manifest Destiny
www.pbs.org/kera/usmexicanwar/dialogues/
    prelude/manifest/manifestdestiny.html

PBS: U.S.-Mexican War
www.pbs.org/kera/usmexicanwar

Westward Expansion
www.snowcrest.net/jmike/westexp.html

National Historic Landmarks (selected)

Henry Clay Home

Lexington, Kentucky

From 1811 until 1852, this two-story brick mansion
    was the residence of Henry Clay (1777–1852),
    the distinguished pre–Civil War political leader,
    statesman, and presidential candidate. Clay
    served as a U.S. senator, speaker of the house,
    and secretary of state. The house was recon-
    structed after Clay's death on the original plan.

Fort Hill

Clemson, South Carolina

This was the residence of John Caldwell Calhoun
    (1782–1850), best remembered for his vigorous
    defense of states' rights. His long political career
    included terms in the U.S. House and Senate,
    service as secretary of war and secretary of state,
    and in the office of vice president.

Mesilla Plaza

Las Cruces, New Mexico

Mesilla was founded in 1848 by the Mexican gov-
    ernment to bring Mexican citizens from terri-
    tory recently ceded to the United States into
    Mexican domain; by the terms of the Gadsden
    Purchase Treaty (1851), the town became part
    of the United States. It still retains the flavor of
    a Mexican village.

San Jacinto Battlefield

Houston, Texas

Here, on April 21, 1836, the decisive battle of
    the Texas Revolution was fought. Nine hundred
    men led by General Sam Houston, commander
    in chief of all Texas forces, surprised the
    Mexican army under the command of President
    Antonio Lopez de Santa Anna, which was
    encamped on the San Jacinto River; in a battle
    lasting eighteen minutes, the Texans routed the
    enemy, killing or capturing many Mexican sol-
    diers. The following day, Santa Anna himself was
    captured and held hostage against further
    Mexican attack.

Index